SEAN STONE

NEW WORLD ORDER

A STRATEGY OF IMPERIALISM

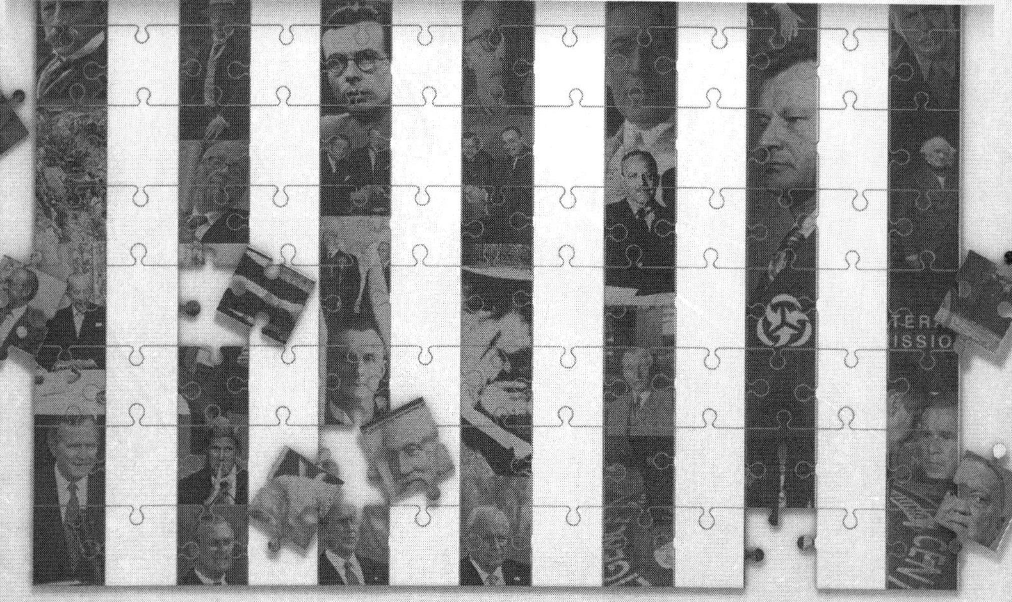

FOREWORD BY RICHARD GROVE

AFTERWORD BY GUIDO PREPARATA

Published by:
Trine Day LLC
PO Box 577
Walterville, OR 97489
1-800-556-2012
www.TrineDay.com
publisher@TrineDay.net

Library of Congress Control Number: 2016950561

Stone, Sean
—1st ed.
p. cm.
Includes references and index.
Epub (ISBN-13) 978-1-63424-091-8
Mobi (ISBN-13) 978-1-63424-092-5
Print (ISBN-13) 978-1-63424-090-1
1. Elliott, William Yandell, -- 1896-1979 -- Influence. 2. Rhodes, Cecil, -- 1853-1902 -- Influence. 3. Rhodes scholarships -- History. 4. World politics. 5. Internationalism. 6. Fugitives (Group). I. Stone, Sean. II. Title

First Edition
10 9 8 7 6

Cover by:
Greg Hardesty
greg@glyph.it

Printed in the USA
Distribution to the Trade by:
Independent Publishers Group (IPG)
814 North Franklin Street
Chicago, Illinois 60610
312.337.0747
www.ipgbook.com

Publisher's Foreword

> *The ghost I saw may be the devil, and the devil has the power to assume a pleasing disguise, and so he may be taking advantage of my weakness and sadness to bring about my damnation. I need better evidence than the ghost to work with. The play's the thing to uncover the conscience of the king.*
>
> – Hamlet, *The Tragedy of Hamlet, Prince of Denmark*, Act 2, Scene 2

Every book has it's own journey – as do we all. Sometimes traveling together, other times alone, we oft come face-to-face with our fears, our foibles and ... our futures. For what will be, is always up to us: Actions begat.

In the *Bhagavad Gita,* Arjuna is distraught about upsetting "cosmic order" (dharma). Wouldn't his overthrowing the establishment cause problems? After all, weren't some of the folks sowing the strife his relations and friends? Yes, they weren't behaving correctly, but if he opposes them, Arjuna worries that he will be defying the natural-order-of-things and committing sin. In the name of dharma, he argues for non-violence, because by attacking and killing so many important men, who are fathers and husbands, it will damage families and communities, which are themselves vital to the wellness of society. How can he, why should he battle?

First, Krishna, Arjuna's charioteer, speaks to him of the eternal nature of the soul, that no action can harm anyone's true self:

> The learned do not grieve for the dead or for the living. Never, indeed, was there a time when I was not, nor when you were not, nor these lords of men. Never, too, will there be a time when we shall not be...

He next explains that action done out of a sense of duty – without attachment – has no karmic effects, and is the correct action.

> Not by nonperformance of actions does a man attain freedom from action; nor by mere renunciation of actions does he attain his spiritual goal.... Do your allotted work, for action is superior to non-action. Even the normal functioning of your body cannot be accomplished through actionlessness...

And we all have different natures, and these differences dictate different duties ... different action.

I met Sean as a guest on his *Buzzsaw* interview show. The topic was my father, who had served in American intelligence for twenty years: OSS, G-2 and CIA. Dad quit the Agency in the late '50s and started to talk to me in the late '60s. He had mostly been an in-house analyst, but during WWII he had also worked in psychological warfare, and then in the early '50s he went covert, even taking the family along as cover.

In 1969 Dad had a profound talk with me. It was the day before my twentieth birthday, and a friend of his, Dr. D.F. Fleming from Vanderbilt, was visiting. My father proceeded to tell me amazing things, all about his intelligence career, before they delved into the issue of psychological warfare. The first thing he told me was that the Vietnam war was about drugs and that there were secret societies involved. He then said that communism was all a sham, and instead, these secret societies were behind it; that it was "all a big game." He also told me that "they" were playing out a "lose-scenario in Vietnam." Hunh?

I had no idea or frame of reference about what they were talking about, but soon began a journey to try to understand what I had been told. Leading me to research, then to write and eventually publish books that no one else seemed willing to do.

After my interview with Sean was over, we continued our conversation and he told me of his college thesis. I asked to read it and found out, as Dr. Peter Dale Scott put it: "I learned a lot by reading it." Not having even heard of his main subject, William Yandell Elliot before, I encouraged Sean to publish, and here we are.

It took me over twenty years to begin to understand what my father told me. A major revelation was the book, *America's Secret Establishment,* by my good friend and mentor, Antony Sutton. He had this to say:

> Watch as events unfold. We are observers. They will destroy themselves. We can help a little, but don't get any bright ideas about overturning the system. They have all the bombs, but we have something stronger – the truth and freedom of spirit.
>
> Be patient, spread the word among friends, do your little bit. The system will self destruct because it is founded on corruption and untruth.

Sean Stone is definitely doing his "little bit." What will you do?

Onwards to the utmost of Futures,
Peace,
RA Kris Millegan
Publisher
TrineDay
August 18, 2016

The political work of the Open Conspiracy must be conducted upon two levels and by entirely different methods. Its main political idea, its political strategy, is to weaken, efface, incorporate, or supersede existing governments. But there is also a tactical diversion of administrative powers and resources to economic and educational arrangements of a modern type. Because a country or a district is inconvenient as a division and destined to ultimate absorption in some more comprehensive and economical system of government, that is no reason why its administration should not be brought meanwhile into working co-operation with the development of the Open Conspiracy.

– H. G. Wells, *The Open Conspiracy*, 1928

Contents

Statue of Cecil Rhodes at Oriel College at Oxford University. He left money to the college on his death in 1902.

FOREWORD

"You never change things by fighting the existing reality. To change something, build a new model that makes the existing model obsolete."

– R. Buckminster Fuller

We have an expression in our English-speaking culture, a metaphorical idiom which represents an obvious *truth*; but recognizing that the *truth* carries with it an obvious risk and/or problems, it thus goes unnamed, unstudied, and undiscussed: that's "*the elephant in the living room*," as the saying goes.

This book provides a rewarding journey for those who don't know anything about the topic, as well as for those who think they already know quite a bit; for the average individual it provides the framework of the "New World Order," and for the academic and serious researcher this book relates a copious amount of real-world facts which are beyond refute, and which must be considered in formulating a holistic understanding of how the world works up to this point in history.

In the turbulent times we live in, I think it's important to focus on the essentials, to refine our priorities, and once in a while – to step back and look at the big picture.

There are two main issues involved when investigating *why* this topic is so prevalent and yet so-little recognized in public: 1) the lack of cogent and coherent learning resources, an issue solved in part by this book, and 2) the fear of ridicule coupled with the fear of wasting time, wherein this book provides a succinct chain of logic to overcome these obstacles. I found it to be a useful tool in comprehending a massive subject of inquiry, and I think you'll likewise find it useful in growing in the "light" direction (aka learning your way forward).

This is a book about freedom and liberty, both intellectual and physical, as it applies to individuals; its contents represent the vanguard of a long chain of contention, continuing back thousands of years. Historically, writing was used *offensively* (to make plans to plunder the production and wealth of others), and *defensively* (to ward off plans of others plundering your production and wealth); in this case the author has accurately recognized a complex plan to use words (as well as weapons) to rob individuals of their liberty, and he has demonstrated intellectual self-defense using words to simplify the complexity, and demonstrate why these plans for global plunder are, by design, intellectually bankrupt and based solely on greed with motives of ever-increasing power.

Writing this book was necessary in order to show why the *"irrational plans"*[1] described herein have been successful, as a method to overcome the dumbing-down of individuals which made the plan possible in the first place. I've studied this topic for more than 12 years; I like to think I've looked into all the disparate puzzle pieces of this story and have built up a strong working knowledge of how all the pieces fit together. I produce podcasts, documentaries and videos to allow the audience to teach themselves about this topic, so it's challenging to find a story (which I think I already know about) to be interesting… unless it's a version of the story which you've never heard, with ramifications which are far reaching. In this case, I was pleasantly surprised by how much I underestimated a few key characters in the story, and the precise organization of facts herein is not offered in any other single book; and for that Sean Stone merits congratulations for publishing a book that is useful to everyone – from the novice reader beginning their journey to cognitive liberty, to the professional with a working understanding of these events. It was gratifying to read such a thorough exposition of the facts which shed light on the prime movers whose efforts helped to convert America from a Constitutional Republic to an Oligarchy. More on how that happened, in a few moments.

Having already had the privilege of reading this book, it's a pleasure to organize some useful thoughts and information to help frame out a showcase for what you're about to dive into. If you're new to this topic, this book is an excellent example of how to begin your self-education, as it provides many sparks to ignite your interest for learning more.

Sean Stone has done a masterful job of addressing the public need for both an overall perspective (in a general sense) and the precise inner-workings of the mainsprings of action (in a specific sense) of this subject matter; he has done this by marshaling the relevant evidence and artifacts in order to provide you with the context and details of a much-talked-about but rarely defined topic. Sean's efforts come to a point, which I think proves to be particularly useful in formulating your own understanding of the world around you, and will aid you in making important choices in your life. In the process of doing so, he takes the existing reality (inaccurate information we've come to believe through our mass media culture) and provides a coherent chain of inter-related facts, which make the common misunderstandings of this topic obsolete.

In many cases, non-fiction books provide windows into the past, to things which have happened before you read about them. In this case,

1. See definition of *parapolitics* on page xxiii

you're reading a non-fiction book which starts in the past, brings you to the present, and with the understanding it imports, gives you an opportunity to make choices and take action as you add your input to a story which is ongoing and unfinished.

For instance, a recent study[2] published by Princeton University revealed how far America has come since the days of "land of the free, home of the brave."[3] "U.S. is an Oligarchy, not a Democracy," is the title of the BBC article published April 17th, 2014 summarizing the findings of the Princeton Oligarchy study for its audience, "'Multivariate analysis indicates that economic elites and organized groups representing business interests have substantial independent impacts on US government policy, while average citizens and mass-based interest groups have little or no independent influence.' In English: the wealthy few move policy, while the average American has little power." What happened between equal representation and being ruled by a group of non-elected rulers? This book thoroughly answers that question, giving you a chance to reverse this trend.

And yet, in spite of this evidence, many people will be happy to tell you that the "*New World Order does not exist.*" Maybe in a way they're right. I can recall a time when I allowed folks to tell me that it didn't exist; I trusted them, and believed that they knew better than I did, so I didn't do my own searching to learn about the topic. Then one day, I decided to start looking for myself, and in the case of this topic, the more you look – if you know how to look – the more you find. The people who say the "New World Order doesn't exist" are usually parroting that perspective because they don't know anything about it – not because there is no evidence of a New World Order in objective reality. It seems most are blocked from becoming informed because of flaws in their philosophy, or their ability to identify truth; and still others have a total absence of philosophy, and thus haphazardly risk their lives daily, by betting on what they believe to actually represent that which exists – instead of using their power of observation.

Defining the New World Order

Much of this book originates with Sean's 2006 thesis for his Bachelor's Degree in American History at Princeton University, titled "The New World Order," in an effort to add much-needed definition, structure, and evidence regarding a subject which was purposely kept

2. "Testing Theories of American Politics: Elites, Interest Groups, and Average Citizens" by Martin Gilens and Benjamin Page, published in *Perspectives on Politics*, September 2014, Vol. 12/No. 3 pages 564-581, © American Political Science Association 2014

3. Lyrics from the "Star Spangled Banner" written by Francis Scott Key during the War of 1812 (September 13, 1814); later adopted as the national anthem of the United States of America in 1931.

amorphous, chaotic, and ambiguous to public knowledge. A few years earlier in 2004, another author who just happened to be the Dean of Princeton's Woodrow Wilson School of Government penned a book titled *A New World Order,* which you can find reviewed on the Council of Foreign Relations' *Foreign Affairs* quarterly magazine website, but it goes out of its way to avoid nearly everything in Sean's thesis to keep its readers in the dark about the true nature of schemes for global governance which are undermining individual liberty. Unfortunately today we don't have a "Committee for Detecting and Defeating Conspiracies" such as George Washington created during his role as spymaster of the American Revolutionary War for Independence from Great Britain;[4] we have to learn how to identify these schemes for ourselves.

The phrase "New World Order" is known to the literary world (via H.G. Wells' 1939 book of the same title) as well as the political (it's been used for decades by some of the most prestigious world planners, including Henry Kissinger and Zbigniew Brzezinski who have advised every Presidential administration in the past 50 years), and you'll find it in books like *Of Paradise and Power: America, Europe and the New World Order* (2007) by Robert Kagan (a Neoconservative[5] cohort of the Bush regime), which bridge both the literary and political spheres. Then there's *Toward a New World Order: The Future of NATO* by George Soros in 1993, a pamphlet which was printed to guide NATO toward its political goal. It's also worth mentioning the 2010 documentary film directed by Jason Bermas titled: *Invisible Empire: A New World Order Defined,* which has an informative 35 minute introduction showcasing the history and usage of the phrase "New World Order" by statesmen and politicians, spanning the last century. In this day of instant-information on everything, how could people be kept in the dark about this topic?

In postulating an answer, I'm reminded of a quote by Allen Dulles, who was fired by John F. Kennedy, and then promptly ended up investigating Kennedy's death. In a transcript published in a 1975 book *The Warren Commission in its Own Words,* we find on page 47 the panel's line of questioning on July 9, 1964, "*Don't you suspect the total mass of data that*

4. *George Washington, Spymaster: How the Americans Outspied the British and Won the Revolutionary War* by Thomas B. Allen, page vii; published by National Geographic (2004). John Jay (for whom a famous school of law and criminal justice is named) headed the Committee to Detect and Defeat Conspiracies on behalf of George Washington.

5. The Neoconservative think tank Project for a New American Century (PNAC) published "Rebuilding America's Defenses" in 2000, citing desires for radical change which just happened to be fulfilled through the 9-11 terrorist attacks. From page 51, "*Further, the process of transformation, even if it brings revolutionary change, is likely to be a long one, absent some catastrophic and catalyzing event – like a new Pearl Harbor.*" According to several sources, "Of the twenty-five people who signed the PNAC's founding statement of principles, ten went on to serve in the administration of U.S. President George W. Bush, including Dick Cheney, Donald Rumsfeld, and Paul Wolfowitz."

is going to be made public is going to be self-evident?," to which Allen Dulles replied, *"But nobody reads. Don't believe people read in this country. There will be a few professors that will read the record..."* to which Mr. Jenner on the panel interjected, *"And a few newspaper reporters who will read parts of it,"* which brought forth the Dulles response *"The public will read very little."* I took the liberty of underlining "*... in this country,*" to point out the philosophical influence of Immanuel Kant[6] and the adverse effects of the Prussian Education System which together transformed Americans from people who asked questions and sought answers, to a collective where self-responsibility is obsolete and individuals obey declarative sentences without question (such as those found in the Warren Commission Report). During its early period, the colonists of America had a literacy rate around 90%, and by the 1840's it was estimated between 91-97% literacy[7], and yet by the time of Kennedy *"nobody reads"* (or more accurately people read *untruths* and can't discern the difference). That's why a revival of reading and asking questions are fundamental to sparking individual liberty and reigniting freedom – because critical thought can't occur without *considering* history. Dulles knew it; the truth is out there, but *not reading* keeps people in the dark, and thus unwittingly submissive to the agenda to which the Dulles brothers subscribed: *internationalism.*

In essence, the New World Order is an agenda to withdraw the freedom and liberty from individuals around the globe, as a means of forming and maintaining a world government without the consent of the people being governed. It's an attempt to roll back the clock a few hundred years, back to the "good old days" of feudalism and slavery ... and according to the aforementioned Princeton Oligarchy study, it has already attained its goals without your consent.

The Problem(s) Resolved by this Book

This book is an accurate description of an organized global hegemony brought about by the field of study known as "Para-Politics," which is a phrase popularized by author and diplomat Peter Dale Scott to describe and refer to what he calls *"a system or practice of politics in which accountability is consciously diminished. It describes at best only an intervening layer of the irrationality under our political culture's rational surface."* Interestingly enough, in searching the word "parapolitics" while writing this (to be sure I was accurate in my description) I found a 1979 book published by Oxford University of same title, *Parapolitics: Toward the City of Man* by Rhodes Scholar Raghavan Iyer. One of my goals by the end of this intro-

6. *The New World Order: A Strategy of Imperialism* by Sean Stone

7. "*Literacy Rates in Early America*" by Soj, 6 December 2003 published by the *Daily Kos*; cites *National Education in the United States of America* by DuPont de Nemours (1812), among other credible sources.

duction is to give you the tools to figure out why that's an interesting synchronicity in context of the subject matter at hand. The purpose of writing about parapolitics is to use logic and reason to consciously expose these topics as a measure to re-establish the connection between the political action and personal accountability for those actions, by identifying and removing the contradictions.

Sean draws out the "intervening layer of irrationality under our political culture's rational surface" through his efforts, chapter by chapter, taking what you think you know, and allowing you to check into the footnotes and references, and begin to understand the details of the overarching story and why power was gained by those who concealed these details right under our noses.

Why doesn't everybody know about these layers of irrationalities already? That question is thoroughly answered throughout this book, but I think the history of WHY deserves a spotlight of attention. The layers of irrationality which comprise parapolitics are by design, well hidden – either in plain sight, or behind classifications of "National Security." If one begins to examine these layers, the system has built-in deterrents – including the use of ridicule by others – in the absence of intellectual defense of the topic.

To wit, the phrase "conspiracy theory" is a non-sequitur which has been used as a short-cut to thinking (or a short-circuit to stop thinking), most commonly thrown down as a sort of all-powerful trump card, to end reasonable discussions, discourage legitimate questions, and to excuse people from engaging in the cognitive processes through observing the facts and performing first-hand inspections of the evidence. In reality the use of the phrase conspiracy theory (to stifle communication) is a practical application of psychological warfare tactics which have been prevalent for the past forty years; it has been a method of keeping the illegal activities of covert operations secret.

The deployment of the phrase conspiracy theory has historically been used to impugn the intellectual integrity of individuals who question the overtly neat-and-clean explanations being peddled (by the "official storytellers") for some of the worst crimes over the past century. As a method of control, conspiracy theory has been leveled to bewilder the audience, and for decades has been a phrase used to stifle legitimate dissent. Many people use the phrase *instead of doing their own thinking,* thereby ensuring the stimulus/response controls instilled through their schooling stay in place. "Conspiracy theory" has become synonymous with "not true" or "not factual." This book offers individuals (who are honestly interested) to identify a cornucopia of facts, evidence, and artifacts which demonstrate that there is a long-term, ongoing conspiracy, and it's no longer a theory.

Where did this trend of conspiracy theory psittacism[8] (the use of phrases without understanding, to parrot) originate and why is it so popular that just about anyone you talk to knows to throw it on the table to avoid looking at evidence?

In an article in the August 1956 edition of *Elks Magazine*, FBI director J. Edgar Hoover (or his FBI ghostwriter) stated: "The individual is handicapped by coming face-to-face with a conspiracy so monstrous he cannot believe it exists. The American mind simply has not come to a realization of the evil which has been introduced into our midst. It rejects even the assumption that human creatures could espouse a philosophy which must ultimately destroy all that is good and decent." Hoover at the time was pointing out what he called a "Communist conspiracy" to rule the planet[9]; but he didn't correctly identify the "elephant in the living room." In hindsight we can see that there was an ongoing agenda to undermine the freedom of individuals and nations around the world, and that agenda used communism as a tool – not as an end in and of itself. Hoover's ability to see clearly was likely obscured by a well-placed smokescreen of propaganda, and thus he misidentified the origin and participants of the effort. Until now, too – few accurate descriptions of this group (of unelected power brokers who determine the fates of nations) have existed.

For more than one hundred years, Americans have been systematically kept in the dark about how their freedom and liberty were actively being subverted, by a few powerful groups who shared a goal of global domination. Over the past century, a few brave professors and professional researchers have authored books describing the so-called "New World Order" (i.e. an agenda to create a world government). These works shined a light into the darkness which exists just beyond the comprehension of the common person. Standing on the shoulders of these giants, Sean Stone has added a perspective which provides definition and description (in a step-by-step narrative); yielding a composition of the facts and evidence which needed to be subverted in order for freedom and liberty to continue to be undermined.

---

8. According to the Oxford English Dictionary, "psittacism" is defined as "The mechanical repetition of previously received ideas or images that reflects neither true reasoning nor feeling; repetition of words or phrases parrot-fashion, without reflection, automatically." (Latin: to parrot)

9. Even if J. Edgar Hoover had been right in identifying it as a Communist conspiracy, he did not have the benefit of Antony C. Sutton's 'Wall Street Trilogy' to understand how western banks and corporations were behind the veil of both Communism and Nazism and funded all sides. This is reiterated by Zbigniew Brzezinski in his book *Between Two Ages: America's Role in the Technetronic Era* via a footnote on page 56. "For impressive evidence of Western participation in the early phase of Soviet economic growth, see Antony C. Sutton's *Western Technology and Soviet Economic Development, 1917-1930* (Stanford, Calif, 1968), which argues that "Soviet economic development for 1917-1930 was essentially dependent on Western technological aid" (p. 283), and that "at least 95 per cent of the industrial structure received this assistance" (p. 348)."

While some are content to think "New World Order ... that's just a conspiracy theory" and go about being willingly incognizant of the part they're playing in a script someone else wrote for them; I offer that by examining the phrase conspiracy theory is enough to make one start asking more questions, not less. Once you start asking questions, and finding valid answers, you're in the driver's seat, and you're writing your own script in life. The ability to ask a question and find the answer is an aspect of freedom which still exists (it is easier today than ever before), and it's a muscle that will be exercised as you read this book.

The term 'conspiracy theory' was systematically popularized in the late 1960's by the CIA. *Isn't that enough of a contradiction to start asking more questions?* I did, and eventually I searched for a curious artifact yielded from a 1976 FOIA request by the *New York Times,* it's known as CIA document 1035-960 "Countering Criticism of the Warren Report" (NARA Record Number 104-10009-10022, released to the public in 1996)[10] and it can still be found by searching the Internet. It's a 53-page memo which observes that author Edward Jay Epstein's then-recent book, *Inquest: The Warren Commission and the Establishment of Truth* (which is found on 20 out of the 53 pages in the memo) was instrumental in sparking public interest in questioning the official story of the Kennedy Assassination. Epstein did so by questioning the integrity of the methods used by the Warren Commission to reach their conclusions. The CIA (in document 1035-960) elaborated on its strategy to stifle dissenting views (regardless of the merit or veracity of the claims), citing: "The aim of this dispatch is to provide material countering and discrediting the claims of the conspiracy theorists, so as to inhibit the circulation of such claims in other countries." This is evidence of a purposeful subversion of the Bill of Rights made legal by "National Security."

Keep in mind, when the *next* investigation of the Kennedy Assassination concluded (1978 United States House of Representatives Select Committee on Assassinations/HSCA report), it was determined that John F. Kennedy and Martin Luther King, Jr. were both likely killed by a *conspiracy* – not lone gunmen – but facts like these are inconvenient truths which don't fit in with the repetitive "news" we're surrounded by, so it falls into the memory hole. What's more, in a 1999 trial resulting from a civil suit against the United States Government, filed by the family of slain civil rights leader Martin Luther King, Jr., the twelve-person jury listened to more than seventy witnesses testify over four weeks and then after deliberating for just one hour, their finding was by unanimous consent: MLK's widow Coretta Scott King held a press conference the day after the verdict relating, "The jury was clearly convinced by the exten-

10. National Archives and Records Administration (NARA) houses the National Declassification Center which handled the FOIA in question

sive evidence that was presented during the trial that, in addition to Mr. Jowers, the conspiracy of the Mafia, local, state and federal government agencies, were deeply involved in the assassination of my husband."[11,12]

JFK's brother, Bobby Kennedy, was – according to L.A. County Coroner Dr. Thomas T. Noguchi, who conducted the autopsy – shot from behind, "less than one inch from Kennedy's head, behind his right ear."[13]

These facts are toxic to the interests who want you to believe *you already have the truth*. The fact that most people have unrealistic views on these types of historical events is not an accident – *that is the conspiracy worth analyzing*. There are interests who want you to continue on, go about your life, and don't ask any questions about such important matters. *They are the experts, and you're to follow their lead... There's nothing to learn that they haven't already taught you.* (Sarcasm implied)

Before we leave this section, I'd like you to read a quote from David Rockefeller in his self-titled *Memoirs* (2002), from page 405: "For more than a century ideological extremists at either end of the political spectrum have seized upon well-publicized incidents ... to attack the Rockefeller family for the inordinate influence they claim we wield over American political and economic institutions. Some even believe we are part of a secret cabal working against the best interests of the United States, characterizing my family and me as 'internationalists' and of conspiring with others around the world to build a more integrated global political and economic structure – one world, if you will. If that's the charge, I stand guilty, and I am proud of it." If you can dismiss that factual statement from a respectable source, you're doing exactly what the CIA and non-elected rulers would want you to do. On the other hand, you can choose for yourself to observe the evidence, weigh the facts, and decide whether or not 'non-elected rulers who govern you without your consent' is attractive to you, or something from which you wish to withdraw your participation. Without such information most people unwittingly participate in the dilution of their rights and removal of their liberties.

At best 'conspiracy theory' is a hypothesis of covert action. What we're studying here are the analytics of covert actions which have already occurred – *parapolitics* if you will – *and the difference is that there is something here to analyze*; therefore it's not about hypothetical events which have not yet occurred.

At this point, I'd like to lay out a brief history of freedom so that we can see where we came from and where we are presently, so we can determine

11. "Court Decision: U.S. 'Government Agencies' Found Guilty in Martin Luther King's Assassination" by *Washington's Blog*, 21 January 2013

12. "Memphis Jury Sees Conspiracy in Martin Luther King's Killing" by Emily Yellin, 9 December 1999, *New York Times*

13. "40 Years After RFK's Death, Questions Linger" by Michael Taylor, *San Francisco Chronicle*, June 3, 2008

where we're going; it's a process not unlike using a compass to find where we are on the map, so we can figure out where we want to go from here.

The Origins and Evolution of Freedom

The struggle of attaining and maintaining individual freedom and liberty is a story as old as written history itself. When I was reading a 1979 reprint of *The Evolution of Civilizations: An Introduction to Historical Analysis* by professor Carroll Quigley (a 1961 text book which points out repeating patterns of rise and collapse of societies over thousands of years), I noticed the logo of its publisher, The Liberty Fund, a symbol which is 4,300 years old, and represents a concept in the language of cuneiform from Sumeria; it is the first appearance of the word freedom (or 'liberty') in any written language. One might ask the question: *what made it necessary to create a word for a concept such as freedom or liberty?* If one persists, one might discover the likelihood of the rise of tyranny, slavery, and other events which violate the right of individuals to live without coercion – a loss of freedom would demand the creation of a word for something they took for granted and didn't bother to give a name, until it was taken away. The problems examined in this book are not relics of the past which are irrelevant to our world, but they do have ancient origins. In my study of history, I have only witnessed a single war, which continues to this day, ongoing; it is the war waged against individuals who express themselves and live freely, and waged by those who seek to suppress the rights and freedoms of individuals in order to collect, assert, and maintain power and control.

To be unaware of this trend in history, and our place in it, is to be unwittingly submissive to that power and under that control. If that's your choice, that's fine; but the evidence first needs to be observed, identified, and weighed in order to make an informed decision. The essence of freedom is diluted when choice (to think or not to think) is abandoned – or denied. History is not just a story of the struggle for individual liberty and freedom over the ages, it has the potential to preserve what matters, and provide us with the history of what men have been; the honor and integrity which enables freedom is based on our sense of history. If you improve your sense of history, you increase the degrees of freedom which you are able to enjoy.

The Emergence of Freedom

Through the ages of tribal warlords and monarchical rule, the concepts of individual liberty and freedom survived slavery, despotism, serfdom, and after 4,300 years, arrived on the shores of North America to begin flourishing under conditions where the kings and queens were separated from their servants by the Atlantic Ocean. The European traders and settlers who arrived in North America found there were differences from their previous homelands; there were no roads, no markets, no city centers to do trade. These intrepid individuals thus had to re-learn what it was like to live in nature. They had to clear their own land, build their own houses, spark their own fires, hunt, trap, and grow their own food; they had to protect themselves from predators – including those among their own species – for there were no 'kings men' to protect them, either from nature, or themselves. This uncharted land demanded something more from its inhabitants, and the potential reward for the people who came from countries ruled by tyrants was learning to be self-reliant and thereby experience the absence of slavery. The early colonists of British North America in the 1600's thus became more and more independent from the historical realms of control in Europe.

By this time in the 17th and 18th centuries, British North America was a place where people from around the world came to escape the monopoly of powers in Europe. America in those days was a very demanding territory, and the grass-roots of what became the United States of America was comprised of hearty and robust individuals, who through hard work learned to be self-reliant – a culture very different from that of Europe with its kingdoms and principalities. The self-reliance built self-esteem, and the ability to do things for themselves coupled with the ability to imagine how to improve technology made America in the 19th century a hotbed of invention and industrial revolutions.

AMERICA VS. THE EMPIRE

Most people think that America's struggle against the British Empire (and their global opium trading monopoly via the East India Company) ended after the American Revolution (1781); a few students of history might cite the cessation of battle after the war of 1812 in 1814. Fewer still realize that while the British Empire focused on subjugating the people of India through the 1800's, it still sought to recolonize America and bring it back into the Empire. While America expanded westward, the British Empire continued to fan the flames of re-colonization, mostly through the complicity of America's Eastern Establishment families (who had built their fortunes on the back of British East India Company opium trading),[14] and aided by robber barons who considered themselves

14. These families are sometimes referred to as 'Boston Brahmins' (including the families of Pilgrims Society founder Joseph Choate, *Washington Post* editor Ben Bradlee, President Franklin Delano Roosevelt, and Senator John Forbes Kerry), a cross-reference between the Brahmin caste of India and the Boston link in the British East India Company's trade routes, which included opium distribution, and of course the tea which got dumped in Boston harbor by the Sons of Liberty. The Boston Brahmin Russell family, which founded Skull and Bones at Yale in 1832, was also an opium merchant (Russell & Co.).

'*globalists*' or '*internationalists*' (recall David Rockefeller and his family's efforts) and found the notion of creating a world government to be attractive. This attempt to use American resources as a stepping-stone to global governance was foreseen by George Washington, who in his farewell address in 1796 mentions the tendency for power to corrupt the foundations laid by the founding fathers, "... they are likely, in the course of time and things, to become potent engines, by which cunning, ambitious, and unprincipled men will be enabled to subvert the power of the people and to usurp for themselves the reins of government, destroying afterwards the very engines which have lifted them to unjust dominion."

By 1902 America was once again in the sights of an enemy, well-funded and fully-cloaked in the camouflage of an ally – an ally with a plan to recolonize America by changing the attitudes, values, behaviors and beliefs as the method of re-integration into the Empire.

America and Great Britain continued to share a great deal in common; both countries spoke English – a language that would become the most dominant on the planet. America's national anthem during this era was "My Country Tis of Thee" (1831) which has a tune practically identical to "God Save the Queen" (1619), the British national anthem. In America we're all familiar with the image of Uncle Sam back in 1917 with his patriotic top-hat, pointing at us, coupled with the words "I Want You for U.S. Army," not realizing that in 1914 an equally iconic image for the British, Lord Kitchener (made famous in the Boer Wars, where he pioneered the use of concentration camps), pointing in the same manner (at the audience), coupled with the words "Britons: [Lord Kitchener] Wants You to Join Your Country's Army – God Save the King." Indeed, we Americans have a lot in common with our British cousins, with a few minor exceptions and one major disagreement: the issue of monarchy. In America we enjoyed a long literary legacy of the evolution of individual liberty, standing upon the shoulders of Locke, Rousseau, Jefferson, Paine, and others; a few individuals who dared to disagree with the history of monarchy. In America, we came to value the equality that is self-evident and granted to all individuals: the rights to property, privacy, and pursuit of happiness, among others; we came to realize that freedom exists when there are no masters, and no slaves; neither above nor below should we consider ourselves, and thus we are equal.

Undermining Freedom

Sean hits heavily upon a point which most other history books of this variety seldom mention: the philosophical engine which powers the tyranny of slavery in a modern sense. He explains how the history of freedom for individuals was on the rise until the philosophy of Immanuel Kant took root, irrationally removing the rights intrinsic to individuals and attributing them to the collective state (which cannot exist without the rights of individuals). This strategy, Kant argued, makes the individual submissive to the collective group, making what's "right" not what one's conscience dictates, but rather "what is best for the group." This idea of "indirect rule" to control human beings in essence makes them automatons of the state or regime in power. Through the 1800's this strategy became the *de facto* philosophical method to control individuals – not enforced by cages or guillotines – but rather by fear and ignorance, and the inevitable result, self-imposed slavery.

This philosophical corruption of self-reliance turns the natural law system upside down, making the strategies which created America obsolete, and in its place mandating that the state has the right to govern without consent. While this concept is antithetical to the concepts of the *Declaration of Independence* in 1776, Kant's ideas flourished in the lands of France, Prussia, and England wherein Kant's ideas were applied through state schools (this is commonly known as the Prussian Education system, created by Kant's acolytes); and then this system jumped the ocean and embedded itself in American culture. In the 1900's Kant's influence was weakening the foundations of freedom as a primer to aid in the rise of collectivism, tyranny, and despotism, globally. If after reading this book you're interested in learning more about how America adopted the Prussian Education System of compulsory indoctrination to systematically remove individuality and self-reliance from students, seek out a copy of *The Underground History of American Education* by John Taylor Gatto, which is an impeccable survey of this phenomenon to undermine self-reliance, and it involves the same participants you'll learn about herein.

With the philosophic foundations of private property, self-reliance, and equal representation being eroded in generation after generation that passed through the Prussian Education System (in America), those who had designs on the re-colonization of America as a stepping-stone to world government, sharpened their pencils. A student of the British Empire, attending Oxford University, wrote down his plan for world domination on behalf of the Empire; his name was Cecil Rhodes. And what I can tell you from my experience is that if school children in America were taught about the life and legacy of Cecil Rhodes, freedom and liberty across the planet would be at much less risk of peril; and as a function of not being taught this story, individuals on every continent stand to lose freedom and liberty – possibly forever. One might even consider reading *The Last Will and Testament of Cecil John Rhodes* by William T. Stead published in 1902 upon Rhodes' death, as you progress in learning about this topic.

What Cecil Rhodes set up was a strategy to re-colonize America; he took the existing desire to do so (on behalf of the British Empire which had desired to do so since 1781, but lacked a viable strategy), added money (Rhodes controlled De Beers diamond mines as well as gold mines in South Africa), a plan for a secret society (funded by Rhodes' *Last Will and Testament* enacted in 1902), and a scholarship fund (Rhodes Scholarships) to ensure that his dream could become reality – without the consent of those to be governed by the effort. On the back of Rhodes' plan, America bonded with Britain through a very 'special relationship' which brought the agenda to the fore, through a strategy of imperialism cloaked in 'democracy'. During his life, Rhodes helped to create massive fortunes through his industrial efforts, on the backs of the African and Chinese slaves he used. Rhodes (with the aid of Kitchener) continued the use of concentration camps, and the system of institutionalized racism known as apartheid.

Not to digress, but to give you some insight into the Chinese slaves used to dig mines and build railroads in Africa for Rhodes and his cartel, many of them died along the way to earning the staggeringly low wage of $.05 per day; though Rhodes and his colleagues insured them each to the tune of $125, thus turning even the downside (of the slaves dying en route) into a profitable endeavor.[15]

After Rhodes' death in 1902, the Rhodes Scholarships were launched in accordance with Rhodes' *Last Will and Testament;* the British imperialists next formed an Anglo-American group called the Pilgrims Society in London and New York.[16] Rhodes' plan was adopted by a wider Anglophile[17] network, including several tax-exempt foundations (such as the Carnegie Foundation, Rockefeller Foundation, and later the Ford Foundation) as his acolytes (in favor of Rhodes' plan for Anglo-American Hegemony) took hold of the American reigns through the Woodrow Wilson presidency. They set up a private corporation called The Federal Reserve Bank (1913) to issue America's currency, and were instrumental in getting America into World War I (and World War II for that matter). They enabled and delivered Lenin[18] and the Bolsheviks, presided over the Versailles Treaty, founded the Royal Institute of International Affairs (1919) and the Council on Foreign Relations (1921), and then proceeded to

15. *Hidden History: The Secret Origins of the First World War* by Docherty and Macgregor (2013), p. 52

16. The Pilgrims Society, according to its founder Joseph Choate (Boston Brahmin), was founded in 1902 *"to promote good-will, good-fellowship, and everlasting peace between the United States and Great Britain."* Members include Henry Kissinger, Walter Cronkite, Thomas Kean (9-11 Commissioner), members of the British Royal Family and Ambassadors between the U.S. and United Kingdom.

17. The Oxford English Dictionary defines "Anglophile" as a noun used to mean "One who is friendly to England"; though in this foreword I use it to mean a fondness for the British monarchy and/or loyal to the idea of the British Empire re-colonizing America (as Rhodes' Last Will mandates).

18. *Wall Street and the Bolshevik Revolution* by Antony C. Sutton

help finance and militarize the Nazis. It was around this time in the 1920's and 30's where Sean describes the activities of William Yandell Elliott, a Rhodes Scholar and member of Franklin D. Roosevelt's "Brain Trust" of advisors shaping American policies. Elliott, whose work clearly reflects a continuity of Cecil Rhodes' *Last Will and Testament,* became a National Security Advisor and had several famous protégés – namely Henry Kissinger (acolyte of Nelson Rockefeller) and Zbigniew Brzezinski (acolyte of Nelson's brother David Rockefeller). Studying this topic surely can teach you about how the world really works, and I always enjoy finding new nuggets of information to help me see the world more clearly.

Just this morning I was reviewing the archive of personal correspondence between Lionel Curtis (a prime mover in Cecil Rhodes' secret society) and Allen Dulles (an internationalist who served the Rhodes agenda while Director of CIA); they were *very close friends* to say the least. Maybe John F. Kennedy thought they were *too* close, or maybe he disagreed with their agenda; it remains to be seen, and maybe history has been waiting for you to throw your hat in the game and join the search for answers.

We in America have a *blind spot*: we think that in order to learn the history of our country, we need only know about the Americans in that story – and that is a formidable error to contend with. As Sean demonstrates, until you understand the 'British angle' of the story (sorry for the pun if you caught it), you're not seeing the big picture. It means learning the names and history of the men left out of the American version of these stories. Aside from Cecil Rhodes and his benefactor Lord Rothschild, it's useful to know the following characters, in case you'd like to look them up before you embark on this line of study: Lord Alfred Milner, Lionel Curtis, L.S. Amery, Alfred Zimmern, William Yandell Elliott, Frank Aydelotte, Sir Edward Grey, Lord Halifax, and Lord Lothian. These men are the focus of a study on the "Inner Circle" of books which I list at the end of this Foreword; learning about them unveils this whole line of research, for their actions have determined the course of the 20th and thus far, the 21st century. A new term, "Democide" (or death of citizens by their own government) had to be coined just to describe how prolific the death tolls were from this group's activities and creations in the 20th century. The "Democide Study"[19] conducted by Rudolph Rummel at the University of Hawaii in 1994 has been updated for the years 1900-1999, a time during which approximately 262 million citizens were killed at the hands of their own government, stating "Just to give perspective on this incredible murder by government, if all these bodies were laid head to toe, with the average height being 5', then they would circle the earth ten times. Also, this democide murdered 6 times more people than died in combat in all the

19. Democide statistics: *Death by Government* (1994) and *Power Kills* (1997), by professor Rudolph J. Rummel, University of Hawaii

foreign and internal wars of the century. Finally, given popular estimates of the dead in a major nuclear war, this total democide is as though such a war did occur, but with its dead spread over a century." History's most evil mass-murderers (Germany's Hitler, Soviet Union's Lenin and Stalin, China's Mao[20], Cambodia's Pol Pot[21], et al.) were enabled, funded, and protected by the participants of the Rhodes agenda.[22,23]

A few interesting books the Anglophiles printed during the early 1900's – which are off the radar of most Americans, and which all just happen to point to the conversion of the British Empire to a World Government – using America as the stepping stone: *The Pan Angles: A Consideration of the Federation of the Seven English-speaking Nations* by Sinclair Kennedy (1915), *The Third British Empire: Being a Course of Lectures Delivered at Columbia University, New York* by Alfred Zimmern (1934), and *Civitas Dei: The Commonwealth of God* (1934) by the utopian socialist and Rhodes group quarterback Lionel Curtis calling for World Government. On the shoulders of those ideas, the architects in charge of manifesting Rhodes' legacy published *The City of Man: A Declaration on World Democracy* in 1940, and Sean shines a spotlight on this book in particular by tracing the consequences of its ideology, which seeded a movement called World Federalism, and these ideas are still in full-force today. During the interim between then and now, Rhodes' agenda was broken up into working groups, and here are the primary books which explain them individually: *Shadows of Power: The Council on Foreign Relations and the American Decline* by James Perloff (1988), *The True Story of the Bilderberg Group* by Daniel Estulin (2009), and *Trilaterals over America* by Patrick Wood and Antony Sutton (1978).

There are also signs that there were a few people within our own government during the past century who tried to call public attention to this story; in 1914 (and again in 1917 when America joined World War I) in an article circulated titled "United States to be British: The Will of Cecil Rhodes," describing Rhodes' secret society, the goal of which was the "Ul-

20. David Rockefeller in his article "From a China Traveler" (10 August 1973, *New York Times*) stated "One is impressed immediately by the sense of national harmony.... Whatever the price of the Chinese Revolution it has obviously succeeded ... in fostering high morale and community purpose. General social and economic progress is no less impressive.... The enormous social advances of China have benefited greatly form the singleness of ideology and purpose.... The social experiment in China under Chairman Mao's leadership is one of the most important and successful in history."

21. "Who Supported the Khmer Rouge?" by Gary Elich, 16 October 2014, via Counterpunch.org; "According to journalist Elizabeth Becker, U.S. National Security Advisor Zbigniew Brzezinski "himself claims that he concocted the idea of persuading Thailand to cooperate fully with China in its efforts to rebuild the Khmer Rouge." Brzezinski said, "I encouraged the Chinese to support Pol Pot... Pol Pot was an abomination. We could never support him, but China could."

22. See Antony C. Sutton's 'Wall Street Trilogy' listed in the Outer Circle of books at the end of this foreword

23. See *The Anglo American Establishment: From Rhodes to Cliveden* by Carroll Quigley

timate Recovery of the United States of America as an Integral Part in the British Empire."[24,25] In the February 14th, 1917, edition of the *New York Times,* congressman Oscar Callaway of Texas warned the public why this important scheme to undermine America wasn't making it on their radar, citing the Rhodes plan in action: "In March, 1915, the J.P. Morgan interests, the steel, shipbuilding, and powder interest, and their subsidiary organizations, got together twelve men high up in the newspaper world and employed them to select the most influential newspapers in the United States and sufficient number of them to control generally the policy of the daily press.... They found it was only necessary to purchase the control of twenty-five of the greatest papers. An agreement was reached; the policy of the papers was bought, to be paid for by the month; an editor was furnished for each paper to properly supervise and edit information regarding the questions of preparedness, militarism, financial policies, and other things of national and international nature considered vital to the interests of the purchasers." If you think that quote is 'too bad to be true', here's what you need to search out for confirmation: Congressional Record of February 9, 1917, page 2947. Last but not least, there's the dozens of pages of testimony entered into the Congressional Record of the 76th Congress, Third Session, by the Honorable J. Thorkelson of Montana on August 19, 1940, which opens with these words: "In order that the American people may have a clearer understanding of those who over a period of years have been undermining this Republic, in order to return it to the British Empire, I have inserted in the RECORD a number of articles to prove this point. These articles are entitled "Steps Toward British Union, a World State, and International Strife." This is part I, and in this I include a hope expressed by Mr. Andrew Carnegie, in his book entitled *Triumphant Democracy*. In this he expresses himself in this manner: 'Let men say what they will, I say that as surely as the sun in the heavens once shone upon Britain and America united, so surely is it one morning to rise, to shine upon, to greet again the reunited states – the British-American Union.'"

These public servants (Callaway, Thorkelson) were pointing accurately at the elephant in the living room, but without the press to disseminate these truths, you're possibly just now learning about this agenda to create world government by piggy-backing on America. That's why it was necessary to buy influence in twenty-five of the greatest newspapers in 1917, so you wouldn't know about this trend of neo-colonialism until now.

---

24. "United States to be British: The Will of Cecil Rhodes" appeared in *Issues and Events* (a weekly magazine) Vol. VI No. 14, New York, April 7, 1917; it was reprinted from the December 5, 1914 *Issues and Events* weekly; this is found in "*Issues and Events, Volumes 4-6*" listed by Google books.

25. *The Last Will and Testament of Cecil John Rhodes with Elucidatory Notes to which are added some chapters describing the Political and Religious Ideas of the Testator* edited by William T. Stead (a Member of the Rhodes Round Table Group), published by *Review of Reviews*, London, 1902

Aside from the aforementioned congressmen, a professor from an esteemed university also caught wind of these events, and attempted to expose their plans to the general public; his name was Carroll Quigley, and after attending Harvard, teaching at Princeton, and consulting the Department of Defense, he published a history book during his time as a professor at Georgetown's School of Foreign Service. Quigley was a professional historian, not a *conspiracy theorist,* and after 20 years of studying the records of the Rhodes legacy (including the archives of the Council on Foreign Relations and Royal Institute of International Affairs) he published *Tragedy and Hope: A History of the World in Our Time,* in 1966. *Tragedy and Hope* contained the seeds of disclosing the Rhodes legacy unfolding in America, and Quigley followed this up with *The Anglo American Establishment,* which is a condensed detailing of how the conspiracy against freedom actually works. Quigley mentored a young Rhodes Scholar named Bill Clinton[26] during his time at Georgetown. Quigley himself was mentored by an earlier Rhodes Scholar (Crane Brinton), and was granted access to the secret records and proceedings of the participants in Rhodes' inner and outer circles because of his acumen for this topic- that is the source material for *The Anglo American Establishment*. Quigley can later be heard, in his own words, in the interview recordings conducted with Rudy Maxa of the *Washington Post,* to write the article "The Professor Who Knew Too Much" published on March 23, 1975. In the interview tapes, Quigley can be heard describing how the printing plates to the book were destroyed by its British publisher, Macmillan (making it nearly impossible to republish *Tragedy and Hope*), how Quigley himself was lied to by the publisher, how *Tragedy and Hope* was cut in half and re-published under the title *The World Since 1939: A History,* which essentially censored the entire first half of Quigley's 1300-page magnum opus, and completely concealed the Anglo-American origins of the story. It's ironic that what I just told you really does *not* make it into Rudy Maxa's *Washington Post* article, *even though it's in the recordings*. I'd like to give you some insight into the difference between the 'controlled press' of the *Washington Post* and the real investigative history being offered in this article "Professor Carroll Quigley and the Article that Said Too Little" by Kevin Cole – who wrote his article directly from the interview's audio recordings:

> "It is during this period of the audio interview that Quigley is preparing to talk about some of the controversy behind the publishing and lack of promotion of "*Tragedy and Hope,*" that he (Quigley) says "I don't know if you want to put this on tape ... you have

26. William Jefferson Clinton thanked Carroll Quigley in his Presidential Inauguration speech, owing his success to his Oxford connections.

> to protect my future ... as well as your own." Quigley states that Macmillan was purchased for 5 million dollars in the summer of 1966 by Collier Books, which he confirms had been a J.P. Morgan company, and that the Morgan interests had bought up the free press.... By 1968, the book was out of print. Collier then brought back the last half of *Tragedy and Hope* as a paperback entitled, *The World Since 1939: A History* all the while continuing to tell everyone that *Tragedy and Hope* was out of print ... he (Quigley) stated they "*had lied to me so many times.*" They "*lied and lied and lied and lied to me*" and also to his publisher Peter Ritner, who had disclosed previously that he thought *Tragedy and Hope* was 'marvelous.'"

I also want to pull another quote directly from the transcript, lest there be some contention on this point: "QUIGLEY: ...if they're out of print or not, you see. And they said 'no,' and so forth. Now, oh, oh, the big thing is. My contract, both, had in it that, if it went out of print, I had the right to recover the plates." RUDY MAXA: "Right." QUIGLEY: "They never got in touch with me offering the plates. I learned in March of this year that they destroyed the plates, of *Tragedy and Hope*. I learned in the summer, 1971, because my wife got mad and called Macmillan on the phone, every week, while I was in England, and finally got from them a letter in which they said the plates had been destroyed. They said 'inadvertently destroyed.'"

I would also offer that the "British angle" is almost always veiled with claims of National Security, and the terms of British secrecy are far longer than the American policies in cases where the "special relationship" is involved;[27,28] might I suggest that the JFK files are still classified because there is British involvement, which allows the U.S. government to conveniently keep those files from public view. Embedded in those conveniently still-secret documents is the Anglo-American Establishment's influence in setting up Saudi Arabia, and its support of proxy armies to act as tailor-made enemies. Recently, after being suppressed for over a decade, the "28-redacted pages" from the *9-11 Commission Report* were released to the public; a disclosure which yields embarrassing details for the U.S., British, and Saudi governments to say the least. It's clear from reading them that the Saudi government was aided in their placement of the hijackers in the U.S.[29] – *aided by those tasked with protecting the rights of American citizens*. One wonders what three characters fit in many of those

27. "Official Secrecy Fostered Coverup" by Len Ackland, *Bulletin of the Atomic Scientists*, Vol. 41 No. 4, April 1985, p. 2

28. "Keeping America Un-Informed: Government Secrecy in the 1980s" reviewed by Gerald Marsh, *Bulletin of the Atomic Scientists*, Vol. 41 No. 4, p. 58

29. "Declassified 9/11 pages show ties to former Saudi ambassador" by Erin Kelly, July 15, 2016 via *USA Today*

redactions – CIA? MI6? *Who is conveniently and consistently protecting the terrorists? Could these redactions protect an agenda in progress?*

Sean takes great care to describe how the British Empire silently transformed from control of territory to more *illusory* stratagems for gaining total control of the planet's resources (both natural and human), such as using the cloak of corporate personhood to create multinational corporations which quietly usurp control of governments around the world. This plan then led to the origin of the World Bank and International Monetary Fund as well as the United Nations to set up the framework – or skeleton – for 'world government' (a.k.a. globalism).

Also worth mentioning is the under-current of the Anglo-American Establishment which was launched after World War II through NATO; often it is called "Operation Gladio," but that's really just the codename for the Italian branch of the operation, which nonetheless has become a slang term for all of the secret armies and operations (around the world) created by Winston Churchill and MI6 and maintained by the CIA throughout the cold war. Initiated in 1940, Gladio was not admitted publicly until fifty years later; even then, recognition of such a top-secret endeavor was begrudgingly tolerated when the Italian Prime Minister Giulio Andreotti revealed it to the world on October 24, 1990. Operation Gladio is often credited with the assassination of Italian Prime Minister Aldo Moro in 1978 (via the Red Brigades), so Andreotti was courageous for making this useful disclosure.

Another disclosure made twenty years after the death of Aldo Moro is the "*Contra Cocaine*" report[30,31] by the CIA's own Inspector General, Frederick Hitz[32], who concluded that the Reagan administration "*tolerated cocaine trafficking into the United States under the umbrella of the contra war in Nicaragua... and that CIA hid the evidence*"[33]

I have read many books related to this topic and specifically to the group of non-elected rulers who Sean diligently tracks throughout this book, but this is the only book which takes a selection of the key players and traces their influence directly to today's world – namely Henry

30. Source Document: *Statement of Frederick P. Hitz, Inspector General, Central Intelligence Agency, Before the Permanent Select Committee on Intelligence, United States House of Representatives: Regarding investigation of allegations of connections between CIA and The Contras in drug trafficking to the United States Volume I: The California Story, Volume II: The Contra Story,* 16 March 1998

31. In paragraph 623 in Volume II, the report details a cable from the Directorate of Operations for CIA, dated October 22, 1982, describing a potential meeting with Contra leaders for "an exchange in [the United States] of narcotics for arms" via *Central Intelligence Agency Inspector General Report of Investigation Allegations of Connections Between CIA and the Contras in Cocaine Trafficking to the United States (96-0143-IG) Volume II: The Contra Story.*

32. "C.I.A. Says It Used Nicaraguan Rebels Accused of Drug Tie" by James Risen, July 17, 1998, via *New York Times.*

33. Source Document: *Lost History: The Contras, Cocaine, the Press & Project Truth* by Iran Contra journalist Robert Parry, p. 243.

Kissinger and Zbigniew Brzezinski – as the conspiracy to control the human resources of this planet continues to unfold. I recently read Kissinger's new book *World Order* (2015), and the book you're about to read is a much more accurate representation of this topic. Kissinger is writing to the uninformed public, as a measure to let them think they know something without learning anything true in the process. His message: "Go Back to Sleep."

Kissinger has top-level access to the real facts, and yet he leads his audience on a pseudo-tour – pointing out everything except that which would be of real interest to readers – how power actually operates in the real world. The bête noire of the mythical tales spun by Kissinger and his ilk are the facts of the Rhodes' agenda, which are readily available for review.

One can only assume that Kissinger can access what you can easily find on the Internet, namely: *Formal Complaint to DoD Inspector General re: JFIC and Congressional Inquiry*[34] (or you can search "FOIA Iron Man Documents 2011") which is a Defense Intelligence Agency response to a Freedom Of Information Act request pertaining to what the U.S. government (and therefore the British government) knew in July of 2000; specifically on page three that the agency held a briefing entitled "The WMD threat to the U.S.," which indicated that "World Trade Centers #1 and #2 were the most likely buildings to be attacked, followed closely by the Pentagon. The briefer indicated that the worst case scenario would be one tower collapsed onto the other. The possibility of striking the buildings with a plane may have been discussed then – it was certainly discussed in the red cell analysis leading up to the briefing ... (redacted) proposed in the red cell analysis that the building could be struck by a jetliner" further relating "the most likely cities to be attacked: New York City and Washington D.C." And yet, the 9-11 terrorist attacks[35] were successful in bringing that meeting's projections to life.

If you, like me, asked the question "*How did the Saudi hijackers do that?*," the roots of that answer begin with understanding the facts and details organized by Sean throughout this book, and are covered in great detail in books #8, #9, and #10 in the "Outer Circle" list at the end of this Foreword. Those are books Kissinger definitely doesn't want you to read.

---

34. "Condi Rice: Here's Your 9/11 Smoking Gun" by Kristen Breitweiser, 9/11 Widow and Activist, 30 October 2015, as published by *The Huffington Post*. Breitweiser notes "As proof, I provide the "Iron Man" documents from the Asymmetrical Threats Division of Joint Forces Intelligence Command (JFIC), also known as DO5, whose task it was to track UBL from mid-1998-mid 2001." (The Iron Man document is linked and you can read it for yourself)

35. The terrorist attacks of September 11, 2001, resulted in the de-verticalization of three world-class skyscrapers in New York City, as well as the recently-reinforced side of the Pentagon which housed the accountants investigating the $2.3 trillion missing from the Department of Defense. See also: "Army history unit piecing together accounts of Pentagon attack" by Milan Simonich, December 16, 2001, via *Pittsburgh Post-Gazette*

The globalists are hoping to enact world government before we learn the true history which will emancipate us from childish myths of how the world works.

In a modern sense of this story, we live in the 'post-9/11 world', where the USA PATRIOT ACT (I'm not shouting, it's actually an acronym for "*Uniting and Strengthening America by Providing Appropriate Tools Required to Intercept and Obstruct Terrorism Act of 2001*") is selectively interpreted in secret to make heretofore illegal violations of our Bill of Rights 'legal' in the name of keeping us safe – instead of securing our rights. This contradiction for the most part goes unchallenged, unless you're a whistleblower.

In 2013 a whistleblower from the U.S. National Security Agency (NSA) disclosed a series of PowerPoint presentation slides, which detailed how American citizens are spied on and their private data collected and catalogued by the government[36]. The slides demonstrated the unfathomable lengths and inestimable budgets involved in conducting mass surveillance. Many of the slides credit the authors: the British "NSA" which is called GCHQ (Government Communications Headquarters), which acts as a *Big Brother*[37] to the NSA. I'm looking forward to learning more about how the history in this book is intersected by Snowden's disclosures, and who benefits from this mass surveillance. I also plan on reading *How America Lost Its Secrets: Edward Snowden, the Man and the Theft* by Edward Jay Epstein, and screening the film *SNOWDEN* by director Oliver Stone; both compositions are slated for release in late 2016.

The agents continuing to carry out the manifestation of Cecil Rhodes' *Last Will and Testament* publish their plans for our future, projecting the path to their world domination in a series of documents known as "Global Strategic Trends Programme" which are, still publicly available on the British Ministry of Defense and American Council on Foreign Relations websites.[38]

James Traub, a member of the Council on Foreign Relations and heir to the Bloomingdale's fortune, recently published a thought-piece in *For-*

36. "New Snowden Doc Reveals How GCHQ/NSA Use The Internet To 'Manipulate, Deceive And Destroy Reputations'" by Mike Masnick, 25 February 2014, published by TechDirt.com. "A few weeks ago, Glenn Greenwald, while working with NBC News, revealed some details of a GCHQ presentation concerning how the surveillance organization had a "dirty tricks" group known as JTRIG – the Joint Threat Research Intelligence Group." At the bottom of the article, note "The Art of Deception" quote alongside the GCHQ logo with a crown over it.

37. In George Orwell's 1949 novel *1984* the term "Big Brother" denotes mass surveillance efforts by the English Socialist (IngSoc) non-elected government described in the dystopian setting.

38. "Global Strategic Trends out to 2045" by U.K. Ministry of Defence, 30 June 2014, part of the DCDC Strategic Trends Programme. Description: "The 5th edition of Global Strategic Trends, published by the Development, Concepts and Doctrine Centre (DCDC), describes a future context for defence and security out to 2045." Also mirrored on the Council on Foreign Relations website.

eign Policy titled "It's Time for the Elites to Rise Up Against the Ignorant Masses: The Brexit has laid bare the political schism of our time. It's not about the left vs. the right; it's about the sane vs. the mindlessly angry." [39]

What ever happened to the 1993 *Toward A New World Order* plan of George Soros? For the past few decades Soros has been busy combining his wealth and influence with the crowd-control techniques of a Bostonian named Gene Sharp. The *New York Times* provided further insight in its article[40] of February 16, 2011, "Few Americans have heard of Mr. Sharp. But for decades, his practical writings on nonviolent revolution – most notably "From Dictatorship to Democracy," a 93-page guide to toppling autocrats, available for download in twenty-four languages – have inspired dissidents around the world, including in Burma, Bosnia, Estonia and Zimbabwe, and now Tunisia and Egypt." The article went on to mention, "In 2008, Iran featured Mr. Sharp, along with Senator John McCain of Arizona and the Democratic financier George Soros, in an animated propaganda video that accused Mr. Sharp of being the CIA agent 'in charge of America's infiltration into other countries,' an assertion his fellow scholars find ludicrous." I'll leave it up to you to make your own decision on Gene Sharp. Personally I don't think he's a conspirator, as Soros uses Sharp's methods for a purpose which seems to be antithetical to why Sharp created them, but I will offer what another *New York Times* article[41] on June 16, 2011 (via Reuters) had to relate, so you can make an informed decision on Soros' participation in popular uprisings around the world:

> The fourth lesson of Central Europe for the Arab Spring came from the founder and chief benefactor of Central European University – George Soros. Mr. Soros, who fled Budapest as a teenager and made his fortune in the United States, suggested that the history of his homeland offered an example for the Arab revolutions that was both cruelly realistic and ultimately inspiring. "Reflecting on the Arab revolutions, one very important factor is that people were willing to sacrifice their lives for a common cause," Mr. Soros said. "That is a memory, a historic event, that will change those countries forever. It is irreversible."

Recently the British people chose to Exit from the European Union (abbreviated BREXIT in modern parlance), which was a move that really threw some obstacles in front of Soros' plan *Toward a New World Order:*

39. "It's Time for the Elites to Rise Up Against the Ignorant Masses" by James Traub, *Foreign Policy,* June 28, 2016

40. "Shy U.S. Intellectual Created Playbook Used in a Revolution" by Sheryl Gay Stolberg, 16 February 2011 via *New York Times*

41. "Lessons From Central Europe for the Arab Spring" by Chrystia Freeland, Reuters 16 June 2011 via *New York Times*

the Future of NATO from 1993. A simple "Soros + BREXIT" search triggers an avalanche of articles where Soros laments the British exit – probably because the European Union was about to militarize and thus take sovereignty away from E.U. nations – and now many countries realize that they could likewise leave the E.U., following the British example. I for one am optimistic that the British voters have started to catch on to the pattern of tyranny unfolding, though I know it will likely be another six months before anything actually happens with BREXIT, and with the cast of characters involved – anything can happen. While we wait on BREXIT, Soros is busy trying to re-kindle the Cold War between the NATO countries and Russia, threatening the planet with the potential for a nuclear war. Why would anyone do this? One quote from the time of Soros' writing *Toward a New World Order: The Future of NATO* (1993) manifesto, which might reflect some of his motivations:

> "It is sort of a disease when you consider yourself some kind of god, the creator of everything, but I feel comfortable about it now since I began to live it out." George Soros, as quoted in *The Independent,* June 2nd, 1993.[42]

As far as the coming presidential election here in America, the 2016 candidates have both taken money from George Soros; according to campaign finance records Hillary Clinton (who is an avowed World Federalist, along with the late Walter Cronkite)[43] has accepted at least $6 million directly from Soros, not to mention his contributions to the Clinton Foundation, and it appears that Donald Trump borrowed up to $160 million from George Soros and two other hedge funds[44] to build Trump Tower in Chicago in 2004. Whatever happens, it won't be too far from the agenda of the New World Order.

With that all being read, the view of this topic as *conspiracy theory* is a model which has become obsolete in the wake of reading this book – such accusations can only occur in a vacuum where the party who wields such phrases has not based their perspectives on objective evidence and facts (now) readily available literally at your fingertips.

---

43. As cited in "The billionaire who built on chaos: Gail Counsell charts the rise of a speculator who considers himself 'some kind of god' " by Gail Counsell, Wednesday 2 June 1993, via *The Independent*

43. It's worth viewing the 17 minute video which results from searching "Hillary Clinton + Walter Cronkite" where they discuss their participation in the *World Federalist* movement and the New World Order.

44. "Big names back Trump tower: Soros, Deutsche Bank said to be in on 90-story building" by Thomas A. Corfman, 28 October 2004, published in the *Chicago Tribune*. "Donald Trump has lined up three New York hedge funds, including money from billionaire George Soros, to invest $160 million in his Chicago skyscraper, a key piece in perhaps the largest construction financing in the city's history, according to real estate sources and public documents."

REVIVING FREEDOM

Collective ignorance does not equal wisdom. This historical information is hidden in order to deny you making informed choices; so that you make serious decisions based on false information, and by the time you find out it's 'too late' to do anything. This situation is reversible, and it begins with learning that the controls enacted against individuals mostly involve stimulus and response – without thinking in between. In my humble opinion, it begins with reading to learn what has been missing from our education.

It's time to outgrow the fear of being called a *conspiracy theorist.* You're smart enough to know that there are important details being left out of the story we're all being told, and you're trying to fill them in by searching out the evidence, observing, and weighing the facts to make your own decisions.

The agenda of the New World Order is in jeopardy, as people are sharing credible information with each other – and this is putting the plans of globalism, internationalism, and world government at risk. Recent articles such as "*With Globalization in Danger, G-20 Double Down on Defense*"[45] and "*IMF Calls on G20 to Boost Positive Image of Globalization*"[46] we are seeing cracks in the façade of the Empire, and our chipping away at tyranny is revealing a struggle for local accountability – freedom and liberty for all individuals. You (and everyone you know) are participating in this story, the least we can do as individuals is become knowledgeable about how it works.

Before you depart for the rest of this book, I want to leave you with a short-list of resources to aid your journey *after* you finish Sean's thesis. The "Inner Circle" of books[47] I find to be of great value if read in close proximity (time-wise) to each other, they all present complimentary views, with very little redundancy (from a variety of sources) of what I'd call the "*British Re-Conquest of America,*" all of which intersect with the history exposed in this book. On the list for the Inner Circle read #1 last, as it's the most challenging book listed.

The "Outer Circle" of books describe the consequences of the Inner Circle's activities, like waves going out on a pond after you throw a stone. And keep in mind, that while you're observing the waves of causality resultant from the secrecy of the agenda, those waves can be canceled out by those who expose those secrets.

---

45. *Bloomberg News,* July 24, 2016

46. *Sputnik News,* July 21, 2016

47. Cecil Rhodes organized his secret society with "rings within rings" to preserve the secrecy of his plan, the Inner Circle of initiates being close to the agenda itself, and the Outer Circle being people who participated in the agenda but weren't necessarily 'in the know' of its real aims.

This reading list will give you a better education on how the world works and a more accurate version of history of the 20th century than any university on the planet can afford to offer. That would definitely be an advantage over anyone who ceases to think for themselves when hearing "*conspiracy theory*," instead of embarking on a personal journey of discovery.

Inner circle:

1. *Tragedy and Hope: A History of the World in Our Time* by Carroll Quigley
2. *Tragedy and Hope 101* by Joseph Plummer (condensed, easy-reading version of Quigley's T&H)
3. *The Anglo American Establishment: From Rhodes to Cliveden* by Carroll Quigley
4. *New World Order: A Strategy of Imperialism* by Sean Stone
5. *Lord Milner's Second War: The Rhodes-Milner Secret Society, The Origin of World War I, and the start of the New World Order* by John Cafferky
6. *Hidden History: Secret Origins of the First World War* by Docherty & Macgregor
7. *Selling War: The British Propaganda Campaign Against America in World War II* by Nicholas John Cull (published by Oxford)
8. *The Irregulars: Roald Dahl and the British Spy Ring in Wartime Washington* by Jennet Conant (author Ian Fleming was one of the British spies in the spy ring working to get America into World War II)

Outer circle:

1. *Wall Street and the Bolsheviks, Wall Street and the Nazis, Wall Street and FDR* by professor Antony C. Sutton (aka 'Wall Street Trilogy' of books by Sutton)
2. *Superclass: The Global Elite and the World They Are Making* by David Rothkopf (brought to you by the Carnegie Foundation and Kissinger Associates)
3. *The Underground History of American Education* by John Taylor Gatto
4. *Fleshing Out Skull and Bones: Investigations Into America's Most Powerful Secret Society* Edited by Kris Millegan
5. *The Double-Cross System: The Incredible Story Of How Nazi Spies Were Turned Into Double Agents* by John Cecil Masterman (former director of British MI6 during WWII; admits they knew about Pearl Harbor prior to the event, and let it happen)

6. *A Man Called Intrepid: The Incredible WWII Narrative Of The Hero Whose Spy Network And Secret Diplomacy Changed The Course Of History* by William Stevenson
7. *NATO's Secret Armies: Operation Gladio and Terrorism in Western Europe* by Daniele Ganser
8. *Dope, Inc.: Britain's Opium War Against the World* by Executive Intelligence Review (EIR)
9. *Secret Affairs: Britain's Collusion with Radical Islam* by Mark Curtis (a research fellow at Britain's Royal Institute of International Affairs)
10. *The Terror Factory: Inside the FBI's Manufactured War on Terror* by Trevor Aaronson
11. *The Hidden History of 9-11* edited by professor Paul Zarembka
12. *Black 9-11: Money Motive and Technology* by Mark Gaffney
13. *Technocracy Rising: The Trojan Horse of Global Transformation* by Patrick Wood
14. Anything published by Peter Dale Scott, F. William Engdahl, Daniel Hopsicker, G. Edward Griffin, and Kris Millegan via TrineDay Publishing

Online Resources:

TragedyAndHope.com provides educational media created to inspire *cognitive liberty,* based on all of the above I just mentioned; conveniently available in podcasts, videos, documentary films, and my interactive *History Blueprint* model which is designed to expedite your learning curve with respect to these topics.

Where to begin? Try *Peace Revolution* episode 082: *The British Elephant in the American Living Room / The Empire Always Listens and Never Forgets.*

You're now prepared to *make the existing model obsolete.* Thank you, for tuning in- and not dropping out!

Richard Grove
Forensic Historian,
TragedyAndHope.com
Hartford, Connecticut, U.S.A.
July 22, 2016

New World Order:
A Strategy of Imperialism

Sean Stone

Professor Antony Sutton

An Introduction to World Order

The Order [of Skull and Bones] is neither left nor right. "Left" and "right" are artificial devices to bring about change, and the extremes of political "left" and political "right" are vital elements in a process of controlled change.[1]

– Antony C. Sutton, *The Order of Skull and Bones*

The phrase "new world order" has struck a chord in both conspiracy theory and popular parlance since at least 1971's publication of John Birch Society member Gary Allen's *None Dare Call it Conspiracy*. Whether blamed on a satanic Illuminati conspiracy, or atheistic communism, the conspiracy theory focuses on the centralization of government and finance for collective global control. The methods used for such a conspiracy are often perceived through the lens of Hegelian dialectic of left-right conflict, ultimately leading to a synthesis of the two extremes. Professor Anthony Sutton, a Fellow at the Hoover Institute where he began research for his groundbreaking books on the American Blueblood secret society of Yale's Skull and Bones, claimed that such a struggle ultimately led to the increased power of the state over its people.

Sutton's thesis may have found an unlikely affirmation in 1992 from former National Security Advisor Zbigniew Brzezinski, who wrote an article for the Council on Foreign Relations' *Foreign Affairs,* wherein he bluntly asserted that the Cold War's premise of freeing the people of Eastern Europe from communism "was a strategic sham, designed to a significant degree for domestic political reasons ... the policy was basically rhetorical, at most tactical."[2] Thus, if the global war against communism furthered the domestic political interests, it might follow that Sutton's argument is accurate, in that secret societies such as Skull and Bones operate to control the left-right paradigm to further government controls over a nation.

However, this book does not intend to argue that the new world order is designed to enhance the power of any single nation, but rather, to transcend the traditional roles played by nation-states. In the words of former Secretary of State and National Security Advisor Henry Kissinger,

> ... the spread of democracy was therefore the overarching goal for international order. Free markets would uplift individuals, enrich societies, and substitute interdependence for traditional interna-

> tional rivalries. In this view, the Cold War was caused by the aberrations of Communism; sooner or later, the Soviet Union would return to the community of nations. Then *a new world order* would encompass all regions of the globe; shared values and goals would render conditions within states more humane and conflicts between states less likely" (emphasis added).[3]

Upon the ending of the Cold War, his successor as National Security Advisor, Zbigniew Brzezinski went further in predicting the demise of the nation-state, for "in the long run, global politics are bound to become increasingly uncongenial to the concentration of hegemonic power in the hands of a single state. Hence, America is not only the first, as well as the only, truly global superpower, but it is also likely to be the very last."[4] For power is an end in itself, and the vehicle to achieve that power has transformed through time, from the rise of city-states to kingdoms to empires, and currently nations. Presiding behind the national government's system of legislative control sits the money-temple that issues the currency by which the state, and the people therein, transact to trade their goods and labor.

It then comes as little surprise that international bankers such as James Warburg would promote the push toward international solidarity in order to control currencies on a global scale. Warburg, a Council on Foreign Relations (CFR) member and son of the investment banker Paul Warburg,[5] declared in 1950, "we shall have world government, whether or not we like it. The question is only whether world government will be achieved by consent or by conquest."[6] In truth, the question should have been, will the American constitutional tradition of its 10th Amendment allow for this new world government; meaning, will "the powers not delegated to the United States [federal government] by the Constitution, nor prohibited by it to the States, [stay] reserved to the States respectively, or to the people"?

History has in fact seen the rise of world governments, in the form of empires, from whose capitols the elite have embarked on mercantile ventures to acquire access to trade. The centers of the empires, even when reflecting a form of representative government for the "homeland," have rarely evinced much concern for the welfare of the peoples in the peripheral domains. Thus, the American experiment in federated government was in truth the progenitor of a novel concept of autonomous states governed from the center in conjunction with the consent of the states that constitute the "United States." Despite America's expansion beyond the initial thirteen states in the 19th Century, Thomas Jefferson's conception of an "empire of liberty" was meant to express a vision of American sovereignty committed to principles of freedom and self-determination against European colonialism. Certainly his decision to extend the new country with the Louisiana Purchase at the start of the 19th Century began a geographic expansion that would end with the protectorate over the Philippines in Asia in 1898. Thus, by the 20th Century, America was confronted with the challenge of ruling as a world power stretched beyond the Pacific Ocean, laying claim to peoples whom America had no intention of incorporating into its democratic processes.

It was upon this landscape, where the British, French, American, Austro-Hungarian, Russian, German, Portuguese, and Dutch empires encompassed the majority of the globe, that a clique of men in England foresaw the evolution of world government, modeled on the American federal system of concentric circles of power. It was, perhaps, the dream of the Novo Ordo Seclorum (New Order of the Ages) stamped by the founding fathers upon the great seal of the United States.[7] But could such a new world order be achieved by conquest, as Paul Warburg stated, without the consent of the governed?

According to William Yandell Elliott (1896-1979), professor of government at Harvard University for almost forty years, it was the French Enlightenment philosopher Jean-Jacques Rousseau who had launched the movement toward popular sovereignty in the 18th Century with his concept of the "social contract" between the ruler and ruled, whereby the consent of the governed would be guaranteed through a democratic process. Rousseau had sown the seeds of political liberalism by contending that only a government chosen by the majority of its people could serve the General Will of the community.

With the Cold War in its infant stages in 1949, W.Y. Elliott edited a political history of the West, wherein he contended that Rousseau's promise to "force men to be free" (through an obligation to respond to the bidding of the General Will) was no better than Marx's "dictatorship of the proletariat," since both lacked respect for the individual's moral responsibility.[8] Elliott thus looked to the skepticism of Immanuel Kant, for "reconciling individual self-interest with moral obligation."

It was Kant's Categorical Imperative, which accepted no *a priori* moral principles, asking instead that each person obey the golden rule by behaving as though his or her action could be universalized. According to Elliott, Kant saved the concept of popular sovereignty by maintaining the right of the individual to "accept or reject the moral values which he was asked by a community to obey," and thus preserving the rights of the minority against the majority's general will. But only by creating moral values for a community, as happens when people develop their own laws in a "constitutional" form of government, can they then arrive at a "shared morality and, through that, the respect for human rights."[9]

From the premise of shared morality under constitutionalism, Elliott surmised that world order would be achieved by constitutional states, in accordance with Kant's supposition that republican (i.e. constitutional) governments could agree upon international laws (from his 1795 essay on "Perpetual Peace"). Kant's ideal of a moral community had apparently been ratified in 1948 with the signing of the United Nations' Universal Declaration of Human Rights by the Western constitutional democracies, while the totalitarian Soviet bloc abstained.[10] The "universalized" moral principles hinged upon the American claim "of the equal and inalienable rights of all members of the human family" and stipulated Rousseau's political legacy that "the will of the people shall be the basis of the authority of government."

The signing of the Human Rights Declaration did not end, however, the "fundamental clash of values" between "totalitarianism and constitutionalism," which would lead inevitably, Elliott contended, to a "hot peace" or a "cold war." So long as totalitarian systems of coercion existed in the world, Elliott believed that a world order based on constitutional laws and agreements could not be secure. On the other hand, it could be argued that the very desire to wipe out totalitarian governments would only lead to what Columbia University History Professor Charles A. Beard called "perpetual war for perpetual peace," since the attempt to exterminate any ideology can only lead to endless wars. Predictably, such warfare would simultaneously transform the very principles of the warring state toward increased authoritarianism.

Such authoritarian tendencies in the United States can be traced to the creation of the National Security Council, Central Intelligence Agency and the consolidation of the Department of Defense under the National Security Act of 1947. Since that time, the United States has engaged in military deployments and foreign coups over seventy times, including military deployments to sequester domestic unrest in urban rioting. Parallel to the waging of wars without Congressional approval, since the declaration of war against Japan following Pearl Harbor, the abuse of constitutional rights on the domestic front has manifested in increased domestic surveillance, such as the post-Patriot Act National Security Agency program of collecting American citizens' Internet communications[11] and phone records,[12] ignoring the 4th Amendment's demand for "probable cause" before "unreasonable searches." The epitome of Executive restrictions on constitutional rights was demonstrated in the post-2012 National Defense Authorization Acts, which gave martial authority to indefinitely detain American citizens, against the 5th Amendment's promise of due process in trial. This mandate, of course, came under the Obama Administration, which had previously targeted an American citizen, Anwar Al-Awlaki, for assassination without due process of trial. He was executed along with three other American citizens in Yemen in 2011.

In the midst of this increasingly authoritarian approach to government, the American people have virtually disappeared from the electoral process, with the lowest voter turnout for the 2014 Congressional elections since 1942, at a time when America was committed to a total war in Europe and Asia. Thus, Elliott's bipolar world-view of constitutional democracies opposing autocratic regimes across the globe must be questioned, as we are left with the "post-Westphalian world" envisioned by Elliott and his intellectual allies, in their attempt to transform sovereign nation-states into universal states whose actions may no longer be circumscribed by national considerations or laws.

Since 1648, the Western political system had organized itself around the principles set forth in the Treaty of Westphalia, ending the 30 Years War between Protestant and Catholic principalities and states. The Treaty of Westphalia lay down terms for peace under the auspices of national self-determination, based on the practice of governments exerting authority only over their own lands and people. While European empires failed to respect the autonomy of colonized peoples across the globe, the concept of internal political sovereignty remained unquestioned throughout the 20th Century. When America challenged the Soviet Union during the Cold War, it was on the premise that Russia had violated the political sovereignty of Eastern European countries, particularly Poland, by absorbing them into a Soviet "Empire." However, the dawn of the 21st Century places the political discourse in an entirely new realm, where national sovereignty itself is in jeopardy.

When the Soviet Union was suffering economic and political collapse in 1991, President George H.W. Bush addressed Congress on the State of the Union to urge war against the Iraqi government, which had invaded its neighbor Kuwait the previous year. Bush stated, "What is at stake is more than one small country; it is a big idea: *a new world order*, where diverse nations are drawn together in common cause to achieve the universal aspirations of mankind – peace and security, freedom, and the rule of law." While the United States had depended upon an international coalition to justify its United Nations defense of South Korea against the Soviet-backed North in 1950, the United States was now untethered from its previous justification for foreign wars: to prevent the expansion of a rival great power.

Instead, the new world order asserted the demand for universal law as a pretense for America to insert itself into the dispute of two countries in the Middle East. From Bosnia, Kosovo and Iraq in the 1990s, to the ongoing military excursions in Afghanistan, Pakistan, Yemen and over 70 countries on a daily basis,[13] the United States is presenting a military show of force predicated on international law and humanitarian intervention, which holds little resemblance to a classical Augustinian "just war" doctrine of self-defense, or last resort. By 2011, when the Obama Administration was waging war, including tactical support and airstrikes on behalf of the North Atlantic Treaty Organization against the Libyan government of Muammar Gaddafi, such action was said to be justified by a United Nations Security Council Resolution "that authorizes the use of force solely to protect civilians and civilian populated areas under attack or threat of attack."[14] Yet, despite the lack of Congressional approval for war, the US-supported NATO campaign led to the ultimate demise of Qaddafi and his government.

This trajectory of US warfare for regime change had begun in 2003 when the United States and Great Britain paved the way to abolishing the old Westphalian world order under the motto of "spreading democracy" by overthrowing the sovereign, albeit autocratic, government of Saddam Hussein's Iraq. As Prime Minister Tony Blair, the man who spearheaded Britain's war against its former colony, explained in 2004,

> So, for me, *before Sept. 11,* I was already reaching for a different philosophy in international relations from a traditional one that has held sway since the Treaty of Westphalia in 1648.... We know now, if we didn't before, that our own self-interest is ultimately bound up with the fate of other nations. The doctrine of international community is no longer a vision of idealism. It is a practical recognition that just as within a country, citizens who are free, well educated, and prosperous tend to be responsible, to feel solidarity with a society in which they have a stake; so do nations that are free, democratic, and benefiting from economic progress, tend to be stable and solid partners in the advance of humankind. The best defense of our security lies in the spread of our values. But we cannot advance these values except within a framework that recognizes their universality. If it is a global threat, it needs a global response, *based on global rules*. (*emphasis added*).[15]

Rather than providing more security and stability, the dissolution of the Iraqi government, namely the Baath Party led by Saddam Hussein, led to a bloody sectarian war in Iraq through the 2000s before spilling over into neighboring Syria via a US-influenced coup effort against the autocratic government of Bashar al-Assad. By 2012, "the CIA-sponsored secret flow of arms from Libya to the Syrian opposition, via Turkey, had been underway for more than a year (it started sometime after [Libyan dictator Muammar] Gaddafi's death on 20 October 2011)."[16] The trouble that soon arose from arming rebel groups against the sovereign government in Syria found a political expression premised on many of the same post-Westphalian politics that the Anglo-Americans were pushing. The self-proclaimed Islamic State (a.k.a. ISIL, or ISIS) gave voice in mid-2014 to Sunni imperial politics, thus drawing recruits and mercenaries from across the Islamic world in an effort to "unite to destroy the present world and create a new-old world of universal justice and peace under the Prophet's banner."[17] In many ways, the movement of the Islamic State reflects the conditions of a community of shared, though often undemocratically forced, morality upon which a constitutional state can be formed.

Whether or not the Islamic State prevails to form a neo-Sunni Caliphate to further weaken the sovereignty of nation-states within the Middle East, it currently serves as a convenient rallying point for the Western powers, including Russia, to unite in their quest for a new world order of homogeneous morality predicated on the globalization of the "free" market. The essential position of the so-called "Middle East" at the axis of Europe, Asia and Africa turns this region into a foothold for socio-political and military access to those continents. Any challenge to corporate homogenization can be targeted by means of a permanent "war on terror" that increasingly violates traditional national borders.

Should the new world order fail to subdue the "rogue" and failed states, which aside from North Korea are centered around the Middle East, it is difficult to fathom the lengths to which the Western power structure might go to achieve that aim. One past proponent of the imperial world order, H.G. Wells, not only foresaw the deployment of nuclear energy for warfare in 1914, he also prophesied a time, such as our own, when warfare between nation-states was becoming so rare that "nothing could have been more obvious to the people of the earlier twentieth century than the rapidity with which war was becoming impossible. And as certainly they did not see it. They did not see it until the atomic bombs burst in their fumbling hands." In Wells' vision, nuclear war between countries would be the final straw to break the back of nation-states, which would then be forced to yield to a world government authority to maintain the peace.

Perhaps the escalation that is currently being centered around Syria, with Russia and the United States on potentially opposite ends of the political spectrum, will one day lead to that moment, where the possession of nuclear weapons increasingly assures their use. Particularly disturbing in such an equation is the possible deployment of a non-state "jihadist" actor to create the final chaos; for, as Wells perceived, "before *the last war* began it was a matter of common knowledge that a man could carry about in a handbag an amount of latent energy sufficient to wreck half a city" (emphasis added).[18]

It is certainly conceivable that World War III, if it were to occur in the Middle East, would be the last war before a unified world order were imposed for the professed security of mankind. But how had America come to this position of globalized militarism, with a military presence in over 100 countries, asserting its notion of security on a global scale? American foreign policy, since its inception, had been established on the farewell address of George Washington "to steer clear of permanent alliances with any portion of the foreign world." Yet during the 20th Century, the United States broke from its historical isolation from European politics to become the inheritor of a new crusade for "freedom."

By reflecting upon the intellectual history of Professor Elliott, we can formulate a thesis about the molding of America's globalist trajectory, along the lines outlined by a dying British empire. Elliott's influence on politics cannot be discounted, not only during his tenure in government positions, including within the National Security Council and Central Intelligence Agency, but while in academia, patronizing future world leaders like McGeorge Bundy, Dean Rusk,[19] Samuel Huntington,[20] and most of all, young Henry Kissinger. Though Elliott's policies were not always adopted in sum, his ideas usually correlated with that of the English and American internationalists promoting increased cooperation between the two nations to form an Atlantic bloc. Following the creation of this "special relationship" after World War II, the Anglophile internationalists further proposed regional economic and military cooperation as a step toward strategic cohesion in the face of disintegrating empires.

Endnotes

1. Sutton, Antony C. *America's Secret Establishment: An Introduction to the Order of Skull & Bones.* Oregon: TrineDay. Updated Reprint. 2002. p. 34.

2. Brzezinski, Zbigniew. "The Cold War and its Aftermath." *Foreign Affairs.* Vol. 71, No. 4, Fall 1992. p. 37.

3. Kissinger, Henry. *World Order.* New York: Penguin Books, 2014. p. 362.

4. Brzezinski, Zbigniew. *The Grand Chessboard.* New York: Basic Books, 1997. p. 209.

5. Founder of the investment firm Kuhn, Loeb & Co., Warburg is often considered the "father" of the Federal Reserve System, the central bank that loans federal banknotes into public circulation.

6. Revision of the United Nations Charter: Hearings Before a Subcommittee of the Committee on Foreign Relations. 81st Congress, 2d Session. U.S. GOVERNMENT PRINTING OFFICE, WASHINGTON. February 17, 1950.

7. The Masonic philosopher Manly P. Hall theorized, in his *Secret Destiny of America* (1944), that "world democracy was the secret dream of the great classical philosophers," preserved by secret societies until it could be realized from the new world, i.e. America.

8. Elliott, W.Y. and Neil A. McDonald. *Western Political Heritage.* New York: Prentice-Hall, Inc., 1950. p. 616.

9. Ibid. p. 623-7.

10. It should be noted that human rights were still blatantly abused by signatories to the Declaration, including by the French, who held colonies in Algeria and Vietnam; the Americans, who permitted discriminatory racial laws domestically; and the British, who engaged in wars in their colonies, such as against the Mau Mau in Kenya. "A former officer in one of the [British] detention camps in 1954-'55 witnessed routine 'short rations, overwork, brutality, humiliating and disgusting treatment and flogging – all in violation of the United Nations' Universal Declaration on Human Rights.'" (See Mark Curtis. *Web of Deceit*. p. 327).

11. Ball, James. "NSA's Prism surveillance program: how it works and what it can do." *The Guardian*. June 8, 2013.

12. Greenwald, Glenn. "NSA collecting phone records of millions of Verizon customers daily." *The Guardian*. June 6, 2013.

13. "In 2011 U.S. Special Operations Command spokesman Col. Tim Nye told me that on any given day, America's elite troops are working in about 70 countries." (See Nick Turse. *The Changing Face of Empire*. p. 81).

14. Cover, Matt. "Obama: UN 'Legitimated' U.S. Action in Libya." CNS News (online). June 16, 2011.

15. Quoted in Steinberg, Jeffrey and Mary Burdman. "London's Blair Pushes Post-Westphalia Chaos." *Executive Intelligence Review*. January 18, 2008.

16. Hersh, Seymour M. "Military to Military." *London Review of Books*. Vol. 38, No. 1. January 7, 2016.

17. Atran, Scott. ISIS is a revolution. *Aeon Magazine*. December 15, 2015.

18. Wells, H.G. *The World Set Free*. London: Macmillan, 1914. p. 103-104.

19. Elliott recommended his fellow Rhodes Scholar Rusk to be President Kennedy's Secretary of State; Elliott became one of Rusk's consultants.

20. When Huntington was denied a professorship at Harvard in 1958, Elliott wrote to Prof. Arthur MacMahon at Columbia University that he "may find it possible to consider him [Huntington] at Columbia." Elliott had known Huntington for ten years at that point and had advised him on his PhD thesis. Huntington was soon welcomed to Columbia, where he became Assistant Director at the Institute of War & Peace Studies. (WYE to MacMahon; Jan. 21, 1958; William Y. Elliott Papers; Box 93, Hoover Institute Archives, Stanford).

Chapter I

The Rhodes Scholarship for Imperialism

There does exist, and has existed for a generation, an international Anglophile network which operates, to some extent, in the way the radical Right believes the Communists act. In fact, this network, which we may identify as the Round Table Groups, has no aversion to cooperating with the Communists, or any other groups, and frequently does so.[1]

– Carroll Quigley, *Tragedy and Hope*

Thus begins a fascinating admission of the influence of a British-originated secret society on American political history, as recounted by Professor Carroll Quigley in his 1966 tome *Tragedy and Hope,* while he was Professor of History at the Foreign Service School at Georgetown University. The Round Table Group referred to by Quigley included the men working with Lord Alfred Milner, the head of the Rhodes Trust from 1902 till his death in 1925. The Group appears to have been an extension of Cecil Rhodes' own conception of a "secret society" to advance a project for the "extension of the English-speaking idea."[2]

The idea of maintaining the integral mass of the British Empire was by no means certain after the loss of its American colony by the Treaty of Paris in 1783. In the nineteenth century a "Little England" movement evolved, which opposed the costs of maintaining the empire. "If the First Empire attracted traders and planters who left Britain to earn their fortunes in the far-flung corners of the imperial domain, its later incarnation is alleged to have appealed to investors who supported entrepreneurs in their attempts to open new markets for the products of British industry and who organized new sources of raw materials for the factories at home."[3] Thus, Great Britain utilized its role as the world's banker, behind the sovereign Pound Sterling, to promote an "informal empire" beyond its physical colonies. Britain had previously used its business interests to gain political ground, as for instance with the British East India Company's trade ultimately leading to India's annexation into the Empire. The same would now occur in southern Africa, through the efforts of the entrepreneur Cecil Rhodes, backed by Lord Nathan Rothschild.

By 1870 the momentum had shifted away from isolationism to a more "liberal imperialism," predicated on financial investments and "indirect rule" of the colonies via local proxies. Ideologically, that year marked the creation of a Chair of Fine Arts at Oxford, which was given to the pre-Raphaelite art professor John Ruskin, who commanded his students that the empire must "Reign or Die." Ruskin "hit Oxford like an earthquake" from the moment he diverted his inaugural lecture from art to empire,[4] lecturing his students that England "must found colonies as fast and as far as she is able, formed of her most energetic and worthiest men .... she must guide the human arts, and gather the divine knowledge, of distant nations, transformed from savageness to manhood."[5]

Ruskin's Inaugural lecture was circulated widely around the Oxford of the 1870s, amongst the likes of Cecil Rhodes (who adhered to Ruskin's call, becoming prime minister of the English Cape Colony in South Africa in 1890), and Rhodes' contemporaries Arnold Toynbee (who advocated social reforms for the working classes), and Lord Milner (whose Round Table Group operated by the principle "that the extension and integration of the Empire and the development of social welfare were essential to the continued existence of the British way of life; and that this British way of life was an instrument which unfolded all the best and highest capabilities of mankind").[6]

Cecil Rhodes' fortune was built on the backs of diamond miners in Kimberley, South Africa, where Rhodes founded DeBeers in partnership with Lord Rothschild. While the legacy of DeBeers continues to this day on the international diamond cartel, Rhodes' impact upon South Africa may have been most felt in the system of apartheid which he institutionalized in the 1880s, first by housing all 10,000 black diamond miners in prison-like barracks, before decreeing that "no native shall work or be allowed to work in any mine, whether in open or underground mining, excepting under the responsible charge of some particular white man as his master or 'baas.'"[7] Rhodes' other legacy would be found in the formation of what he referred to as a "secret society." In his 1877 "Confessions of Faith" he had alluded to it:

> I look into history and I read the story of the Jesuits I see what they were able to do in a bad cause and I might say under bad leaders. At the present day I become a member of the Masonic order I see the wealth and power they possess the influence they hold and I think over their ceremonies and I wonder that a large body of men can devote themselves to what at times appear the most ridiculous and absurd rites without an object and without an end. The idea gleaming and dancing before ones eyes like a will-of-the-wisp at last frames itself into a plan. Why should we not form *a secret society with but one object the furtherance of the British Empire and the bringing of the whole uncivilised world under*

> *British rule for the recovery of the United States for the making the Anglo-Saxon race but one Empire.* (emphasis added)

Whether or not Rhodes' secret society was ever formalized, Lord Milner was initiated into Rhodes' ultimate vision for the empire, becoming his heir apparent. At the time of Rhodes' death in 1902, Milner was still working as High Commissioner of South Africa, a position which Rhodes helped secure for Milner in 1897. As High Commissioner, Milner was perfectly placed to help incite the Boer War which Rhodes had been hoping to provoke in order to unite South Africa under British rule, thus thwarting the political independence of the Dutch Boer republics.

After the successful Boer War (1899-1902), Milner incorporated the Boers' Transvaal and Orange River Colony into South Africa with the aid of his political disciples called the "Kindergarten," who constituted the main body of the subsequent Round Table Group, which seems to have played the role of Rhodes' intended secret society. After Milner left a united South Africa under the leadership of his Round Table ally General Jan Smuts in 1910, Milner returned to England with his Kindergarten to pursue Rhodes' dream, by furthering the imperial federation of the Empire into a "Commonwealth." That year, the Rhodes Trust was used to launch *The Round Table*, a journal on Commonwealth Affairs.

According to John Buchan, one of Milner's disciples from South Africa and a peripheral member of the Round Table Group, he "dreamed of a world-wide brotherhood with the background of a common race and creed, consecrated to the service of peace... It was humanitarian and international; we believed that we were laying the basis of a federation of the world."[8] Thus, the initial endeavor of Imperial Federation intended to retain the English loyalties of the expatriate white colonists in South Africa, Canada, Australia and New Zealand.

These federalists were fundamentally Nationalistic Imperialists who believed that "the British State must follow that [Anglo-Saxon] race... wherever it settles in appreciable numbers as an independent community." Thus Milner and his fellow federalists hoped that the "white man's burden" would serve to bind "the citizen[s] of the Empire" because their race would be more amicable to a common jurisdiction under the Crown.[9] This emphasis on the federation of the Empire into a Commonwealth of Nations became the guiding mission of the Round Table Movement from its formation until the creation of independent Dominions for South Africa, Ireland, Australia, Canada, and New Zealand in 1931. Yet a further, and more ambitious, elaboration for the Empire was also stirring by the early twentieth century.

Meeting between 1902 and 1908, Milner and his political protégé L.S. Amery engaged in discussions with Liberal Party members like Secretary of State Edward Grey and Round Table affiliate Lord Robert Cecil "to discuss the future of this perplexing, promising and frustrating Empire" of England. The direction of the Empire's long-term achievement of a federated global government was not yet clear to this group of "Coefficients," according to participant H.G. Wells, the Fabian Socialist writer. As Wells described the internal cleavages, Amery and Milner tended to accept Imperialist and "Monarchist forms" as a vehicle for achieving the "world commonweal," while Wells was disgruntled at the continuation of any sort of nationalism.[10] Nevertheless, Milner "knew we had to make a new world,"[11] and though the Coefficients may have diverged on the means, they believed that a new international order was in the making.[12] As Wells described the situation,

> The British Empire ... had to be the precursor of a world-state or nothing.... It was possible for the Germans and Austrians to hold together in their Zollverein (tariff and trade bloc) because they were placed like a clenched fist in the centre of Europe. But the British Empire was like an open hand all over the world. It had no natural economic unity and it could maintain no artificial economic unity. Its essential unity must be a unity of great ideas embodied in the English speech and literature."[13]

While Milner may have differed from Wells as a "Nationalist" rather than a "Cosmopolitan" in his imperial outlook,[14] his personal sentiments were insignificant to the ultimate destiny of the Empire, which would not rest with a unification of the English-speaking races and the creation of the British Commonwealth after 1926, or even an alliance with the lost colony of America. Instead, the English-speaking alliance was considered a mere precursor to the greater internationalist project of world governance through international financial controls and supranational legal agreements and treaties.

For instance, while Rhodes willed in 1877 the "colonisation by British subjects of all lands where the means of livelihood are attainable by energy, labour and enterprise, and especially the occupation by British settlers of the entire Continent of Africa, the Holy Land, the Valley of the Euphrates," the colonization of Africa and the Middle East did proceed through World War I, with the British adding mandates over Palestine and Iraq to their African interests. By the time the British laid claim to Palestine in 1920, Rhodes' disciple Lord Milner, and his secretary L.S. Amery, had already crafted the declaration committing Britain to the creation of a Jewish homeland in Palestine. "The document that emerges is handed to Baron Rothschild by British foreign secretary Arthur Balfour, and thus becomes known as the Balfour Declaration [of 1917]." As historian Robin Brown points out, Rhodes' Trustee and Biographer Lewis Michell had already amended Rhodes' wording for the empire in 1910 to envision "the Holy Land secured for the Zionists." Given Lord Rothschild's role as a Trustee of Rhodes' will, it seems he played a role in influencing the ultimate goal for Palestine, though custodianship would first need to pass through British hands before it could be turned into the Jewish state of Israel. Thus, despite Milner's commitment to his Anglo-Saxon race, he was not beyond alliances with groups like the Zionists to achieve the ultimate destiny of Britain's global empire. Yet as the 20th Century would prove, the empire would not stop with Britain.

A few years after Milner's death in 1925, H.G. Wells was as committed as ever to the goal of world commonwealth, but he believed that nationalism would have to be swept away first through revolutionary reconsiderations. Refining his idea on a global movement toward world socialism, he described the end-goal in *The Open Conspiracy: Blue Prints for a World Revolution* (1929). The "objective of the Open Conspiracy" would be met by increased socialization of international controls on raw materials, a centralized world banking system,[15] "a world pax, a world economic control, and a restrained population."[16] As Wells understood the openness of the conspiracy, though there may be "a convergence of many different sorts of people upon a common idea," the means of achieving this vision of managerial socialism would not be accomplished through any "sort of simple organization." It would require a "common spirit," but "between many of its contributory factors there may be very wide gaps of understanding and sympathy."[17] Nonetheless, so long as the goal of a world commonwealth of laws under international governance remained the same, the endeavor could be described as an "open" conspiracy, transcending time and personnel.

Wells, for example, never met W.Y. Elliott, but their aims were still largely the same thanks to the "common spirit" guiding the conspiracy's agents and its various infrastructures (i.e. the Round Table Group, the Royal Institute of International Affairs, the Council on Foreign Relations). Whilst in the context of the greater "open conspiracy" toward globalization Elliott is scarcely remembered by modern scholarship, he was certainly one of the agents reinforcing the paradigms that transformed the nationalistic political and economic structures of the nineteenth century into the supranational corporate and legal superstructures of the twentieth.

It would be at Oxford, while studying as a Rhodes Scholar, that Henry Kissinger's mentor William Yandell Elliott developed his sentiment for world law and international controls. He maintained his Anglophile connections while as a Harvard professor of politics and U.S. government official throughout his career. As he explained to his fellow Rhodes scholar W.E. Sikes in 1951, "I believe we strike a very happy balance in keeping up with what our British allies are doing and sometimes understanding it a little better than those who have not the exposure we had at Oxford and afterwards."[18]

Although Elliott's policies were not always adopted in sum, his ideas usually correlated with that of the English and American internationalists promoting increased cooperation between the two nations to form an Atlantic bloc. Following the creation of this "special relationship" after World War II, the internationalists further proposed regional economic and military cooperation as a step toward increased cohesion of the world in the face of disintegrating empires.

Endnotes

1. Quigley, Carroll. *Tragedy and Hope*. New York: The Macmillan Company, 1966. p. 950

2. Quigley, Carroll. *Tragedy and Hope*. p. 131

3. Davis, Lance and Robert A. Huttenback. *Mammon and the Pursuit of Empire*. Cambridge: Cambridge University Press. 1986. p. 71

4. Quigley, Carroll. *Tragedy and Hope*. p. 130

5. Birch, Dinah. *John Ruskin: Selected Writings*. Oxford: Oxford University Press, 2004. p. 202-3

6. Quigley, Carroll. *The Anglo-American Establishment*. New York: Book in Focus, 1981. p. 29

7. Roberts, Janine. *Glitter and Greed*. New York: Disinformation, 2003. p. 21

8. Buchan, John. Buchan, John. *Pilgrim's Way: An Autobiography*. New York: Carroll & Graf Publishers, Inc., 1968. p. 120-1

9. Milner, Viscount Alfred. "Key to My Position." *Questions of the Hour*. 2nd Ed. London: Thomas Nelson and Sons, Ltd., 1925. p. 211 - 214

10. The ultimate aim of the Round Table Group was to unify "the greater capacity of the English-speaking peoples" based on their higher culture to act "as the torch-bearers of internationalism" and bring under the control of an international government the means "in developing and securing a just distribution of the world's resources; in fighting the common enemies of mankind, poverty, hunger and disease; in raising to the highest level the standard of life of the masses of the people, and in setting up in place of the present system of industrial autocracy a new system of industrial democracy; and finally, in encouraging education, promoting the interchange of students and teachers, and developing facilities such as transport and communications, upon which depend the fine flowers of internationalism – the spiritual, cultural and social relationships between peoples." (See H. Duncan Hall. *British Commonwealth of Nations*. p. 359-60).

11. The Milner Group described this goal as "not in our lifetime" or "not in the present century." (See Carroll Quigley. *The Anglo-American Empire*. p. 150).

12. Wells, H.G. *Experiment in Autobiography*. Boston: Little, Brown, and Co., 1962. p. 650-653.

13. Ibid. p. 652.

14. Brown, Robin. *The Secret Society*. p. 106-107). Milner termed himself "a British Race Patriot.'"

15. The last element of the "Open Conspiracy," population "restraint," was the only element that

did not arise in Elliott's writings. Yet his protégé, Henry Kissinger, as Sec. of State in 1974 issued National Security Council Study Memo 200 on "Implications of Worldwide Population Growth for U.S. Security and Overseas Interests." The memo named thirteen developing countries as "strategic targets" for population control efforts. (See William Engdahl. *A Century of War*. p. 148)

16. Wells, H.G. *The Open Conspiracy*. Montana: Kessinger Publishing, 2004. p. 68

17. Ibid. p. 42.

18. WYE to W.E. Sikes; July 11, 1951; William Y. Elliott Papers; Box 6, Hoover Institute Archives, Stanford.

Dining Hall, Balliol College, Oxford University

Chapter II

An Education on the "Informal" Empire After Versailles

> *Two centuries ago, the philosopher Kant predicted that perpetual peace would come about eventually – either as the creation of man's moral aspirations or as the consequence of physical necessity. What seemed utopian then looms as tomorrow's reality; soon there will be no alternative.*
>
> – Secretary of State Henry Kissinger; Address to UN General Assembly, 1973

In 1919 W.Y. Elliott was selected to earn his doctorate in politics at Oxford University thanks to a Rhodes scholarship. Though still in his early twenties, he was already a veteran of World War I and held degrees from Vanderbilt University and the Sorbonne in France. Yet Elliott's subsequent education at Balliol College, particularly under his tutor Alexander Dunlop Lindsay, would integrally develop his philosophy of democratic government as an expression of individual freedom within pluralistic group organizations; the evolution of these ideas found formulation in his first book, *The Pragmatic Revolt in Politics* (1928), which spelled out a supra-national political theory that he would emphasize throughout his life.

The Rhodes Scholarship was established upon Cecil Rhodes' death in 1902 by the Rhodes Trust, the principal of whose Trustees was then Lord Milner. The Scholarships were intended "to be a kind of religious brotherhood like the Jesuits, 'a church for the extension of the British Empire'" by training young men to foster the aim of Rhodes' secret society and its imperial purpose. Consequently, "until the 1950s – perhaps later – its leading figures [amongst the Rhodes Trustees] showed a deep faith in the idea of the British Empire as a global community bound together by common loyalties and racial sympathies.... They believed that they stood for a modern and enlightened imperialism, best disseminated through teaching, research, and other forms of 'public education.'"[1]

Milner's Round Table Group that emerged in the 1910s and '20s accepted that the extension of the British Empire through liberal imperialist tactics would depend on a supra-national allegiance to a "common ideology" in uniting "the peoples of the United Kingdom, the Empire, and the United States." The subsequent options of an "imperial, Anglo-American, or world" federation of governments would then be achieved through the coordinated policies of their disciples, influenced by their liberal education in English ideals.[2] Thus, in bringing young scholars from the United States each year to Oxford, the group was particularly intent on cultivating the thinking of young Americans in the tradition of Cecil Rhodes' prescription for economic and theoretical bonds of empire.

Elliott's time as a Rhodes Scholar was spent at Balliol College, where fellow Professor H.W.C. Davis noted that "a very high proportion indeed of Rhodes scholars in those years [after World War I] were pressing hard to get into the College."[3] Davis gave no explanation for their interest, though it is clear that members of Milner's Round Table Group practically ran the college in the early 20th Century through its numerous fellows, including Milner, L.S. Amery, and Balliol's Master A.L. Smith.

In 1906 A.D. Lindsay was invited to a fellowship at Balliol to teach Classics and Philosophy. Lindsay became an affiliate of the Round Table Movement throughout his career, though he was never an official member. Lindsay's involvement with the Movement can be ascribed to his friendship with fellow Fabian Socialist (and confidante of Lord Milner) A.L. Smith, who shared with Lindsay a commitment to "uplifting the working classes and preserving the Empire."[4] These two endeavors were not mutually exclusive, according to John Ruskin's exhortations to young Milner and his friend Arnold Toynbee at Oxford in the 1870s that the Empire would only be perpetuated if the working class could be persuaded into the Empire's noble traditions "of education, beauty, rule of law, freedom, decency, and self-discipline."[5] In turn, the major organization to which Lindsay committed himself throughout his life was the Workers' Education Association (WEA), founded in 1903 as a continuation of Cambridge and Oxford's university extension programs in adult education.

The reason that workers' education played a role in the Round Table's bid to consolidate the Empire was that the labor groups in the British Dominions feared the idea of a leviathan super-state, as well as the "grossly uneven distribution of wealth." Labor felt that an imperial federation would jeopardize the democratic functions of local homogeneity, thus indicating the need for "a network of strong voluntary associations, or groups, to perform functions which the state cannot safely be entrusted to perform, to safeguard the interests of the individual, and to stand between him and the overwhelming power of the state."[6] The extreme form of group strength at the expense of the state became known as syndicalism. Yet a more mild form of group life could be encouraged across national boundaries to foster common spiritual and social purposes supra-nationally. This issue of encouraging individuality and group organization at the expense of the nation-state became a prime focus for Lindsay, and later his pupil Elliott, in the discussion of democratic politics.

The large number of Round Table members and affiliates congregating around Oxford in the early twentieth century testifies to the intellectual atmosphere of the institution and its professors' espousals of social consciousness and internationalism. The role of international voluntary associations like the W.E.A. or the Round Table Groups established by Lionel Curtis in the English Dominions (Canada, New Zealand, Australia, South Africa) was considered integral by the Round Table Movement in encouraging inter-imperial cooperation and forums for the circulation of common ideas. Thus, when Lindsay's lifelong friend J.H. Oldham founded the World Council of Churches at Oxford in 1937, he claimed to have been inspired by the leaders of the Round Table Movement, Lord Lothian and Lionel Curtis. According to Oldham, "The Round Table group were [sic] my great educators in matters of *constitutional principles"* (emphasis added).[7] Likewise, Lindsay, "through his contacts with Oldham" and Oxford Professor A.E. Zimmern[8] (of the Round Table Group), was "in touch with those who… were trying to keep open the international links of the Churches" as part of supranational organizing in the face of burgeoning nationalism on the Continent just before World War II.[9]

It is not difficult to imagine how the Round Table's influence, particularly on supranational "constitutional issues" may have equally influenced Lindsay as they did his collaborator Oldham. He had certainly adopted the Round Table's desire for international legal structures by the time he wrote for Round Tabler H.W.C. Davis' pro-war pamphlets in 1914 justifying Britain's *War Against War* "on the grounds that … international law to be upheld by the nations as 'takers-up of suits.'"[10]

From a purely legalistic point of view, the German Empire was considered the aggressor in its attack upon France via the neutral country of Belgium, which England claimed to be defending by its declaration of war on Germany. Of course, the legalistic view, ending with Germany bearing economic war "guilt," failed to take into account the English balance of power policy on the Continent that led to its encircling alliance system that created an anti-German coalition even with Germany's great trade partner Russia. While the Russians were exporting foods and raw goods to Germany in exchange for finished goods, "World War I effectively removed Russia's major trading partner, eliminating the source of roughly half of all its imports."[11] Such disruption would play into the economic crisis that would precipitate, along with the brutality of the war itself, the downfall of the Czar and the formation of the Soviet Union.

From the British perspective, the war against Germany was necessary, and while "endless discussions ensued about Britain's obligation to defend Belgian neutrality under the Treaty of 1839, those who made the decision saw clearly that the real reason for war was that Britain could not allow Germany to defeat France."[12] Of course, the British had not intervened to defend France against Germany less than 50 years earlier when Prussia swept into Paris in 1871. Yet now that Germany had consolidated to become an imperial power, the British Empire could no longer permit a precipitous shift in the continental balance of power in favor of its chief naval competitor's rivalry on the seas, permitting Germany's increased access to colonial markets. Indeed, *The Round Table*'s first issue in 1910 dealt with the "threat from Germany," fretting that Britain had "no means of marshaling the whole strength and resources of the Empire effectively behind its will" in case of war.[13] Accordingly, England had secretly committed to a naval convention with France in 1912, and "unbeknownst to the Houses and most ministers, Lord Grey of the Foreign Office exchanged with Paul Cambon, the French ambassador in London, a series of letters in which, on the basis of classified military conventions drafted by the General Staff of both countries, Britain, in case of war, pledged intervention on the side of France."[14]

It was only a matter of time before war would arrive on the continent, as President Woodrow Wilson's advisor Colonel Edward House admitted in May 1914, a month before the assassination of the Austrian Duke Franz Ferdinand would ostensibly catalyze war, that "whenever England consents, France and Russia will close in on Germany and Austria."[15]

When W.Y. Elliott arrived at Balliol in 1919, in the shadow of the Versailles Peace Conference, the English Round Table Movement had shifted its emphasis away from a federal union of the Empire, under the imperialism of the Crown, towards the Commonwealth system, which would be formalized in 1948. The Commonwealth meant a family of allied but independent Dominion states, free to pursue their own domestic policies but expected to cooperate with inter-imperial affairs and security. The Round Table Group's acceptance of international conferences and mandates to replace the imperialistic world of the pre-World War I era was evidenced by the creation of the League of Nations in 1919, whose Charter was drafted mainly by Sir Robert Cecil, A.E. Zimmern, and General Jan Smuts, all of whom were part of Milner's Round Table.

Its Charter ultimately denied the League of Nations any decisive executive authority or jurisdiction over foreign countries' sovereign affairs, thus indicating that the Round Table Group remained suspicious of a coercive super-state. Instead, the League was designed as a forum for international cooperation through discussion in attempts to reach consensus. The Commonwealth historian H. Duncan Hall, a disciple of the Round Tabler A.L. Smith (A.D. Lindsay's friend and predecessor as Master of

Balliol), further noted in his book *The British Commonwealth of Nations* (1920) that the future of the British Empire as a supranational sovereign lay in its ability to foster cooperation amongst its Dominions through the independence of their parliaments from Britain's federal legislation. The fact that the Dominions were entered into the League of Nations as separate nations formalized their autonomy from Great Britain.

Hall hoped that inter-imperial voluntary associations would not only heighten the socio-political ties within the Empire but would also extend to America so as to draw her "as close to the nations of the British Commonwealth as these nations are to one another." Of course, Hall's book came on the heels of American entry into the World War on behalf of the Anglo-French allies. Despite the American republic's historical antagonism to Great Britain, the Woodrow Wilson administration had sided with the Empire, under the pretext of combating Germany's unrestricted submarine warfare.[16] Following the war, America's relationship with England would have to be fostered, per Hall, on the pretext that as a former colony, it shared a "fundamental identity" with other Anglo-Saxon peoples "in language, institutions, laws, ideas, and traditions."[17] This basis for an international moral (i.e. cultural and political) community would be adopted by Elliott as the main focus of his emerging philosophy as a Rhodes Scholar, and thereafter.

Elliott's doctoral thesis at Oxford in 1923 was extended into book form in *The Pragmatic Revolt in Politics* by the time he was an assistant professor at Harvard in 1928. He decided that the book "owed a great part of its tone and temper to my old tutor A.D. Lindsay."[18] According to Lindsay's understanding, the populace of the European and American democratic states since the industrial revolution had grown too large and diversified to satisfy the individual voter's will. Instead of national unity, the Industrial Revolution of the nineteenth century had created an era of unprecedented economic interdependence (not least of which was the dependence of the industrial nations on raw materials for the manufacturing of finished goods), so much so that "men increasingly find their fortunes affected by the governments of men whom they do not know and over whom they have no control."[19] He described this international distention and insecurity as being exacerbated by the fact that national governments were determining the fates of millions of men through mechanized, detached, and "total" wars (i.e. involving all of society's manpower and productivity).

Lindsay deduced that in order to assure the "peace and order" of the international scene, greater centralization of power amongst governments would be necessary. Yet a single host government would not suffice to amalgamate cultures or standardize rules across different civilizations. Instead, Lindsay favored the democratic organizations evidenced by smaller national and international groups, i.e. trade unions, Workers Education Associations, and guild meetings. Consequently, Lindsay was outlining a paradoxical theme of both "greater centralization and greater decentralization of government." This would be possible if the citizens were made to feel part of their communities, while the normalization of economic and democratic conditions across countries would make international sub-groups more relevant in their purposes and principles.[20]

To Lindsay, a Labour Party socialist, the idea that society was a diverse and organic phenomenon "imbued his socialism, which was not obsessed with the idea of identical equality, because it was based on the reality of democratic experience in the small group – "democracy by discussion." In mass democracy men are units who must be as far as possible identical, but organically real societies like families or colleges are rich because all their members are different but all count and all contribute."[21] This was the main theme of W.Y. Elliott's first book, wherein he offered a remedy to resurgent nationalism through an emphasis on group organization derived from common interests and liberal values.

Surveying the international landscape of the 1920s, Elliott theorized that pragmatic, and unprincipled, politicians and strongmen threatened the European rule of law embodied in constitutional democracy. Elliott wrote *The Pragmatic Revolt in Politics* as a warning to "the smug sense of security in the post-war democracies which led to a eat, drink, and be merry psychology," in the face of rising fascist and communist political organizations.[22] In "Il Duce," the fascist prototype dictator Benito Mussolini who had suspended democracy in Italy in 1925, Elliott saw all he despised in the totalitarian principle of state sovereignty. "Fascism represents the last stand of the theory of the absolute sovereignty of the nation-state;" it also represented the civilian unrest in states like Italy, which had grown impatient with the inertia inherent in parliamentary democracy.[23]

Fascism, with its political adherents spread throughout Western Europe and America, presented an anti-idealistic proposal for "an hierarchically organized and functionally integrated nation under efficient dictatorship."[24] In this sense, the dictator would represent himself as the (Rousseauian) will of the people and then act decisively. In fact, A.D. Lindsay contended that Rousseau's conception of a general "will" of the people is pure "mythology" in the democratic state because "the great mass of the people can only *consent* to what government or some other organized group of people proposes to do" (*emphasis added*).[25] Should real choice be offered to the people in decision-making, Lindsay believed that the leader would have to utilize persuasive propaganda to normalize political opinion in order to manufacture a consensus, thus uniting the democracy through tyranny. Therefore, Lindsay argued that the essence of democracy was not universal suffrage or the right to *choose* the legislator (since one's vote is not necessarily for the elected legislator) but rather, democracy lies in the freedom of expression, for "if the discussion is at all successful, we discover something from it which could have been discovered in no other way."[26] Thus, the trouble with "organic" fascism was its determination to channel the energy of the group to purposive ends without accounting of individual freedom for moral choice.

In the 1920s, the contending political extreme opposing "capitalistic fascism" proved to be syndicalism, propounded by political philosophers like England's Harold Laski. Syndicalists proposed that in contrast to fascism's ultra-nationalism, the nation-state should be distilled in its authority toward a pluralistic society. Syndicalism, as a socialist extension of the Marxist "dictatorship of the proletariat," denies the authority of the state as inherently superior to that of any other interest group, i.e. labor unions or associations. It is important to note that whereas Lindsay did support pluralism in the sense of strong group organizations, as a Fabian Socialist he ultimately respected the super-ordinate power of the state.

Between the two extremes of fascism and syndicalism emerging in the 1920s, Elliott believed republican constitutionalism to be the soundest historical route to maintain individual freedom as well as group purpose. He termed his concept of the group "co-organic," implying that there existed "a common group end," which represents the economic and organizational structure of the group; yet there also existed a "moral consensus as to a common value or purpose for which the group stands." Such moral cohesion presupposed "a basic psychological unity" of "an enduring and shared value" within the group.[27] The group would thus have economic and moral factors bonding its members, but while the "shared cultural purpose" would tend to limit the group's area of interests to its state or region, Elliott saw no reason that the co-organic group life could not be developed through a common economic and moral purpose internationally. After all, nationalism was but a Platonic "Myth" that had developed historically (and pragmatically) to meet the needs of government. In this context, Elliott perceived the establishment of the League of Nations as "a great step toward limiting anarchy," but so long as nations existed as enclaves of "cultural communities," there could be no international consensus on the imposition of international laws.[28]

Essentially, Elliott esteemed the English tradition of the rule of law, made consummate in constitutional governance, as preclusive to a sustainable world order. The rule of law made it possible for communities to test the feasibility of their laws and values, and so, although the constitutional community could change its opinions and aims, it could not abolish the ultimate authority of those laws, which made the community "constitutional." Toward this end, Elliott rejected syndicalism as not offering constitutionalism, for it denied the authority of the state, which must be the arbiter of the laws. Elliott believed that the concept of right could only exist as stipulated by law, and though laws are "not static," their very existence conferred upon the citizens in constitutionally-sovereign nations the "moral responsibility" of obligation to the nation's ends because this "moral loyalty" is "freely given" through democratic means, rather than coerced as in the totalitarian state.[29] Elliott's main point was that in a "co-organic" state, "final control of his decisions is retained by the individual."[30] On the other hand, the dominant group's "attitude toward property rights and social obligations" would inevitably be reflected in the legislation; but Elliott contended that the essence of constitutionalism would still uphold the freedom to associate, discuss, and pragmatically test the viability of the legislation.[31]

Ultimately, Elliott's emphasis on sub-national groups and organizations serving "moral purposes" was intended to draw individuals away from traditional nationalism's idea of serving "the state as an end in itself." By decentralizing power into various domestic organizations, Elliott hoped to offer people the "dialectic of choice" in regards to group and moral affiliation, but at the same time, the higher morality of constitutionalism as a form of politics could transcend nation-states and concentrate power in international bodies and the rule of law.

Writing in the 1920s, Elliott still hoped that the League of Nations, and the World Court, could diminish the role of the nation-state in international affairs. By assuming more "coercive strength" based on the commonality of having only republican regimes within the League (at the time of its founding), Elliott contended that the League and World Court could "prove their necessity to a new world order."[32]

Despite the aims of the Round Table Group and its ideological adherents, the world order then forming was found in the burgeoning nationalism and agitation for self-government in the colonial world, particularly in the wake of President Woodrow Wilson's Fourteen Points Doctrine, which included national self-determination. In 1928 Elliott predicted "the only possible way in which a colonial empire, political or economic, may now be held without perpetual violence and repression, is under the actual practice of a trusteeship for the peoples who make too painful a botch of the job of governing themselves. And trusteeship implies accountability to a third party – an outside tribunal." Whether it would amount to a continuation of the imperial mandates system or a new form of international trusteeship of the colonies, Elliott did not believe that the majority of the world from Asia and the Near East to Africa and Latin

America was capable of self-government in a constitutional manner. Consequently, until the "savage, semi-savage, and politically immature communities" were imbued with enough "moral" responsibility, Elliott feared the continuation of "the usual bankruptcies of imperialistic control."

On the other hand, should the European empires unite with America to form "a co-organic world society of states, linked into a truly federal state" in the League of Nations, the united world could work through the League of Nations to organize a "mandates system, under the final sovereignty and supervision of a workable League."[33]

Elliott seems to have derived his co-organic mythos from the Round Table Group's hope for shared ideals to cohere nations to serve a larger superstructure: the English Commonwealth.[34] Elliott was asserting that through co-organic organization, the League of Nations could be made into a federally sovereign state. Lord Milner and his Round Table Movement had intended to federate the English Empire through the Commonwealth, with a common "defence and high policy," using taxes and representatives from the colonies. To the Round Table ideologue Lionel Curtis, writing in *The Commonwealth of Nations* (1916), "A Commonwealth no less than an autocracy is, in the last analysis, despotic in its claims." This language only served to polarize the more liberal Britons and colonists, particularly those of the Labor Party, who were anathema to the stretch of the Imperial state. Thus, Elliott's attempt to reconcile the two positions became his prescription for a "co-organic" philosophy of shared values and purposes without denying the freedom of the individual.[35]

In 1931, the Statutes of Westminster effectively achieved the Round Table Group's mission of granting to South Africa, Ireland, New Zealand, Australia, and Canada independent Dominion status under the British Commonwealth, which then constituted about one-quarter of the earth. The Dominion nations would maintain formal ties to the Empire in inter-imperial affairs, while enjoying domestic sovereignty, including the right to secede from the Commonwealth.[36] Elliott in turn devoted his next book to the British Commonwealth. Yet back in America, Elliott's description of co-organic group activity seems to have had its own influence on the attitude of his old friends, the Fugitives/Agrarians, and their conception of sectionalism in the 1930s.

Endnotes

1. Darwin, John. "The Rhodes Trust in the Age of Empire." *The History of the Rhodes Trust*. Ed. Anthony Kenny. Oxford University Press, 2001. p. 463.

2. Quigley, Carroll. *The Anglo-American Establishment*. P. 150.

3. Davis, H.W. Carliss. *A History of Balliol College*. Revised by R.H.C. Davis & Richard Hunt. Oxford: Basil Blackwell, 1963.

4. Quigley. *The Anglo-American Establishment*. p. 97.

5. Quigley, Carroll. *Tragedy and Hope*. p. 130.

6. Hall, H. Duncan. *The British Commonwealth of Nations*. London: Methuen & Co. Ltd., 1920. p. 211-12.

7. Quoted in Chaitkin, Anton. *Treason in America*. 2nd Ed. Washington D.C.: Executive Intelligence Review, 1998. p. 556-7.

8. Zimmern, a friend and collaborator with Lindsay on League of Nations projects, had given intellectual clarity to the mission of the Round Table Movement in 1911 with his history of *The Greek Commonwealth*, wherein he described the Athenian Empire of the fifth century as "the child of necessity" which used the watchword of "Freedom" against the Persian Empire to cull the necessary funds from its allies into its own Imperial Exchequer, which ultimately went toward the beautification of Athens. Zimmern then clearly stated the case for the Round Table Group against the "Little Englander" movement: "Athens could no more step back than most Englishmen feel they can leave India. She had woken up to find herself an Empire and was resolved to play the part." (p. 185-6; 194).

9. Scott, Drusilla. *A.D. Lindsay*. Oxford: Basil Blackwell, 1971. P. 263.

10. Ibid. p. 77.

11. White, Christine A. *British and American Commercial Relations with Soviet Russia, 1918-1924*. Chapel Hill & London: The University of North Carolina Press, 1992. p. 24.

12. Quigley, Carroll. *Tragedy and Hope*. p. 225.

13. Brown, Robin. The Secret Society. p. 288-289.

14. Preparata, Guido Giacomo. *Conjuring Hitler*. London: Pluto Press, 2005. p. 19.

15. Ibid. p. 20.

16. Much of the American public's anti-German sentiment had been stoked by the 1915 sinking of the British passenger-liner *Lusitania* by a German submarine. Though the *Lusitania* was indeed carrying armaments, the killing of civilians, including more than 100 Americans, outraged the public. But a most intriguing historical allegation is that British intelligence provided the Germans with the information about the *Lusitania* carrying weapons through an agent – none other than the notorious OTO "black" magician Aleister Crowley. (See Richard B. Spence. *Secret Agent 666*. p. 82-84).

17. Hall, H. Duncan. p. 370.

18. Elliott, William Y. "The Pragmatic Revolt in Politics: Twenty Years in Retrospect." From *The Review of Politics*, Vol. II, No. 1. (January 1940) Reprinted in The Pragmatic Revolt in Politics. New York: Howard Fertig, 1968.

19. Ibid. p. 177.

20. This extract of Lindsay's philosophy comes from *The Modern Democratic State, Vol. 1*. It was written for the Royal Institute of International Affairs (founded in 1919 by the Milner Group, particularly Robert Cecil and Lionel Curtis, with A.D. Lindsay's former pupil, the historian A.J. Toynbee, as its first staff member). At the beginning of WWII the Institute relocated from Chatham House to Balliol College (until 1943). Though Lindsay wrote *The Modern Democratic State* as late as 1941, it was culled from twenty years of lecturing on the subject.

21. Scott, Drusilla. p. xv .

22. W.Y.E. to G.A. Borgese; September 4, 1940. W.Y. Elliott Papers, Box 147, Hoover Institute, Stanford.

23. Elliott, William Y. *The Pragmatic Revolt in Politics*. New York: Macmillan, 1928. Reprinted 1968 by Howard Fertig. p. 335-36.

24. Ibid. p. 221.

25. Lindsay, A.D. *The Essentials of Democracy*. Philadelphia: University of Pennsylvania Press,

1929. p. 32.

26. Ibid. p. 37.

27. Elliott, William Y. *The Pragmatic Revolt in Politics*. p. 354-5.

28. Ibid. p. 356 - 358.

29. Ibid. p. 368.

30. Ibid. p. 374.

31. Ibid. p. 407.

32. Ibid. p. 490.

33. Ibid. p. 486-91.

34. The Round Table's "proposals for imperial cooperation had as their basic principle the assumption that communities which had a common ideology could pursue parallel courses toward the same goal merely by consultation among their leaders." (See Carroll Quigley. *The Anglo-American Establishment*. p. 151.)

35. Hall, p. 216-7.

36. However, it should be noted that the British Crown still owns the majority of the lands of the Commonwealth, or nearly 7 billion acres. (For more, see Cahill, Kevin. *Who Owns the World*. New York: Grand Central Publishing, 2010.)

This book, released in 1928, represents the selected verse of eleven poets who published a journal called the *Fugitive*.

Chapter III

Political Sectionalism in America Between the Wars

Act only according to that maxim whereby you can at the same time will that it should become a universal law without contradiction.

Act in such a way that you treat humanity, whether in your own person or in the person of any other, never merely as a means to an end, but always at the same time as an end. Therefore, every rational being must so act as if he were through his maxim always a legislating member in the universal kingdom of ends.

– Immanuel Kant's three formulations on the Categorical Imperative

Before Oxford, Elliott's years as an undergraduate at Vanderbilt University were spent discussing philosophy and poetry with a group of young men who became recognized in the 1930s as Agrarians. In the late 1910s, though, John Crowe Ransom, Allen Tate, Donald Davidson, Elliott, and later Robert Penn Warren were known for their poetry journal, *The Fugitive* (1922-1925). Although Elliott never adopted the mantle of Agrarianism, he maintained an affinity for his student-friends' movement and remained close to them throughout his life.[1]

In 1930 the Agrarian writer Allen Tate noted in the *New Republic* that the words *sectionalism* and *regionalism* were appearing "in almost every essay on the relation of literature to American society that I have read in the last three years."[2] Tate would have respected this phenomenon, for over the previous decade he and his fellow Fugitive poets had been attempting to rekindle a uniquely *Southern* literary tradition through their publication.

By 1928, John Crowe Ransom and Tate had begun to broaden their political horizons by preparing a polemic with some of the former Fugitives called *I'll Take My Stand* (1930). This book, made up of twelve essays by the self-proclaimed "Southern Agrarians," was intended to promote the idea of "Agrarian versus Industrial." The Agrarians believed that the Southern way of life, culturally as well as economically, would be swallowed up by the industrialization of the North, even in agricultural production, in which the South's rural lands specialized.

In many ways, the Agrarians' emphasis on self-sufficient production and ending industrial capitalism's "unrelenting war on nature" prefigured the environmental movement of the 1960s and '70s.[3] According to critic William Tucker, "this book is often cited as one of the most Quixotic episodes in American literary history – the effort of a small group of Southern academics to resurrect a romanticized antebellum South.... They excoriated the efforts of science and scorned the fruits of technology. Indoor plumbing, farm machinery, and paved roads, they said, were only the manacles of an encroaching industrial misery."[4] Yet the Agrarian movement's claims of a culturally-distinct and land-oriented Southern tradition were also steeped in Anglophile influences.

In *I'll Take My Stand,* the Agrarian leader Ransom, himself a Rhodes Scholar (1913), was not shy about announcing the "Anglophile sentiment" in the South, which derived its desire for fixed traditions and socio-economic order from England's "seasoned provincial life." The South that Ransom and his fellow Agrarians romanticized and wished to preserve had "aristocracy, a kind of serfdom, a ritualized religion... in short, it was a stable, organic, and spiritually unified society like the Middle Ages."[5] The Victorian Medievalists like Thomas Carlyle and John Ruskin who preferred feudalism's pre-industrialism served as ideological parents for the Agrarians. To Ransom in particular, the Medievalists' fear that industrial society's theory of scientific and economic progress would destroy the social and aesthetic fabric of pre-industrial communities had "been realized... with almost fatal completeness in America."[6]

Yet the Agrarians' search for tradition did not end with the Victorians, for they had a more modern inspiration from the English poet T.S. Eliot,[7] whose own articulation of the "proper Christian community rejected the presence of Negroes and Jews because they divided the monolithic social unity." If W.Y. Elliott's "co-organic" community depended upon a commonly shared value system, it could have been conceivably construed to permit the exclusion of those who did not fit, per the morality of the community. Some of the Agrarians, like Ransom and Tate, seem to have imbibed this "cultural relativism" in order to adopt "the feeling of the community in which you lived."[8] Consequently, the import of regionalism, or sectionalism, was that it allowed for the socio-economic integrity of communities, the sum of which defined a region.

In 1935 W.Y. Elliott, then a professor of government at Harvard, wrote a justification of the New Deal in his book *The Need for Constitutional Reform*. The book advocated a centralization of authority in the hands of the Executive, but in terms of the federal system as a whole, he paradoxically hoped that the states would be redistributed as "commonwealths." These regional commonwealths were in fact envisioned as a means of centralizing administrative bureaucracy in order to reduce and streamline "the number and functions of local (particularly county) government areas."[9] Elliott proposed that the states be replaced by "natural" (i.e. historical) regions like New England, New York, the South Atlantic Seaboard, the lower Mississippi Valley, the Pacific Coast, et al., each with its own unicameral legislature. "The Commonwealths should have the duty of carrying out federal laws as the provinces have in Canada," but the fifty states would then remain as a more localized administrative unit.

The creation of regions would theoretically sap the power of the populations concentrated in a few cities in Northern states by distributing and equalizing the represented populations grouped into more culturally homogeneous regions. These regions would then be free to conduct their domestic legislation without federal interference, just as the British Dominion states now had "home rule" on domestic matters; yet the American commonwealths would "be required to carry out the laws of the federal government, and should be subject to federal supervision and inspection." All in all, the strength of the commonwealths would "stop the plethoric growth of bureaucracy in Washington," which would streamline the President's power to initiate policies of national concern while the commonwealth governments would have more autonomy in their own affairs.[10] Elliott's Agrarian friends certainly respected this acknowledgment of the local autonomy of the commonwealth, or region, as integral to preserving local culture.

Since sectionalism was already a theme for the Agrarians since at least the 1920s, it seems likely that Elliott derived some of his conception of an American commonwealth from his former friends. Two years before Elliott's tract on Constitutional reforms, the Agrarian Donald Davidson had published an article for *Hound and Horn* magazine on "Sectionalism in the United States" (1935). With chauvinistic Southern loyalty, Davidson accused liberals of being "under the delusion that the United States *are* a compact and well unified body."[11] Donaldson was using the language of the antebellum South Carolina "nullifier" Senator John C. Calhoun when he referred to the United States as a plurality with "a semblance of unity." Davidson claimed that in fact America was still divided by antebellum regions of capitalism (in the East), independent farmers (in the West), and "landed aristocracy" (in the South).[12] He was convinced that "national unity" would only emerge if decentralization allowed each section to unify itself through cultural history in order to avoid the Spenglerian decline of America through the "standardized massing of humanity void of social structure, and uninspired by any common interest."[13]

Elliott himself had recognized the dangers of what he perceived to be the massing of citizens into cities as a consequence of industrialization, particularly after World War I. In 1928, just before the country's financial crash, Elliott wrote discouragingly to his friend, the American Secretary of the Rhodes Trust Frank Aydelotte, of "the development of interdependence in modern political society, due to the growth of industrial[ization] and urbanization with the consequent emphasis on duty. This results in an emphasis upon the social solidarity and the functional relations of the individual, both to his own group (occupational, professional, etc.) and to the entire body politic.... Personally, I very much resent the tendency toward Fascism and *the cooperative state,* which is pretty evident in this country" (emphasis added).[14] Apparently Elliott was discouraged by industry and the urban settings' dissolution of the "co-organic" community, replacing it with a heterogeneous socio-economic life. The concentration of people in a few cities also helped the idea of national unity, which Elliott resented as sublimating individuality and community independence. Essentially, Elliott's thesis for strong executive strength over "co-organic" commonwealths was intended to prevent industrialization's absolution of pastoral independence.

After Elliott published his commonwealth argument in *The Need for Constitutional Reform,* Frank L. Owsley wrote the Agrarians' "clearest political statement" for *American Review,* "The Pillars of Agrarianism" (1935). Therein he noted Elliott's contribution to the movement, for between Elliott's proposal to reform the courts to eliminate all concurrent powers between the state and federal governments, "his plan is essentially what Agrarians have urged constantly."[15] Owsley seems to have been further influenced by Elliott's critical discussion of the "Supreme Court as Censor" in *The Need for Constitutional Reform.* In the book, Elliott criticized the Court's role "as censor of social and political policy" by using the 14th Amendment's Due Process Clause to overturn state legislation, beginning in the Reconstruction Era.[16] Elliott preferred that the Court "return to the tradition that it maintained on the whole from [Chief Justice] Taney's time [i.e. the 1830s] down through the Granger Cases" of the 1880s; this tradition referred to the Court's deference from interfering in social legislation for the sake of pragmatic experimentation.[17]

In fact, Elliott was merely echoing his affinity for English governmental structures in his criticism of the Court's "right to censor social policy," for in the British Commonwealth, "British theory has relied upon responsible political rather than upon judicial control in this sphere. The danger, plentifully apparent in our system, that the courts would misuse their censorial powers to prevent radical social experiments of any character has not existed in the British Dominions, where parliamentary supremacy was acknowledged."

According to Elliott, the Judiciary could not be as responsive to communal needs as the Executive and Legislature, so it should not work to censure those branches' "social experiments," including the numerous federal agencies established under the New Deal.[18] The Agrarian Frank Owsley followed up with "The Foundations of Democracy" in *Who Owns America?* (1936), insisting that since the Court could rule on the Constitutionality of government actions, the American people were subject to the undemocratic whims of an elite body. Instead, Owsley took a line from Elliott that America needed "a new Constitution which will reconstruct the Federal Government from center to circumference. Such a reconstruction must take into consideration the realities of American life, past and present; and one of the greatest realities is sectionalism and regionalism."[19] Owsley, like Donald Davidson before him, then couched his argument for sectionalism in its historical relation to early American divisions between North and South before the Reconstruction period attempted national unification.

Elliott's thesis for Constitutional reforms, including regionalism, was so influential among the Agrarians that their Distributist ally Herbert Agar invited Elliott to contribute an essay to the joint Distributist-Agrarian book, which Agar was editing with Allen Tate, *Who Owns America?* (1936). Distributism, which John Crowe Ransom had studied in England in 1932, was a movement advocating small property ownership and a return to the Medievalist guild system to counteract the "Servile State" of industrial capitalism, which took away the individual's ownership of property, i.e. the fruits of his own labor.

Who Owns America? even included an essay from Distributist leader Hillaire Belloc, and was intended to influence the realization in America of a genuine "property state" where the "majority of families own real property." Elliott demurred from contributing an essay on the legislative means for realizing this state, citing a heavy workload, though he may have in fact disagreed with the economic premise.[20] Nevertheless, Elliott and Agar remained in contact, as they both served on the Editorial Board for *The City of Man: A Declaration on World Democracy* (1940). In fact, the "historic American plan," according to Agar (future head of Freedom House), implied a Jeffersonian limited government based on his "vision of an agrarian democracy with limited restraints on individual freedoms and with even these restraints emanating from remote sources of power," a vision which W.Y. Elliott seems to have shared in his analysis of "co-organic" voluntary associations and the reorganization of American states into commonwealths.[21]

This quest for regional and communal autonomy was continued by both men in their 1940 publication, *The City of Man*, where the question of economic organization was again broached, this time to advocate a pluralist economy, or an "extensive economy," which included Medievalist "home industry and individual artisanship," with the consequent suburbanization of American life. It was considered an evolution beyond industrial collectivization that production might be "for use instead of for financial returns" as exemplified in "public works and institutions of welfare and learning, pointing to a society not wholly expressed in terms of money." Thus the Distributist-Agrarian alliance for self-sufficient production and socialistic structures of distribution found expression in the authors of *The City of Man*'s charge of "Capitalism-Communism as enemy brothers."[22]

While most people might find it difficult to comprehend the notion of capitalism and communism co-existing in an economic system, it should be pointed out that monopoly capitalism, i.e. when a handful of major corporations dominate distribution in a region, plays essentially that role. Thus, when historian Antony Sutton assessed the relationship of international finance, especially centered around JP Morgan's Guaranty Trust Company, in supporting the Bolshevik revolution in Russia, he believed it was based upon the bank's desire that "the gigantic Russian market was to be converted into a captive market and a technical colony to be exploited by a few high-powered American financiers and the corporations under their control.... In other words, we are suggesting that the Bolshevik Revolution was an alliance of statists: statist revolutionaries and statist financiers aligned against the genuine revolutionary libertarian elements in Russia."[23] On the other hand, the Bolshevik revolutionaries may have been statists, but they were also anti-German enough to satisfy the Western Allies; as President Wilson's advisor Colonel House pointed out, the Russian revolution "contains within it ... great motives of serious danger to German domination: [for example], anti-capitalist feeling, which would be fully as intense, or more intense, against German capitalism."[24]

While the Bolshevik regime remained officially unrecognized by the U.S. government until 1933, it is interesting to note that American trade was not obstructed by official government animosity. In fact, the Soviet and American interests were conducting business as usual thanks to Armand Hammer's Allied American Corporation, which acted as commercial agent for at least thirty-eight American companies in the USSR in the 1920s, including Ford Motors, U.S. Rubber, and Westinghouse Electric. JP Morgan's Guaranty Trust provided credit for many of the American businesses operating there, and "direct trade was further facilitated by an agreement between the [Soviet] State Bank of the RSFSR and the Guaranty Trust Company, whereby the latter had agreed to act on behalf of the State Bank in the United States."[25]

In the following decade, W.Y. Elliott would make the argument in his book *The Need for Constitutional Reform* (1935) that the U.S. federal government must continue with its New Deal policies of centralizing control of the rules by which big business operated. Elliott's metaphor compared the federal government to a "referee" or a "joint-stock company" working to conserve public property for private capital, thus preventing the excesses of laissez faire that had led to the Great Depression. Elliott recognized as inexorable the federal government's influence in American life, but he recommended that service and merchandising industries be left free to compete, while the concentrative industries like steel, automotive and textile should see their resources conserved through voluntary cartels.[26]

Elliott's views were hardly alien to the ruling elite; for example the "seven sister" major oil companies had come together with the Achnacarry Agreement of 1928 to determine that "high prices and production limits [on oil] were justified on the basis of conservation." In fact, through the 1930s the Federal Trade Commission deduced that "conservation became the cartel's slogan at a time when a rising flood of international production threatened to depress world prices."[27]

Rather than leaving the cartels free to collude, W.Y. Elliott advocated that the extractive industries be subject to regional controls by the national government to normalize the rate of extraction of raw materials as well as their use in production. Consequently, when his Agrarian friend Donald Davidson acknowledged Elliott's contribution to the argument for sectionalism in *Who Owns America?*, Davidson astutely differentiated between his own antagonism to centralized power and Elliott's thesis for a strong, though "responsible," federal government. Elliott's commitment to the strong executive power was intentional, though, for its thesis was derived from the English Empire and its emerging model for its Commonwealth.

Endnotes

1. Both Allen Tate and John Crowe Ransom became editors of the Elliott-Kissinger run Harvard journal *Confluence* in the 1950s. Elliott presided over the Fugitive reunion at Vanderbilt in 1952 even though he had mainly been "Editor in Abstentia" of the magazine while he was away at Oxford.

2. Karanikas, Alexander. *Tillers of a Myth: Southern Agrarians as Social and Literary Critics.* Madison: University of Wisconsin Press, 1969. p. 100.

3. Quoted in Duncan, Christopher M. *Fugitive Theory*. Lanham: Lexington Books, 2000. p. 143-4

4. Tucker, William. *Progress & Privilege*. New York: Anchor Press, 1982. p. 8.

5 Karanikas. p. 8.

6. Ibid. p. 81-2.

7. Allen Tate is generally acknowledged as having "discovered" Eliot for the Fugitives, but it was in fact W.Y. Elliott who had befriended T.S. Eliot while in Paris sometime after WWI. At Oxford, Elliott promoted *The Fugitive* around campus, especially to the author Robert Graves. T.S. Eliot then assisted his friend Graves in getting J.C. Ransom's second book of poetry, *Grace after Meat*, published in 1924.

8. Ibid. p. 91-2.

9. Elliott, William Yandell. *The Need for Constitutional Reform.* New York: Whittlesey House, 1935. p. 9.

10. Ibid. p. 198.

11. Davidson, Donald. "Sectionalism in the United States." *The Southern Agrarians and the New Deal.* Ed. Emily S. Bingham and Thomas A. Underwood. Charlottesville: The University of Virginia, 2001. p. 51.

12. Ibid. p. 55.

13. Ibid. p. 73.

14. WYE to Aydelotte; Nov. 8, 1928; Box 159, Hoover Institute, Stanford.

15. Owsley, Frank L. "The Pillars of Agrarianism." *The Southern Agrarians and the New Deal.* p. 209.

16. Elliott, William Yandell. *The Need for Constitutional Reform.* P. 157-9.

17. Ibid. p. 205.

18. Elliott, W.Y. "The National Powers under the Constitution." *Proceedings of the Academy of Political Science*, Vol. 16, No. 4. January 1936. p. 4-5.

19. Owsley, Frank Lawrence. "The Foundations of Democracy." *Who Owns America?* Ed. Herbert Agar and Allen Tate. p. 58.

20. Herbert Agar to WYE; Sept. 17, 1935; William Y. Elliott Papers; Box 162, Hoover Institute Archives, Stanford.

21. Karanikas, p. 57.

22. Agar, Herbert, et al. *The City of Man: A Declaration on World Democracy*. New York: The Viking Press, 1941. p. 91-2.

23. Sutton, Antony. *Wall Street and the Bolshevik Revolution*. Western Australia: Veritas Publishing Company, 1981. p. 173.

24. Preparata, Guido Giacomo. Conjuring Hitler. p. 35.

25. White, Christine A. *British & American Commercial Relations with Soviet Russia, 1918 – 1924*. p. 196.

26. Elliott, William Yandell. *The Need for Constitutional Reform*. p. 120.

27. Gibson, Donald. *Wealth, Power, and the Crisis of Laissez Faire Capitalism*. New York: Palgrave Macmillan, 2011. p. 162.

Chatham House in London, home of The Royal Institute of International Affairs, was founded by Lionel Curtis who, along with Lord Milner, established Rhode's Round Table Group. Chatham House originated the anonymity rule known as the Chatham House Rule, which provides that guests attending a seminar may discuss the results of the seminar in the outside world, without discussing the attendance or identity of the speaker.

The Chatham House Rule evolved to facilitate frank and honest discussion on controversial or unpopular issues by speakers who may not have otherwise had the appropriate forum to speak freely.

Chapter IV

A Commonwealth of Nations – the 1930s

The strongest is never strong enough to remain forever master unless he transforms his power into right and obedience into duty.

– Jean-Jacques Rousseau

When W.Y. Elliott published his book on *The Need for Constitutional Reform* in 1935, it was in response to President Roosevelt's "pragmatist" style of navigating through Congress novel legislation, in the greatest display of Executive activity in American history. The New Deal, in sum, "imposed regulation on Wall Street [by creating the Security and Exchange Commission], monitored the airwaves [via the Federal Communications Commission], rescued debt-ridden farmers and homeowners, built model communities, transformed home-building, made federal housing a permanent feature [under the United States Housing Authority], fostered unionization of the factories, drastically reduced child labor, ended the tyranny of company towns, wiped out sweatshops, established minimal working standards, enabled thousands of tenants to buy their own farms, built camps for migrants, introduced the Welfare State [through the creation of Social Security] with old-age pensions, unemployment insurance, and aid for dependent children and the handicapped, provided jobs for millions of unemployed [in fact, the Works Progress Administration made the Federal government the largest single employer in the country]."[1]

Such Executive authority, in the face of the greatest depression America had ever suffered, inevitably led to conservative reaction, including from the Federal Judiciary itself, which invalidated the National Recovery Administration (NRA) in a Supreme Court ruling of 1935. The Court deemed that the Executive's attempt to set prices for labor and goods in large corporations' intrastate commerce was unconstitutional. W.Y. Elliott's response to the constitutional crisis was to advocate Constitutional Conventions that would give the Executive branch more authority to implement its policies by populism, thus bypassing the unelected Judiciary's obstruction.

While much of FDR's New Deal could be described as experimental and expedient toward resolving an economic crisis, Elliott noted that the American political emphasis had shifted from the laissez-faire liberalism of "free association" to "social security." Yet Elliott did not oppose this fundamental shift, advocating instead for a pragmatic approach to reshape the Constitution and meet the needs of modern America under an Executive-led government. By 1940, Elliott and his co-authors in *The City of Man* could reflect positively on the New Deal as confirming that "some form of collectivism and socialized democracy, is with us to stay" thanks to the introduction of "a nucleus of planned economy into the loosened texture of free enterprise."[2] The lesson of the 1930s was that a strong Executive, which responds to the needs of the people, was necessary for federal governance, since authority, "atomized among too many, becomes elusive or vanishes altogether."[3]

To Elliott, a strong Executive could act more decisively as a representative of "a national community" than could a divided Congressional body.[4] Too often the federal government had been rendered shiftless in national concerns due to party politics. National matters not only included interstate legislation but also international concerns like the 1930 Smoot-Hawley Tariff passed by Congress, or even the treaty-making powers of the Senate which obstructed President Wilson's designs for America to join the League of Nations in 1920. On the other hand, in order for the Executive not to assume dictatorial powers, Elliott's co-organic thesis implied that the communities within the nation remain committed to the overarching federal policies.

Ultimately, Elliott imagined a federal commonwealth for the United States along the lines of Canada, with "a strong national government of a British rather than an American model, provided it is also a responsible one." When Elliott compared America to Britain, he understood that their major difference lies in the absence of a Constitution in Great Britain. Instead, British legislation is created ad-hoc, though predicated on prior law, much like the U.S. Supreme Court's decisions. Thus, in a sense, Elliott had no qualms with advocating for the abandonment of the United States Constitution, so long as the political class were said to be responding to the demands of the democracy.

Elliott's argument for stronger Executive powers was merely intended to streamline the legislative goals of the democratic community, for "a representative system must represent community and not special interests."[5] While it has certainly been the case that Congress finds itself riddled with "special" local interests, resulting in pork-barrel politics and irrelevant "rider" attachments to bills, it must be recalled that what distinguishes a republic from a democracy is the protection of special, or minority, interests in spite of the majority.

Elliott addressed the Senate with even more vitriol than the House of Representatives. To Elliott, the Senate was made up of an elitist body without party discipline, tending to serve the interests of "lobbying pressure groups."[6] The Senate offered unequal representation by giving every state, regardless of its population size, the same number of delegates, while Senators then sat for overlong six-year terms. The House better represented the will of the people because its members were proportionally distributed, but he believed that four-year terms for House representatives, coinciding with the Presidential elections, would force the citizens to choose politicians of both branches based on the same national issues. Elliott hoped that forcing representatives to run concomitantly with the Presidential candidates would force greater party discipline, which might bring one party into power in both branches of government.

Rather than respecting the system of checks and balances created by a bicameral Congress, separated from the President, Elliott advocated for a powerful Executive based on the party discipline by simultaneously controlling Congress. Accordingly, he preferred the British parliamentary system, where the ruling party of the House names the Prime Minister who then generally enjoys Parliamentary support. Elliott's quarrel was really the same as that of Round Table Group organizer Lionel Curtis who claimed in 1934 that the American Constitution had failed by creating "an elective monarchy" in a President who sits "on the throne" for four years; "in the interval the safety of the state may be jeopardized by a deadlock between the executive and legislature."[7] Elliott mused that the American Constitution could be reformed to allow the President the right of the British Prime Minister to call a national referendum at least once during his term to decide if the citizens would stand behind his platform or Congress' in the case of controversial legislation. This national election would act as a kind of recall vote on the President and would acknowledge a real democratic voice arising from the public.[8]

If Elliott was encouraging the authority of the Executive to avoid the Congressional "pork-barreling" of local interests into national bills,[9] he also recognized that America needed a more efficient and experienced Executive branch to carry out its policies. In 1936 Elliott began his career in government as a member of the President's Committee on Administrative Management, chaired by Louis Brownlow. The Brownlow Committee produced a study, which "inspired" the Reorganization Act of 1939 and created the Executive Office of the President.[10] The Reorganization Act accomplished much of the bureaucratic reconstruction that Elliott had advocated in *The Need for Constitutional Reform*, giving the President authority to restructure the federal government's machinery "to increase efficiency," "to eliminate overlapping and duplication of effort" by grouping agencies, and to abolish superfluous ones. The first Reorganization Plan established ten Executive Departments such as the Federal Security

Agency (with the Social Security Board and Civilian Conservation Corps grouped within that Agency).

As Elliott advocated for the Reorganization Bill's passage by Congress, whether preparing for "a war on poverty or a war against external enemies," the national government needed strong Executive leadership and a trustworthy staff to carry out its policies.[11] But while FDR certainly culled a "Brain Trust" to serve as advisors and administrators, Brownlow even noted in his autobiography of 1958 "that he was quite certain that FDR, when creating the Executive Office, 'had not in his wildest dreams' envisioned the expansion that later occurred,"[12] including the creation of the National Security Council in the Executive Office.

Ever since President Jackson's "spoils" system, civil servant appointments had been at the discretion of the incoming president, thus preventing a permanent civil service from taking shape. With the expansion of the federal agencies and personnel during the New Deal, W.Y. Elliot now argued that the American government was in ever greater need of a British-style "expert civil service, and that civil service cannot be effective unless, as we say, it is somehow taken out of politics," i.e. taken out of the democratic process.[13]

Elliott's advocacy of the expert civil service was clearly adopted from the English model, particularly echoing Elliott's mentor at Oxford A.D. Lindsay and his Platonic argument that *shipbuilders* were needed to build ships; in this case, political experts were necessary to steer the ship of state. According to Lindsay, "what is needed and what is most difficult, is to combine the technical knowledge of the expert with the practical experience and understanding of the common life of the ordinary public. The expert has to be sensitive to public opinion."[14]

In representative democracies like those of America and England, the representatives are assumed to respond to the pressures of their electorate. On the other hand, Elliott hoped that civil servants, as in England, would enjoy more insulation from public opinion while being able to efficiently organize and run their departments. He noted, "it would seem incredible to an Englishman that there is no permanent head to any department of the government of the United States. Not even the Treasury or the Department of State is an exception."[15]

Essentially, Elliott was frustrated by the haphazard approach of American policy, which changed with the presidency and lacked a discernible objective. He subsequently predicted the corporate model of government that would become commonplace at the end of World War II, proposing in 1935 "an efficient administrative mechanism and a permanent non-political bureaucracy."[16] In the Cold War years, politicians would become more permanent as they rotated from one department to another, or remained as advisors to executive committees and administrations. Elliott himself avoided party affiliations, serving on Roosevelt's Business Advisory Committee and War Production Board, Truman's Office of Civilian Requirements, Eisenhower's National Security Counsel and Office of Defense Mobilization, and as a special consultant to Kennedy's Secretary of State Dean Rusk. What Elliott was arguing for American government had previously been espoused by the Round Table Group founder Lord Alfred Milner, whose own "distaste for party politics" had led him to advocate the "managerial revolution" in Britain in the early twentieth century,[17] turning government personnel into managers who ran posts within government, regardless of the ruling party.[18] Of course, such a political class was said to represent the enemy of American freedom in the form of the Soviet Politburo, which ruled the country autocratically.

If Elliott derived his concept of a permanent civil service from the British, he would have understood the import of governmental organization while visiting England at the turn of the decade. In the years after his political statement of 1928, *The Pragmatic Revolt in Politics*, Elliott returned to England to research the British Empire with the help of Ray Atherton, Counselor to the American Embassy in London. Elliott would likely have also used his Rhodes Trust contacts like Lord Lothian, then head of the Rhodes Trust, whom he met by at least 1929. For example, when he was preparing his book on *The New British Empire*, Dr. Thomas Jones of Balliol (PM Ramsay MacDonald's private secretary) toured Elliott around London, "giving [him] an insight into the workings of the British Government that never gets into textbooks." Jones would hold discussions with department personnel in order to make "a cumbersome machine like the civil service gear into the Prime Minister's office." One of the staple "bureaucrats" at these meetings was Round Table Group member Maurice Hankey, secretary for the Committee of Imperial Defense.[19]

Elliott's research into the British Commonwealth culminated in a series of lectures delivered at Lowell House, Harvard in early 1931; these lectures were then adapted into book form as *The New British Empire* (1932). The "New" Empire implied its peaceful transition to "Commonwealth," as initially intended by the Round Table Group and then articulated by the Balfour Declaration of 1926 as well as the official Statutes of Westminster in 1931. Accordingly, by 1931 the Dominion states (Australia, Ireland, Canada, New Zealand, and South Africa) were given "equal" and autonomous status as nations, "united by a common allegiance to the Crown." To Elliott, this model of a workable, liberal commonwealth could serve as a guide toward world organization through spiritual and political unity.

As the English Round Table Movement sought to politically unify the Dominions within the Empire in the 1920s, the movement faced the pressure of counteracting liberal support for the "grandiose experiment in communism" taking place in Russia since 1917. To understand the nature of the "cold war" between Russia and the West spanning the twentieth century, it is important to recognize that both the British and Russian Empires were in search of international order in the 1920s and '30s; whereas the Russians ostensibly sought a "classless world order," the British sought a presumably democratic order of national cooperation through constitutional legalities.

In the wake of England's extension of national sovereignty to the Dominions, Elliott spoke of England's "democratic experiment" as an attempt "to counterbalance Russia ... on an even larger scale, of transforming the British Empire from a centralized system, under either British hegemony or direct rule, into a League of Allied States."[20] Unlike Russia's *Comintern,* which exported "communist *nationalization*" (*emphasis added*) programs through revolution, England was attempting to secure an international order based on "nationalist cooperation" through conferences.[21]

Looking toward a future international federation, or even alliance, built upon "kindred states," in contrast to the contemporary League of Nations (whose nations were not linked by common language, tradition, race, or history) Elliott hoped that the English Commonwealth could successfully create normative standards "for problems like the internationalization of raw materials, the adoption of common professional standards of legislation in shared interests ... citizenship, naturalization, shipping, courts of admiralty and copyright."[22]

By standardizing the legal apparatus of international regulation, Elliott was advocating for a type of international federalism not far removed from American federalism. Such regulations would require a strong and centralized legislative authority drawing ministers and representatives from the Commonwealth nations to participate in drafting the international controls, much like interstate controls drafted by the federal government in the United States. In 1928 he had already noted that U.S. federalism could serve as a model for international federalism: "The existence of the United States for a century and a half under a constitution that preserves to each state inviolably its equal representation in the Senate shows the possibility of international organization in which the sovereignty may be assigned by a constitutional agreement to fit the limits of the international community of purpose."[23] Yet this community of purpose presupposed a commonality of political, economic and moral values.

Like his emphasis on regional "commonwealths" to be drawn in the United States based on cultural affinities, within the English Dominions there already existed an Anglo-Saxon ruling class which shared "a common language and sentimental and racial ties which predispose experts toward more intimate collaboration" on international regulations.[24] It is important to note that England had only given Dominion status to the nations ruled by Anglo-Saxon majorities (even if the population was mostly black, as in the case of South Africa), entrusted to maintain their allegiance to English traditions and customs. The colonial nations from Egypt to Malaysia and India (though it was promised eventual Dominion status) were given no such autonomy. Instead, a system of "trusteeship" developed in the colonial countries, whereupon the British were said to be governing "in trust for the natives." In the meantime, with British colonization efforts serving as an outlet for its excess population into the more scarcely populated Commonwealth, the English proclaimed their intention of cultivating the natives for self-government in a liberal democratic tradition, so as to eventually grant them "responsible government" status.

As Elliott articulated England's hold over the Empire, it "depends on moral force, on the hold of institutions, on the subtle uses of venerable symbols, and on a gradual transformation of traditions that retain their spiritual essence."[25] Presumably this meant that the English hoped to gradually transform the Commonwealth into a unified system of legal and moral terms, though the "spiritual essence" of the natives would be permitted. In order to command the allegiance of the Empire's citizens, though, Elliott referred to the importance of the Round Table Group conferences, as "'Imperial' Conferences are multiplied, and 'experts' are brought from the ends of the earth, not alone for the tangible results their meetings accomplish but to fill them with the spirit of cooperation on which the Commonwealth depends.

"The great apostle of this form of imperialism was Lord Milner, and after him Mr. L.S. Amery [Milner's lieutenant at the Colonial Office after World War I] ... because this Rome, though it may diminish, will hardly be destroyed. In the most dire event, like Rome its monuments would be more enduring than marble or bronze, for its laws and its social habits will have stamped more of the human race with their impress than any civilization the world has seen."[26] Thus Elliott was referring to the intangible components of the English Imperial tradition like "education, beauty, rule of law, freedom, decency, and self-discipline," the apostle of which was John Ruskin, who so profoundly excited the Oxford of Cecil Rhodes, Lord Milner, and their Victorian imperialist cohorts. Elliott obviously admired England's imperial influences through education and law.[27]

On the other hand, Dominion nationalists like the Southern Irish and the Dutch Boers of South Africa, let alone the Indians, had a strong resentment toward British rule, making the allegiance of the Dominions to Great Britain a tenuous matter. South Africa and Ireland still asserted their right to remain neutral in war; and the unity of the British Commonwealth had yet to be tested by war.

As early as 1920 H. Duncan Hall, the Balliol College historian of *The British Commonwealth of Nations,* had articulated England's uncertainty about the cohesiveness of the Commonwealth in a time of war. When war finally did break out in Europe in 1939, the major imperial threat to England was not posed by Russia but by Germany. In early 1940, Elliott began working on a book, *The British Commonwealth at War,* with his friend Hall, whose 1920 history was considered by Elliott to be "for many years the outstanding work on the British Commonwealth."[28] In the intervening years Hall had worked at the League of Nations in charge of opium control and then as a liaison officer with the Commonwealth Nations. Hall would soon assume most of the responsibility for editing his and Elliott's book, which was eventually published in 1943, for Elliott was diverted by his work with the government's Office of Production Management. Nevertheless, Elliott helped Hall collect information through his contacts at the Round Table Group's Royal Institute of International Affairs, through its Director A. J. Toynbee, as well as other Round Table contacts such as Britain's Ambassador to the U.S. Lord Lothian (until his death in 1940), A.D. Marris,[29] and H.V. Hodson.[30]

By 1943, in the midst of an apocalyptic world war, the British Commonwealth now appeared "the most successful international organization that has yet been fashioned", according to at least one critic who gleaned the message of Elliott and Hall's book.[31] Elliott and Hall may have exaggerated any trepidation that "members of the British Commonwealth can be neutral in respect of one another," when in fact Ireland declared itself neutral and closed its ports to English ships during the war. However, the author's essential point proved correct when the rest of the Dominions carried on the war against the Axis powers.[32]

Presaging the international operations of the United Nations' "blue helmets" after World War II, when a Canadian force arrived in Hong Kong in 1943, Canada's Prime Minister declared that "defense against aggression, actual or threatened, in any part of the world is today a part of the defense of every country which still enjoys freedom."[33] On the other hand, the English desperately needed to preserve access to their Empire for geo-strategic purposes of waging the war, which in turn now required a vast "quantity and variety of raw materials and manufacturing skills," which could not be provided by any one nation. Fortunately, these economic ties would be reinforced by British conscription of soldiers from across its Commonwealth, on the premise of "the strong psychological bonds that unite the members of the Commonwealth to one another. It is in these bonds that the secret of the British Commonwealth lies."[34]

Hall was astutely differentiating between the Commonwealth's successes in providing mutual security against aggression, and the League of Nations' failures. Whether the English colonies were indeed "free" was irrelevant, for such loyalty to the Crown's assets by the Dominions exemplified for Hall the British Commonwealth's psychological conception of itself as a "family of nations." In this sense, the Commonwealth nations, including "most of the sixty millions of colored peoples in the colonial Empire," were united by a "common citizenship" through their respective nations and their constitutional body of laws which made their political systems compatible. Even though waging the war compartmentally, the Dominion field officers were responsible for their regional commands like "localized systems of defense in a world-wide complex."[35] The Dominions were thus living up to the League of Nations' aspirations for collective security, which had never been previously realized in the face of Japanese, Italian, and German expansion in the 1930s.

Hall's argument that the English Empire was psychologically bound obviously exaggerated the affinity of the colonial subjects toward the "family of nations." Yet this propaganda was intended to encourage an American alliance with the British Commonwealth as part of their shared democratic heritage. Before America's direct entry into the war, Elliott was eagerly promoting aid to England in the battle to preserve the "freedom of the seas" under British naval control because that freedom "means the maintenance of the British Commonwealth of Nations as our own front line."[36] So long as the British Empire was spread upon every region of the globe, America was not directly threatened by the Axis powers.

More importantly, Elliott believed that the English Commonwealth's vast extent would furnish the basis for creating a new international order after the war. "That Empire as a world empire holds the key to world control" along an economically and politically liberal philosophy that could still be coordinated with that of the United States.[37] Historically, Elliott noted the British complaint about America's unreliability as a political partner because "the Senate is always there. Your [i.e. American] diplomacy cannot deliver its promises, since one-third of your anachronistic Senate can always block the executive on international agreements."[38] This sentiment would seem to have been aggravated by the Congress' intransigence in joining the League of Nations in the 1920s, or committing to an alliance with England after the First World War.

Elliott's proposed constitutional reforms from 1935-'38 to curb the power of the Senate in restraining the president's treaty-making power never came to be; nonetheless, the centralization of Executive powers in America during the 1930s had laid the foundation for a strong Executive to guide the foreign policy of America after the next World War. Thereafter, the Republican majority in Congress surprisingly supported the Democratic President Truman's economic initiatives in aiding Europe with the Marshall Plan and military initiatives to replace England's traditional role in Greece and Turkey starting in 1947.

By far the most important step toward initiating Executive control on a permanent basis was the 1947 National Security Act, creating the Central Intelligence Agency and a National Security Council (under the President) which would be instrumental in keeping America engaged in international reconnaissance on a permanent basis. The government had certainly yet to solve the "warfare between the Executive and the Legislature," for the Legislature maintained control of the fiscal purse which would determine the viability of Executive foreign and domestic policies, but the realization by Congress and the President that America had an economic and political stake in the world order allowed America to pursue a protracted "cold" war for the first time in its history. It is imperative to understand how novel a course this was in American history; for such entrenched imperial supremacy across the globe had formerly been the conduct of the British, with their machinations for balancing power.

Endnotes

1. Leuchtenber, William E. *Franklin D. Roosevelt and the New Deal, 1932-1940*. Cited in Gibson, Donald. *Wealth, Power, and the Crisis of Laissez Faire Capitalism*. p. 96.
2. Agar, Herbert, et al. *The City of Man*. p. 90-3.
3. Ibid. p. 79.
4. Elliott, W.Y. "Getting a New Constitution." *Annals of the American Academy of Political and Social Science*, Vol. 185. May 1936. p. 120.
5. WYE to William F. Buckley, Jr., p. 2; Oct. 25, 1960; Box 77, Hoover Institute, Stanford.
6. Elliott, William Yandell. *The Need for Constitutional Reform*. p. 32.
7. Curtis, Lionel. *Civitas Dei*. London : Macmillan, 1934. p. 273-4.
8. Elliott, William Yandell. *The Need for Constitutional Reform*. p. 33.
9. Elliott seems to have initiated the idea of a Presidential line item veto for riders to bills, so as to give the Executive final say over the federal government's expenditures. Such unilateral power was ultimately implemented by the Line Item Veto Act of 1996, before being deemed unconstitutional by the Supreme Court in 1998.
10. Gentile, Richard H. "Elliott, William Yandell III." Dictionary of American Biography. Supplement 10. Ed. Kenneth T. Jackson. New York: Charles Scribner's Sons, 1995.
11. Elliott, William Yandell. "The Crisis of the American Constitution." p. 12
12. Relyea, Harold. *The Executive Office of the President: An Historical Overview*. CRS Report for Congress. November 26, 2008. p. 11.
13. Lindsay, A.D. *Essentials of Democracy*. p. 54.
14. Ibid. p. 82.

15. Elliott, W.Y. *The Need for Constitutional Reform*. p. 227.

16. Ibid. p.9.

17. Hence the appearance of Round Table members in various civil servant posts within Liberal, Conservative, and Labour governments all the way through World War II.

18. Quigley, Carroll. *The Anglo-American Establishment*. p. 85.

19. WYE to Jones; June 5, 1939; W.Y. Elliott Papers; Box 136, Hoover Institute.

20. It would appear that Elliott recognized in the British Commonwealth the inception of a real possibility for *Perpetual Peace* as Kant had proposed in the late-eighteenth century.

21. Elliott, W.Y. *The New British Empire*. 1st Ed. New York: McGraw-Hill Book Co., Inc., 1932. p. 3-4.

22. Ibid. p. 26

23. Ibid. p. 490-1..

24. Ibid. p. 27.

25. Ibid. p. 170.

26. Ibid. p. 131.

27. Quigley, Carroll. *Tragedy and Hope*. p. 130.

28. WYE to Henry Allen Moe (Secretary of the Guggenheim Memorial Foundation and fellow Balliol Rhodes Scholar); Dec. 8, 1939; Box 136, Hoover Institute Archives, Stanford

29. The son of Round Table Group founder William Marris, A.D. was at the British Embassy in Washington D.C. at the time.

30. Hodson wrote the *Proceedings* of the 1938 Round Table Conference on Commonwealth Affairs and knew Elliott through mutual friends in Ottawa, Canada. Hodson also figured prominently on *The Round Table* journal.

31. Commager, Henry Steele. "The Dominions Stand Firm." *The New York Times*. Aug. 1, 1943

32. Elliot, W.Y. and H. Duncan Hall, Ed. *The British Commonwealth at War*. New York: Alfred A. Knopf, 1943. p. 25.

33. Ibid. p. 73.

34. Ibid. p. 80.

35. Ibid. p. 60.

36. Ibid. p. 8.

37. Ibid. p. 8.

38. Elliott, W.Y. "A Joint Policy for Britain and the U.S.A." *The Political Quarterly*, Vol. 9, No. 2. April 1938. p. 180.

William Yandell Elliott at WBOS (Boston) microphone, circa 1940.
Courtesy Elliott family

Chapter V

The Crisis of World Order – On the Brink of World War

The word Fascism has now no meaning except in so far as it signifies "something not desirable"... It is almost universally felt that when we call a country democratic we are praising it: consequently the defenders of every kind of regime claim that it is a democracy, and fear that they might have to stop using that word if it were tied down to any one meaning. Words of this kind are often used in a consciously dishonest way. That is, the person who uses them has his own private definition, but allows his hearer to think he means something quite different.

– George Orwell, *The Politics of the English Language* (1946)

In 1938, England was still the pre-eminent power in the world, the only empire to have gained, territorially, from World War I on the spoils of the Ottoman and German Empires. Yet England had also become a net debtor, while America had replaced it as the world's creditor nation. On the other hand, England's imperial Commonwealth still amounted to about a quarter of the earth's land (and a quarter of its peoples). This massive base of human and natural resources made England content with the international status quo. According to the English delegates at the 2nd Unofficial Conference on Commonwealth Relations in September 1938, "a war in any part of the world, even if she [the British Empire] was not involved, would threaten her interests."[1]

This unofficial conference, which included all the Dominion nations, as well as India, was sponsored by the Round Table Groups in the Dominions. The conference was held in the midst of Prime Minister Neville Chamberlain's appeasement of Hitler's absorption of the Czechoslovakian Sudetenland into Germany. England's delegation to the Commonwealth Conference was headed by Lord Lothian, a chief architect of the appeasement policy, coordinated with England's Foreign Secretary Lord Halifax and her Ambassador to Germany Sir Neville Henderson. Lothian, as a member of the House of Lords, had met with Hitler in 1935 and agreed with him that in order "to stabilize Europe for 10 years the League of Nations should be dominated by [Cecil] Rhodes' view – USA, England and Germany would together preserve peace of the world."[2] This attitude was consecrated by the Anglo-German Naval Agreement of that year, setting the size of the German Navy at 35% the size of the Royal Navy, thereby setting the tone for Germany's rearmament through 1940.

England's appeasement of German militarization had become blatant by 1938, to an extent that many of the Dominions had grown critical of England's policy. According to Lord Lothian, the emphasis of the Unofficial Commonwealth Relations Conference was to retrieve "a tolerable international order," after the failure of the League of Nations system, involving "the maintenance of the British Empire as a bastion of liberty and peace in the world, and close collaboration with the United States, whose history and interests were so closely linked with those of Great Britain."[3] Essentially, the failure of the League would be blamed on American "isolationism," when in fact America had historically always maintained its independence from European imperial politics.

This 1938 Conference was not in fact an ordinary meeting of government officials, for it was a continuation of the Round Table system of conferences, wherein the Dominion branches of the Institutes of International Affairs (IIAs) chose the delegates to the conference. The IIAs were established by the Dominion members of the Round Table Group between 1927 and 1936, fashioned on the Royal Institute of International Affairs (RIIA), which was established largely by Lionel Curtis, the Oxford Colonial historian and agent of the Milner Round Table Group, immediately after World War I.

The intention of the RIIA, which also published *International Affairs* magazine, was to promote international cooperation within the Empire through "the holding of discussion meetings, the organization of study groups, the sponsoring of research, and the publication of information and materials based on these."[4] Curtis had been one of Lord Milner's first disciples in the South African Kindergarten, but by 1922 his elaborate writings on a federated world commonwealth seemed far from being achieved through the League of Nations, to which he devoted his attention in the 1920s. By 1925, after Milner's death, Lord Lothian, already the publisher of *The Round Table* journal, took a leading role within the Group and assumed Milner's place as administer of the Rhodes Trust; naturally, the Rhodes Trust sponsored the Round Table's Unofficial Conference on Commonwealth Relations in 1938.

If Curtis' ideal of a federated British Commonwealth, let alone a federated world commonwealth, seemed unrealistic by 1922, when the British Dominions had entered the League of Nations as separate members, then by 1931 when the Statutes of Westminster gave the Dominions independence, the Round Table Group felt that "what was necessary was the creation of a British-minded internationalism not a British super-nationalism;" i.e. imperialism.[5]

In meeting with Aldoph Hitler in 1935, Lothian had emphasized his internationalist position by deferring to Germany's pre-eminence as the Continental power. This meeting alone would not have given Germany the go-ahead to rearm, but when Hitler did seize the Rhineland, in violation of the Versailles peace settlement, the English made no quarrel. Essentially, Lothian, L.S. Amery, and other Round Table members, also known as "the Cliveden Set," adopted a "three-bloc world" policy of an Atlantic bloc (England and America), a Continental bloc (Germany and France) and Russia, which would in turn be restrained in the East by Japan. The key to the situation was that Germany and Russia never reach the Aegean or Adriatic seas to the south, which would be maintained by the Atlantic alliance.

At the same time, the Germans would be given Austria, part of Czechoslovakia, and the Polish Corridor;[6] this eastward thrust would put Russia and Germany in contact, providing a "front-line bulwark against the spread of Communism."[7] As England's White Paper of 1935 explained appeasement, "in the short run, Britain's policy is the avoidance of European conflict; in the long run, her policy continues to aim at recreating the conditions for world order where force is no longer the arbiter between states."[8]

In June 1938 *The Round Table* expanded on this temporary balance of power equation in Europe, by emphasizing that the League of Nations' ideal of collective security against aggression had failed in 1931 with the Japanese seizure of Manchuria, and then again in 1935 when Italy claimed Ethiopia. Accordingly, it was ineffective to hope for collective security in a world without super-ordinate laws and enforcers, so "the best security for peace is that *the world should be divided into zones* within each of which one of the great armed Powers, or a group of them, is clearly preponderant" (emphasis added).[9]

This balance of power was not readily acceptable to those Round Tablers who still believed in the ideal of world commonwealth based on a single international law and order. Lionel Curtis had been the perceiver of such a one-world doctrine when he promised the end-goal of the movement as "the organization of all human society in one state based on the principle of the *commonwealth*."[10]

When the Commonwealth delegates convened in 1938, with a Round Tabler from Australia chairing the Conference,[11] a great deal of discussion centered around the organization of a "new world order,"[12] Would the new world order stem from the organizational base of the English Commonwealth, the only transnational system of government to have yet proven effective? Or would the new order require a new world government? These questions generated numerous answers from the delegates, as well as one response from a group of Anglophile intellectuals in America who were concurrently expressing their vision for a renovated world order.

After the English appeasement of Germany in September 1938, a group of intellectuals in America began formulating their objections, including University of Chicago President Robert M. Hutchins,[13] Professor G.A. Borgese, his father-in-law Thomas Mann (the German novelist) and Distributist-supporter Lewis Mumford. It was not until May 1939, three months before Germany and Russia's joint invasion of Poland, that this group coalesced its thinking into a memorandum, which then circulated to other intellectuals, stating that the "Western Powers, perhaps fortified by a more or less ambiguous alliance with Russia, will resist the forthcoming challenges of Nazism and Fascism" or else suffer the demise of Western Europe.[14]

While Germany's absorption of Austria and the Czech Sudetenland in 1938 had been seen as permissible by the British Round Table, the group still expected Hitler's methods of expansion to be peaceful and patient, so as to avoid arousing British public opinion. Instead, when Hitler violently occupied Bohemia and Moravia in March 1939, the Milner Group shifted its policy from appeasement to a "Grand Alliance" of Poland, France, and tentatively Soviet Russia[15] (as mentioned in the Hutchins-group Memo circulated two months later). In the meantime, the Milner Group still hoped to maintain peace by letting Hitler dominate the European Continent, so long as Germany did not violate Turkey or Greece, which would have jeopardized England's maritime hold on the Aegean and Adriatic Seas.[16]

Lord Lothian, who had prominently supported the appeasement of Germany, now prepared the public Milner group position of a "Grand Alliance Against Aggression" in an anonymous article for *The Round Table.*[17] Shedding crocodile tears, Lothian lamented that Germany's "drastic and brutal subjugation of Czechoslovakia" in March went far beyond the pacifistic limits expected by the legalistic British when they had conceded to German acquisition of the Sudetenland. Lothian had recently been appointed British Ambassador to America (where he would remain until his death in 1940), and as he proceeded to America in 1939, he conceded that a balance of power strategy would no longer suffice to maintain peace. In words echoing Lionel Curtis', Lothian confessed the Round Table's true ambition of a world government, for "the only way in which you can secure the reign of morality in the international sphere is by Federal Union. Until you do that, power will reign and the practical choice between statesmen is not right or wrong but the lesser of two evils."[18]

In America, Hutchins' and Borgese's memo led to the convening of a conference in late May 1940, held by the self-proclaimed "Committee on Europe." The product of the group's deliberation, *The City of Man: A Declaration of World Democracy* (1940), was a book that seemed reminiscent of the Round Table's Commonwealth Conference of 1938. Now in

1940 it was the Americans, led by such Anglophiles as Frank Aydelotte (former Rhodes Scholar and current American Secretary of the Rhodes Trust), the American Distributist leader Herbert Agar, Lewis Mumford (Knighted in 1943 for service to the British Empire), and W.Y. Elliott,[19] who determined that "universal peace can be founded only on the unity of man under one law and one government."

Some of the Round Table delegates to the 1938 Conference had intimated that "the British Commonwealth may be the means to that end [of world government]."[20] Likewise, the Committee on Europe accorded England premier status in organizing the world, for "Europe with Britain – and with the nations of the British Commonwealth – is already the world."[21] Indeed, between the empires of England, France, Portugal, and the Netherlands, the majority of the world served as a colony for the European powers.

According to the opening speaker on the issue of the "Commonwealth as a Co-operative Organization," at the 1938 Round Table Conference, human beings would have to "develop the sense of duty… to all others," intimating a world commonwealth. This created allegations by other delegates that normal men could not readily accept political affiliations of too wide a sphere, for "man remained a small-scale animal. Life in a small community was, and always would be, more natural to him…"[22]

In 1940, the Committee on Europe thus discerned that the movement toward world government must be both "centripetal and peripheral," for just as the world government gains centralizing authority, "regional decentralization will effectually distribute power to the smallest local unit, the city and the village, down to the elemental unit which is the family, while world-wide authority will make cooperation possible among them all." Their antipathy to national organization emphasized a specific opponent: Germany, the nation which had only recently managed to centralize its industries in order to develop its economy and arms production to a place of asserting itself once more as an imperial power; "all centralizing structures – and not Germany alone … must fall into smaller federal units."

The Committee on Europe was fundamentally declaring war on the nation-state, to balkanize it into a "deflated and disciplined," and thus manageable proportion of local groups and organizations, "under the law of the world-state" for the so-called "peace" of tomorrow.[23] Likewise, the Round Table delegates had discussed the implications of a future world order in a League of Nations structure, strengthened by "the surrender of national sovereignty, the pooling of security, economic co-operation," etc. The nation-state, with its assumption of national sovereignty, was indeed inimical to the Committee's plans, as the group even intimated an eventual end to American national sovereignty once it had played its part in creating a world government,[24] for "the Pax Americana is [but a] preamble to the Pax Humana."[25]

When the Committee on Europe spoke of a "Pax Humana," they were suggesting the adoption of a system of legal authority acceptable to all governments as part of their commitment to the world order. To the Committee, this peace for all humanity could be achieved through peaceful means of alliance, just as the British Commonwealth had been formed through independent cooperation, while ignoring the prospect of further wars to force other governments into conformity with the legal codes imposed upon them by this new world order.

At the end of World War I, the English imperial federalists of the Round Table Movement had first broached the issue of building within the Empire "an Imperial super-State which perhaps in alliance with the United States would be powerful enough to impose peace upon the world." On the other hand, the more level-headed imperialists recognized that such a super-state would only "perpetuate international rivalry" and would probably alienate the isolationist-prone Unites States. Consequently, the Round Table Groups of the Dominions adopted a course for establishing the British Commonwealth "as a group of free 'allied' states" to encourage rather than coerce cooperation.[26] In a similar vein, the Committee on Europe intended to adopt a method of creating moral cohesion.

Years before the United Nations' 1948 platform for a Declaration of Human Rights, the Committee on Europe advocated the adoption of "a universal law first promulgated to all humanity, entrusted to the good will of those groups and communities that are progressively disposed to adopt it, *then enforced on the rebels*, finally to become the common peace and freedom of all the people of the earth" (emphasis added).[27] In other words, the Western democracies needed to first determine the economic and moral values that would unite mankind, and then spread this platform through allies to coerce the "rebels," or rogue states and players, into accepting the platitudes.

The Committee recognized in 1940, before the greatest destruction of the century had yet to occur, that in order to spread this universal system of values, "the area of destruction must probably spread before the path is clear for the new order." These men believed that the new order could not be born except from chaos, for the world's peoples were not all governed by any single religious, social, or economic tradition, nor a singular legal ethic. In order to create a homogeneous intellectual milieu for the formation of a "Universal Parliament" representing all of humanity, the colonized and undemocratic ("barbarian") peoples would have to be "educated to the full responsibility of their coming freedom."[28]

According to the Committee on Europe, the twenty years between World Wars had seen "the plight of democracy" due to an "education adrift in a relativity that doubted all values" save "material delights." The Committee accused "science" of shirking "the spiritual issues" to the point that a "pragmatic" philosophy developed, focusing more on material ends than on the moral and spiritual means.[29] Pragmatism and the "philosophy of intuition" were based on assumptions that life is "constant flux and change," impressionistic and irrational. These attitudes were prominent in pre-war Europe where the intellectual avant-garde like author Van Wyck Brooks (a contributor to *The City of Man*) had spent time. By War's end in 1919, even that generation's "rebellious optimists became despairing nihilists," according to the Committee, and pragmatism's distrust of rationalism and idealism had swept aside faith in democracy as a means of permanently ending war.[30]

Now, like the Jacobins of the French Revolution, the Committee hoped to indoctrinate the people of the world with "the highest religion" – Democracy. In the democratic community, freedom no longer meant the "corrupted liberalism" of individuality and national autonomy afforded to states, for the citizens and their nations should find "harmony subordinated to a plan."[31] A plan for the Universal State could be found in "the law of common wealth," intimating social duties for the political and economic welfare of all.[32]

The Round Table's 1938 Conference opening speaker on Commonwealth Co-operation had proclaimed "the object of human existence was to develop the sense of duty in each man to all others… An international sense of duty, which would make international law a reality, could only be exercised and developed in an international Commonwealth."[33] Following this argument, the Committee on Europe considered the New Deal to be "the most important example" of economic remodeling of a society in consideration of the general welfare; this implied that the Committee believed democracy to mean the collective duty of citizens to contribute to the "common wealth."[34] Consequently, though democratic communities were innately assured freedom of thought and representation, the Committee held that democracy deserved one imposition – faith in democracy. Allegiance to democracy would in turn become an allegiance to a process of democratization, rested upon the faith that "there is no liberty but one: the right, *which is a duty*, of making one self and others free through absolute allegiance to the final goal of man" (*emphasis added*).

The Committee did not explicate the "final goal of man," but they clearly believed that only democracy, as a political vehicle, would allow people to achieve the goal of "common wealth." Accordingly, "the City of Man" meant the achievement of democratic communities under the rule of a "Universal

Parliament" devoted to the "highest religion"; the democratic faith's power lay in political participation based on rights and the subsequent feeling of duty to the democracy.[35] Unfortunately, the City of Man failed to reconcile how democracy, or the vote of the majority, might in fact conflict with the rights and benefits of the minority, or even the goals of the common wealth. After all, Nazi Germany and fascist Italy were consequences of democratic platforms and processes that brought Hitler and Mussolini to power, respectively. In effect, they had elected dictators

Ignoring the failures of democracy to prevent war in Europe, the Committee saw the leadership for the project to create "the City of Man" inevitably coming from "The New World," which "is the United States."[36] In this venture they hoped that America would adopt her imperial heritage from Britain, as the Romans had evolved the world empire of the Greek's.[37]

Even amidst the Great Depression, America was still the foremost economic power in the world, thanks to the massive debts owed it by the European belligerents of World War I. On the other hand, America's history demonstrated its uneasy attitude toward European affairs, for the American tradition of foreign policy since President Washington had stipulated its independent disposition from any "entangling alliances" in European affairs. Of course, America had colonies in the Pacific since the expansion of its Empire all the way to the Philippines at the end of the nineteenth century, but traditionally America was committed to the Monroe Doctrine of 1823, preserving the Americas as independent of European colonialism.

The memory of World War I and Britain's pro-war propaganda from its leading authors, including H.G. Wells, was still fresh in the minds of most Americans. And the 1934-'36 Nye Committee's implications that America was dragged into war for the profits of international arms-dealers and bankers (particularly J.P. Morgan) made the prospect of another war in Europe all the more unappealing. Thus, in November 1940 "at a moment when tentative plans for appeasement and rumors of even greater drives for 'peace' and appeasement to come [were] being circulated with increasing boldness" in America, the Anglophile Committee on Europe offered a bold prediction of a non-isolationist future where America would actually lead the way in redesigning the world order.[38]

The authors' admiration for England was apparent in their appraisal of it as the country "where modern man first rose to his dignity" because of its long tradition of parliamentary representation, but there are other indications of Anglophile connections within the group.[39] As already mentioned, the ideology of the declaration correlated to the Round Table Group's aspirations for a system of world governance, which even the British government's Defence White Paper of 1935 articulated as "the peaceable development of that tradition of freedom and co-operation which is its outstanding contribution to civilization."[40] On the other hand, the means for attaining world governance had yet to be unanimously resolved by the Round Table Group, which even seemed to splinter over the issue of appeasing Germany.

W.Y. Elliott was one such critic of appeasement, at least by late 1938, and when Professor Alfred Zimmern, one of the intellectual architects of the Round Table Movement in the 1910s, came to visit him at Harvard, Elliott criticized him for "pussy-footing" around. On the other hand, appeasement "did not altogether run along with [Zimmern's] own views. So he professed afterwards."[41] Zimmern, an attendee at the 1938 Round Table Conference on Commonwealth Relations, seems to have remained loyal to the vision of a strong League of Nations with federal powers of enforcement to ensure world order, rather than weakening the League for the sake of Continental peace under German hegemony. As for Elliott, he made his own efforts to obstruct the promulgation of appeasement in 1938 and '39 by "several times thwart[ing] [the Cliveden Set's] machinations when they were trying to turn the policy of the *Christian-Science Monitor* [in America] in this direction and in other maneuvers."[42] The Cliveden Set, named after Lord Astor's English estate, referred to the circle around Round Tablers Lord Milner, Lothian, Halifax and others who were actively promoting the appeasement of Germany, "in that they sought to contain the Soviet Union between a German-dominated Europe and an English-speaking bloc."[43]

Meanwhile, Elliott's anti-fascist pedigree led him into collaboration with two of the most prominent Italian expatriate intellectuals, Giuseppe Borgese and Gaetano Salvemini (both contributors to *The City of Man*). Borgese was actually the main scribe of *The City of Man*, and his antipathy to fascism soon put him, as well as Salvemini, in contact with the Office of Strategic Services (OSS, the forerunner to the CIA), which began running a recruitment program in 1942 to prepare for the invasion of Italy. Yet, before America's involvement in World War II even began, Elliott was already cooperating with the Mazzini Society, a group of Italian émigrés including Salvemini, Count Carlo Sforza, and Max Ascoli.[44]

The society was coordinating anti-Fascist activity in America, but as the Italian newspaper *La Notizia* charged, it was "financed by the British to smear the patriotism of Americans of Italian origin by labeling them as fascist and paid agents of the fascist government."[45] Indeed, Elliott's introduction to Salvemini's 1940 pamphlet for the American Council on Public Affairs undemocratically demanded that if "Italy expels Americans ruthlessly[; l]et us do the same in return." He justified his call for a neo-Alien and Sedition Act by charging that all Italian fascist sympathizers were "Mussolini's agents," perhaps justifying *La Notizia*'s allegations about the Mazzini Society. Most disconcertingly, Elliott did not concede the freedom of speech integral to democracy when he begged the federal power of deportation of fascist sympathizers.[46]

The other crucial connection for Elliott and the Mazzini Society was the Society's relationship to British intelligence. According to Max Corvo, an OSS officer involved in the Italian expedition from 1942, "in order to maintain a high degree of control and to monitor anti-Fascist activities in the United States, the British relied on their connections with the Mazzini Society."[47] It would not be surprising if Elliott, the former Rhodes Scholar and friend of the historian/British intelligence agent A.J. Toynbee,[48] was one of their intelligence contacts in America. Toynbee was the director of the Royal Institute of International Affairs when it merged with British intelligence's Foreign Office in 1939. To securely conduct intelligence gathering and planning, the intelligence apparatus moved to Balliol College, Oxford, whose Master, A.D. Lindsay, had mentored both Toynbee and Elliott.[49] In sum, the Anglophile nexus involved with *The City of Man* in 1940 makes it a curiously propagandistic text for world government,[50] though the book itself received little attention from the public.

As for Elliott's British-backed Mazzini Society, their attempts to regain power in Italy proved unsuccessful because the Society's "key men were reported to have contacts with the British intelligence service which was believed to support a postwar retention of the monarchy."[51] Many Italian émigrés, particularly of the labor movement, were intensely hostile to the Italian monarchy, and when the British sent a refugee, Dino Gentili, to America to encourage the establishment of a government-in-exile under the old aristocrat of the Mazzini Society, Count Sforza, the American State Department refused to support it.[52] After FDR's death at the end of the war, the CIA (perhaps taking its cue from British intelligence) was not opposed to running clandestine operations in 1948 to influence the elections against the Communist Party candidate and secure a victory for the pro-Western Christian Democrat, Luigi Einaudi.

Through various clandestine schemes of the CIA after World War II, along with overt Congressional allocations of financial and military aid, the American government abandoned its tradition of non-interference in European national affairs (beginning with military aid to Greece in 1946), as predicted by the Committee on Europe. America proceeded to adopt the imperialist attitude of interfering in foreign countries' internal affairs, often under the auspices of protecting democracy. W.Y. Elliott's own collaboration with American government anti-communist propaganda activities will be discussed in Chapter Six. Yet, beginning in 1940, whether Elliott's collaboration with the Mazzini Society made him a collaborator with foreign British intelligence would ultimately prove immaterial to his vision for a constitutional world order, to be reached, in the words of Winston Churchill during his 1946 "Iron Curtain Speech," "if the population of the English-speaking Commonwealths be added to that of the United States with all that such co-operation implies in the air, on the sea, all over the globe and in science and in industry, and in moral force."

In this endeavor, Churchill and his British counterparts, like Elliott and his Anglophile collaborators, were imitating the ideology of Cecil Rhodes, whose various wills were essentially "inspired by the same idea," according to Rhodes' principal Trustee from 1925-'39, Lord Lothian, for "the extension and stabilization of civilization throughout the world on the basis of the political ideals embodied in the British and American constitutions."[53] To realize this project, Rhodes had allegedly established a secret society with Milner in 1891, "The Society of the Elect," whose ultimate aim was "the extension of British rule throughout the world... the ultimate recovery of the United States of America as an integral part of a British Empire, the consolidation of the whole Empire, the inauguration of a system of Colonial Representation in the Imperial Parliament... and finally the foundation of so great a power as to hereafter render wars impossible."[54] The endeavor may have taken more than a generation, but by the late 1930s the adherents of this open conspiracy had begun to make progress in the reincorporation of America into a "special relationship" with England.

Endnotes

1. *The British Commonwealth and the Future. Proceedings of the Second Unofficial Conference on Commonwealth Relations*. Ed. H.V. Hodson. New York: Oxford University Press, 1939. p. 23.

2. Transcript of conversation quoted in Chaitkin, Anton. *Treason in America*. 2nd Ed. Washington, D.C.: Executive Intelligence Review, 1998. p. 557-8.

3. Hodson, H.V. p. 117-8.

4. Quigley, Carroll. *The Anglo-American Establishment*. p. 182-5.

5. Kendle, John E. *The Round Table Movement*. Toronto: University of Toronto Press, 1975. p. 289.

6. Quigley, Carroll. *Tragedy and Hope*. p. 643.

7. Ibid. p. 619.

8. Quoted in Hodson, H.V. p. 24.

9. Quoted in *The Anglo-American Establishment*. Quigley, Carroll. p. 282.

10. Curtis, Lionel. *Civitas Dei*. London: Macmillan & Co., 1934.) p. 277.

11. T.R. Bavin; other Round Table Group delegates of note were Lionel Curtis, A.E. Zimmern, Vincent Massey, and the editor of the *Proceedings* H.V. Hodson (all of whom, save Curtis, were known affiliates of W.Y. Elliott).

12. Hodson, H.V. p. 199.

13. In 1948 Hutchins, as University President, would sponsor "a program for a World Republic," including national surrender over expropriation rights, the power of taxation, regulation of trans-

portation, etc. (See Wormser, Rene. p. 34).

14. Agar, Herbert, et al. *The City of Man: A Declaration on World Democracy.* New York: The Viking Press, 1941. p. 97-8.

15. Quigley. *The Anglo-American Establishment.* p. 292.

16. Quigley. *Tragedy and Hope.* p. 643.

17. "The Grand Alliance Against Aggression." *The Round Table: A Quarterly Review of the Politics of the British Commonwealth.* No. 115. June 1939.

18. Quoted in Butler, J.R.M. *Lord Lothian (Philip Kerr).* New York: St. Martin's Press, 1960. p. 256.

19. Only Borgese, Agar, Mumford, and Elliott served on the Committee's Executive Board.

20. Hodson, H.V. p. 229.

21. Agar, Herbert, et al. *The City of Man.* p. 23-4.

22. Hodson, H.V. p. 241.

23. *The City of Man.* p. 23-26.

24. In 1957 the Foreign Policy Research Institute launched *Orbis*, a foreign policy journal with W.Y. Elliott on the Editorial Board, with an article declaring that "The mission of the American people is to bury the nation-state, lead their bereaved peoples into larger unions, and overawe with its might the would-be saboteurs of the new order... It is likely that the accomplishment of this mission will exhaust the energies of America and that, then, the historical center of gravity will shift to another people." (Strausz-Hupe, Robert; "The Balance of Tomorrow"; p. 26).

25. *The City of Man.* p. 66.

26. Hall, H. Duncan. *The British Commonwealth of Nations.* p. 218.

27. *The City of Man.* p. 95.

28. Ibid. p. 26.

29. *The City of Man.* p. 17-8.

30. May, Henry F. "The Rebellion of the Intellectuals, 1912-1917." *American Quarterly*, Vol. 8, No. 2 (Summer, 1956). p. 114 - 126.

31. Ibid. p. 33..

32. Ibid. p. 85-6

33. Hodson, H.V. p. 241.

34. Ibid. p. 93.

35. Ibid. p. 29-33.

36. Ibid. p. 13.

37. The *City of Man* authors invoked for America a Roman tradition where "Rome did not spread upon the world; the world spread upon the Romans," who represented Civilization to the "barbarians." (p. 64).

38. Poore, Charles. *Books of the Times. The New York Times.* Nov. 30, 1940.

39. *The City of Man.* p. 13..

40. Hodson, H.V. p. 24

41. WYE to A.D. Lindsay. Jan. 31, 1939. William Y. Elliott Papers; Box 161, Hoover Institute Archives, Stanford.

42. WYE to Samuel Beer; August 25, 1961; William Y. Elliott Papers; Box 77, Hoover Institute Archives, Stanford.

43. Quigley, Carroll. *Tragedy and Hope.* P. 581.

44. Ascoli was the first President of the Society; he had known Elliott since 1931 when he first came to Harvard as a visiting professor.

45. "La Notizia." April 7, 1945; as reproduced in letter from Einaundi to WYE; May 26, 1945;

William Y. Elliott Archives, Harvard University.

46. Elliott, William Yandell, Introduction. "Why Tolerate Mussolini's Agents?" From *Italian Fascist Activities in the U.S.* By Dr. Gaetano Salvemini. American Council on Public Affairs: Wash. D.C. 1940. p. 1-2.

47. From Corvo, Max. *The O.S.S. in Italy, 1942-1945*. New York: Praeger, 1990. p. 28

48. Toynbee, the nephew of the Oxford professor Arnold Toynbee (Lord Milner's mentor), became an outstanding member of Milner's Round Table as director of its think-tank, the Royal Institute of International Affairs.

49. While a young professor at Oxford from 1907-1916, Toynbee was described as the "protégé" of A.D. Lindsay during those crucial developmental years. (See Williamm H. McNeill. *Arnold J. Toynbee*. p. 25).

50. Furthermore, in 1942 Toynbee was brought to America by the Rockefeller Foundation where he met with his American colleagues like Wall Street lawyer John Foster Dulles, to whom he proposed the need for a world government, "independent of any nation or group of nations, and those who determine from time to time its powers and personnel must come to include those who are now neutrals and enemies." (McNeill, p. 183-4).

51. *The O.S.S. in Italy, 1942-1945*. p. 20.

52. Ibid. p. 29-30.

53. Quoted in Butler, J.R.M. *Lord Lothian (Philip Kerr)*. p. 128.

54. Quigley, Carroll. *The Anglo-American Establishment*. p. 33.

William Yandell Elliott served six U.S. Presidents.

Courtesy Elliott family

Chapter VI

A New Economic Order – World War II

The colonial system means war. Exploit the resources of an India, a Burma, a Java; take all the wealth out of these countries, but never put anything back into them, things like education, decent standards of living, minimum health requirements – all you're doing is storing up the kind of trouble that leads to war.

– Pres. Franklin Roosevelt, quoted by his son Elliott in *As He Saw It* (1946)

If the American-led international order that emerged after World War II could be called the "new world order," then the previously existing order must refer to British international hegemony since the end of the Napoleonic Wars in 1815. The consummate myth of that century was that the English-dominated balance of power in Western Europe had led to "an epoch of unprecedentedly rapid growth," supported by the "relative prevalence of harmony over inconsistency, of order over disorder."[1] This harmony, initially embodied in the balance of power between Russia, Prussia, Austria, and England, known as the Concert of Europe, was reinforced economically and militarily by Britain's domination of the seas, ensuring the imperial access to colonial markets, as well as by England's horde of gold and silver to back its credit system.

According to the myth of a liberal world order, the nationalist economics arising from Germany by the 1830s imperiled the order by "seriously impair[ing] the efficiency of the international economy," which had formerly "relied principally upon the automatic forces of private markets, supplemented by inconspicuous and largely informal central authority exercised from London."[2] However, British liberalism, even under the appearance of harmony, was imperialistic and recognized as such by men like Friedrich List of Germany, who helped found the *Zollverein* customs union in 1834 as a federation amongst German states to protect against English dumping of refined goods. List proved to be an economic nationalist like his American brethren Henry Clay and Henry Carey, with whom he had worked to enact the protectionist tariffs and government-led industrial growth of the 1820s.

List's book, *The National System of Political Economy*, proved his commitment to economic nationalism by the contention that "European nations... must commence with the development of their own internal manufacturing powers... Should they be hindered in these endeavors by

England's manufacturing, commercial, and naval supremacy, in the union of their powers lies the only means of reducing such pretensions... Every war which the powers of the continent have waged against one another [in the last century] has had for its invariable result to increase the industry, the wealth, the navigation, the colonial possessions, and the power of the insular supremacy," i.e. Great Britain.[3] The Continental Europeans continued to play into the imperialist warfare taking place between Britain and its sometime rivals, sometimes allies, like Turkey, France, Russia, and Germany, in order to control the geographic circumstances of this international order.[4]

The nineteenth century was in fact dominated by private market forces in England, like the banking and merchant interests of the East India Company, whose policies of "free trade" justified two Opium Wars with China, using government force to open China's markets to British trade, including the forced legalization of opium. On the other hand, the geographic grasp for natural resources by the European imperialists came to a head during the 1880s in the "scramble for Africa," though it had been private companies like Rhodes' British South Africa Company that had spearheaded Britain's move into Africa, and precipitated wars in South Africa to secure its hold.

Yet England's national economy (as opposed to its private corporate and banking interests) had begun to decline by the 1870s, beginning with the depression of 1873. "The lack of capital investment into British manufactures was evident already at the International Exhibition of 1867... Export of British iron and steel, coal and other products declined in this period. It was a turning point in British history which signaled that the onset of 'free trade' some three decades earlier, with the repeal of the Corn Laws, had doomed English industrial technology to decadence in order that finance assume supremacy in the affairs of the Empire."[5] While Britain's "buy cheap, sell dear" mercantile policy had sacrificed the health of its domestic industries and agriculture, the Empire persevered thanks to "the City" in London (i.e. the private financial houses, which in turn owned the Bank of England), which acted as the world's creditor for international trade and investments. Meanwhile, the British colonial experience on the whole proved that "imperialism can best be viewed as a mechanism for transferring income from the middle to the upper classes."[6]

By the end of the nineteenth century the English nation's economic health was clearly threatened by two burgeoning industrial nations, America and Germany. When England declared war on Germany in 1914, on the pretense of its alliance with Belgium, the nation was near bankruptcy and had to abandon the gold standard in order to inflate its currency to debt-finance the war effort. It could be argued that Britain and France also staked the war on accessing the oil resources of Germany's ally, the Ottoman Empire, in the Middle East (via the 1916 Sykes-Picot Agreement).[7] As the war dragged on though, it was the American Anglophile J.P. Morgan Bank, through its houses in England, which would largely subsidize England and France's effort to the tune of over $1 billion until America's entry in 1917 secured Morgan's investment.

The nineteenth century's international economic order had collapsed as England ceased to be the world's largest creditor nation, replaced now by the United States. Yet to the American Anglophiles of the Morgan bank, with its agents and allies in the new Council on Foreign Relations (founded in 1921), America needed a broader international policy to accommodate its global financial interests, which coincided with England's financial assets.

According to W.Y. Elliott, the idea of commonwealth, as proposed by Cicero in *De Republica,* was "a consensus of agreement on the basis of law – what today we call a constitutional system – and also upon a community of utility or *shared economic interest*" (emphasis added).[8] After World War I, in order to manipulate public opinion within the British Commonwealth and in America toward closer collaboration and internationalism, the Round Table's Lionel Curtis proposed the formation of Institutes of International Affairs in the Dominions and the United States.[9] Consequently, the Royal Institute of International Affairs was founded in 1919, with the American counterpart, the Council on Foreign Relations (CFR) established in New York City in 1921 with Thomas Lamont of J.P. Morgan and former Rhodes Scholar Whitney Shepardson heading the American branch.

W.Y. Elliott became a member of the CFR in 1934 and remained a member through the 1960s. From its founding, the CFR's select members consistently promoted an internationalist role for America, in contrast to the isolationist tendency of America's Congress after the war. The CFR's Research Committee director in the 1920s and '30s, Isaiah Bowman, compared America's economic interests to Britain's, embracing the "east and west from China to the Philippines to Liberia and Tangier." But unlike Britain's territorial empire, America's would be a commercial empire based exclusively on the trade of foreign raw materials in exchange for American-made goods.[10]

By 1931, however, the hope for an Anglo-American alliance, even informally, was far from realized. Instead, Congress had recently adopted the highly protectionist Smoot-Hawley Tariff of 1930, while the worldwide depression had ruined the Anglo-American debt system of the Dawes and Young plans (1924-'31), wherein America had loaned money to Germany to repay its debts to England, thus aiding England's financial recovery.

Amidst the depression, even England's now independent Dominion nations were pursuing increasingly nationalistic economic programs of industrialization, to the detriment of Great Britain, by excluding "any real sharing of public wealth, either by common taxes, or tariffs, or ownership of natural resources."[11] England was even rebuffed at the Imperial Conference of 1930 when it tried to convince the Dominions to lower their tariffs in order to alleviate the early stages of the depression. Thus, not only was British merchant finance threatened by nationalization platforms in its own Dominions, but now the Soviet Union epitomized nationalist economic policies, since Lenin's New Economic Policy of 1921, that could encourage other nations to follow its course of rapid industrialization behind state protections.

At the start of the 1930s, W.Y. Elliott remarked, "standing squarely across [England's] imperial path in many exploitable resources, notably wheat, oil, timber, minerals, and to some degree cotton also, now stands the Soviet Giant. He is useful to the Empire only in that he threatens the Dominions economically and makes them more dependent on British favors." Under state capitalism mechanisms, Russia could cheaply produce exportable goods that could then be "dumped" on the international markets at below-production cost, much in the same way that England had utilized its own manufacturing technology to dump its goods on underdeveloped nations in the nineteenth century. Russia's empire was also extremely resource-rich and had natural access to oil for industry. According to Elliott, this competition could be used to draw the Dominions closer to England in a cohesive economic bloc by offering each other trade benefits. On the other hand, the Commonwealth's main targets for trade were resource-rich countries like India and China, whom the Russians were now advancing upon with their new industrial products.[12]

On the whole though, England still enjoyed a preponderance of trade with all of its Dominions in 1931, save Canada, which had industrialized most rapidly and was importing heavily from its industrialized neighbor, America. In fact, the U.S. had become England's chief "rival" in trade with the Dominions. As an American, Elliott should have had little to fear from economic nationalism in a country as resource-rich and technologically advanced as America. As Elliott pointed out in 1931, "so long as her natural riches are not exhausted" America could recover from the Great Depression with its industrial capacity still intact.[13] Nevertheless, Elliott linked America's relationship with the British Commonwealth to trade with Canada. According to Elliott, "the development of the British league is of more importance than almost any other contemporary problem," and so Canada's friendship should be courted by reducing America's tariffs to encourage trade between the two nations, guaranteeing "the future security of Anglo-American relations."[14]

Elliott recognized how invaluable an asset England's "informal empire" would be for the international stability of economic order. He suggested in 1931 that the Dominions should remember that "access on favored terms to [England's] immense colonial dependencies may one day be very valuable to the Dominions in the struggle of raw materials or markets."[15] As for England, its "one hope" for overcoming its problems of dwindling production and nationalist competition would be for England to "organize the democratic nations of Europe and the west, inviting collaboration of America, for concerted economic action through Geneva [i.e. the League of Nations]... Though it calls itself Socialist, at heart [the ruling Labor Party] is content to put off "nationalization" indefinitely and rely upon international finance for help. If, therefore, the British Empire can transform itself into a workable league of nations within the world League, on a purely consultative and co-operative basis, divesting itself of a mercantilist philosophy of exploitation wherever that status is not based on consent, it may afford more effective leadership to the great democracies of the West in the coming struggle with the *common enemy*, autocratic Bolshevism" (emphasis added).[16] Perhaps the Soviets were considered the common enemy because of their non-democratic Communist Party rule, but they had also defaulted on foreign debts after seizing power in 1917, and their economics of state-regulated production and trade remained outside British financial control.

Instead of taking the leadership position Elliott had suggested, in 1931 the English Labor government under PM MacDonald dissolved and formed a National government with the Conservatives and Liberals as a reaction to the Great Depression, putting the English economy behind protectionist trade barriers and creating a cartelized socialism, including the consolidation of private utilities in public hands. Although Elliott opposed the protectionism of the English government in the 1930s, he did agree with the centralizing socialist economic measures taking place in both England and America as a means toward ultimately "freeing international trade."[17]

As a New Dealer, Elliott's 1935 text on *The Need for Constitutional Reform* had encouraged the American government to begin stockpiling resources for the nation's industrial future, even as he denounced the "complete socialism of Russia." Elliott distinguished democratic socialism from nationalistic socialism by claiming that the state should act as a partner *with* capitalism by controlling the "fiscal, credit, and banking systems" in order to create secure conditions for capitalist relations.

In order to avoid the exploitative and monopolistic capitalism of the pre-Depression era, Elliott advocated that the state assume "a type of holding-company control" on American utility companies and natural resources industries.[18] The models for this type of management were the Royal Dutch Shell and Anglo-Persian Oil Companies, whose major stock-holder was the British government, which then had an effective method of "controlling the development of a vital industry" for national and international consumption.[19] Quite probably, Elliott detested Soviet economic nationalism because it did not allow foreign (i.e. British or American) capital to develop and exploit its resource assets and industrial potential, though he encouraged the American state to protect its own capitalistic mechanisms through governmental conservation and allocations. In the long run, he envisioned that the joined Anglo-American territory's resource assets would be enough to allow for "a planned world economic system" using an internationally-organized fiscal and banking system. Though Elliott treated the idea of the internationally "planned" system as "Utopian" in 1937, he cryptically asserted, "Utopias themselves are not without their uses."[20]

In a sense, the British Agricultural Marketing Act of 1931, which centralized control of certain crop distributions, was a national version of Elliott's suggestions, beginning in 1931, for *international* control of commodity and resource distribution, though his definition of "international" remained vague. It seems that Elliott intended for some sort of strengthened League of Nations superstructure to regulate the distribution of resources and commodities in order to partition them amongst the various industrial nations. Elliott's internationalist project despised economic nationalism because it restricted free access to foreign nations' natural resources. When nations raised tariffs, they generally did so to build up their domestic industries using domestic resources, creating competition with the already industrialized nations like England and America for manufactured goods.

The international order of the nineteenth century had succeeded in limiting industrial development to a few European imperial powers (as well as America and Japan) with preponderant access to natural resources and scientific know-how. In fact, even under British hegemony Elliott admitted that the world had hardly experienced real "free trade" because whenever an Empire had come to dominate a large portion of the world market, "the capitalist groups have become nationalistic and consequently exclusive" so as to preserve their privilege of exploiting these resources.[21] In a truly "international" capitalist order, nation-states would have no inherent claim to property, which should only be subject to ownership and exploitation by (corporate) capitalist forces at large, though not entirely free of the global state's regulation.

According to Elliott's understanding of history, wars have been produced by nations seeking to promote their national economic interests by creating protectionist barriers against foreign goods or by seeking to augment their territory through military force. Presumably, once nationalism could be replaced by international financial controls and resource allocations, states would no longer fight from economic motivations to insure growth in GNP. Access to foreign resources and markets had long been the rationale for imperialism, and as Elliott noted forebodingly in his 1937 book on *International Control in the Non-Ferrous Metals*, nationalistic claims to resources "would probably produce imperialistic wars to secure political control over these sources of the most vital raw materials for modern armaments."[22]

Elliott was ahead of his time when he completed this work on international resource allocations in 1935 (only to have publication delayed by two years). By 1937, however, fascists were fighting communists in Spain, Japan was invading China, and Germany had illegally seized the Rhineland in its bid toward expanding its resource base for rearmament. Japan, Italy, and Germany had withdrawn from the League of Nations, thus destroying the hopes for collective security. In April of that year, Elliott addressed the prospect of "Peace or War" if the economic "have-not" powers of Germany, Japan, and Italy could not be satiated in their desires for economic independence. They were "have-nots" because they were dissatisfied with their territorial allotment of resources and thus emphasized a Machiavellian philosophy of "expand or perish," an imperialist bid against the existing international framework laid down by the British Empire.

Yet Elliott also faulted England for its exclusive control of the world's tin and rubber supply as "lending color to the claims of the 'have-not' powers, and is wounding a great and powerful friend in the United States."[23] Elliott was intimating that England should share her loot with America, as well as making tin and rubber more easily accessible for the "have-nots." In any case, "Great Britain is not able to watch the struggle on the continent of Europe without realizing that a victory for either communism or fascism would have disastrous effects upon the British Empire."[24] Both systems would assure the continuation of imperialistic nationalism in a world that Elliott believed, echoing the sentiments of H.G. Wells at the turn of the century, should become more internationally-controlled.

In 1937, Elliott hoped that England would not cut herself off from America by pursuing nationalist policies at America's expense. In March, Elliott sent a letter to Lord Lothian, then head of the Rhodes Trust and a member of the House of Lords. Amidst the concern over Germany's rearmament and its Eastern territorial ambitions, Lothian had addressed the House advocating the three-bloc policy of British neutrality in Continental affairs while encouraging an Atlantic alliance based on "British-American co-operation." Elliott conceded that "such co-operation seems to be the best hope for peace," but Elliott argued that Britain's bilateral trade pacts with countries like Argentina had "hampered the [Secretary of State Cordell] Hull policy" of multilateral pacts.[25] Elliott sincerely believed that trade and openness were the best policies to preserve peace between the major powers. Britain made no effort, however, to dilute its bilateral agreements, and by early 1938 Elliott understood that the American isolationist attitude in world affairs was tantamount to England's "pro-Halifax" (and Lothian) group of pacifists "willing to make any concession whatever to Germany's ambition in Central or Eastern Europe."[26]

Due to America's historical ambivalence toward international affairs, Elliott proposed "indirect co-operation" between the two powers involving the American and British governments "buying up all the available strategic minerals under the control of British or American producers," as well as settling war debts "by stock-piling tin and other commodities on government account" in an effort to "restore [sic] pressure for debtor [i.e. British and German] morality."[27] The effect of this stock-piling program would inevitably serve as an international regulation on "have-not" powers' industrial [28]development. Toward this end, he believed that peace could be ensured "by a real willingness to accept disarmament, or international scrutiny of armaments," thus rendering national sovereignty nearly obsolete.[29]

Of course, the other American internationalists, such as those within the Council on Foreign Relations, likewise understood that America and Britain could together enforce the "security of a world safe for democracy" (in Elliott's words).[30] In an insightful letter from CFR President Norman H. Davis to fellow CFR member Elliott in February 1938, Davis explained that he had "been arguing for some time that since Great Britain and the United States between them still control the seas, the raw materials, the gold, and so forth, of the world, they have the power – provided they have the vision and intelligence to use it wisely – to remove the menace of international anarchy, and to bring about an era of confidence and security which would solve most of the problems that now harass the world. There are constantly two difficulties in the way of Anglo-American cooperation. One is that the British Tory can hardly conceive of any kind of cooperation that does not mean playing the British game, and the other, that the American isolationist is so blind as not to see the advantage of any kind of cooperation."[31]

As Davis noted, it seemed as though the British were following their own scheme for global order through balance of power policies in 1938, as PM Chamberlain was preoccupied with appeasing Germany. Yet Elliott was perspicacious enough to understand that German expansion would transform it from a "have-not" into a "have" power. He seems to have recognized the balance-of-power machinations of the British government taking place in 1938 when England was conceding Austria and the Sudetenland to Germany, so he developed a "theory that Germany's Eastern expansion will make her almost self-supporting, at least as long as her peace time trade with other parts of the world is not seriously curtailed."[32] Elliott realized, however, that in order for a three-bloc world to be effective, Russia would be necessary to restrain Germany on the Continent.

In truth, this may have been the British strategy all along, as evidenced by the Governor of the Bank of England, Montagu Norman, in his intriguing relationship with the Nazi party. Norman had been corresponding intimately with Hjalmar Schacht, since he was selected president of Germany's

Reichsbank in 1923, but when Adolf Hitler, backed by certain German industrialists with banking ties to Wall Street,[33] became Chancellor in 1933, Norman had Schacht appointed Minister of Economics for the new regime. Norman's Bank of England began advancing the new Nazi government credit that had previously been withheld amidst Germany's debt default in 1931, and Norman personally visited Berlin in 1934 "to arrange further secret financial stabilization for the new regime."[34] Not only was Germany allowed to default on 90% of its debts owed in 1932 but "by the end of the decade, Nazi Germany was Britain's principal trading client."[35] Thus, throughout the 1930s England seems to have adopted Round Tabler Lord Lothian's approach to dealing with the Continent by strengthening Germany as a bulwark against Soviet Russia, in a continuation of the British balance of power game, which tended to pit neighbor against neighbor across the continent.

By May 1939, after England had rebuffed the Russian's suggestion of March to hold an international conference for a united front against aggression, Elliott criticized England for conceding too much to Germany and "making the usual mistake with Russia… that is an extremely important element in the whole situation. There will surely not be a very restraining influence if Russia's weight is definitely *outside the balance*" (emphasis added).[36] Indeed, all of the British maneuverings to push Hitler east and to form "cartels dividing the world's markets," beginning with coal in January 1939 and a general agreement on British and Reichsgruppe Industrial cooperation in March 1939, was in effect forcing the Soviets toward a truce with their fascist arch-enemies.[37]

After the sack of Czechoslovakia in March 1939, Germany was preparing to take the Polish Corridor with force, despite England's secret overtures for Hitler to have patience and expand by cooperative means, as had been attempted with the partition of Czechoslovakia at the Munich Conference in September 1938. As former German Chancellor Heinrich Bruening expressed to Elliott in June 1939, England's overtures to Hitler were only making England appear all the more feeble; "I am sure that the ill-timed new feelers for secret conversations with the Nazis which were put forward last week have only strengthened the Radicals in Germany to persuade Hitler to take greater risks than he apparently was willing to do four weeks ago."[38] Sure enough, in September 1939 Germany and Russia shocked the West by jointly dividing Poland, thus forcing Britain into a precarious situation because of its public commitments to Poland's defense.

With the onset of war in Europe, America was committed to its Neutrality Act of 1935, passed in response to Italy's invasion of Ethiopia and prohibiting the sale of arms to belligerents. Curiously, though Germany attacked Poland on September 1st, Elliott waited until September 19th, two days after the Soviets had invaded Poland, to appeal to his Congresswoman Edith Nourse Rogers of the Foreign Affairs Committee to repeal "the mis-named 'Neutrality Act.'" Whether Elliott was deliberately taking the anti-Soviet tact of the British is not clear, but he astutely argued that the Neutrality Act prevented victim nations like Poland from arming against aggressors like Germany. Instead, he supported a "cash and carry" policy, which would allow merchant nations like Britain to buy from the States using their gold reserves, or trading their natural resources for cash. Roosevelt's cabinet urged similar amendments to the Neutrality Act, which was fully replaced by the "cash and carry" policy in November. Furthermore, Elliott urged America to arm the British Commonwealth's bulwark in North America, Canada, as part of the "Monroe Doctrine" of defending the continent. On the other hand, Elliott did not yet favor direct American engagement in the war, perhaps not yet clear on to how to proceed, as his British allies waited out the "phony war" of winter.[39]

Through the winter of 1939, the British government did not come to the aid of Poland and was still not sure whether to fight German fascism or Russian communism. When Russia invaded Finland in late 1939, the British and French prepared a joint expeditionary force of up to 57,000 men to aid Finland, although the two nations had done nothing in respect of Poland or Czechoslovakia's destruction by Germany. All the way until March 12, 1940, when Finland and Russia signed a peace treaty, the British awaited a formal Finnish request for help, which did not arrive.[40]

Around this time in mid-March, Elliott drafted a "Program for Action" which he presented to President Roosevelt and Secretary of State Cordell Hull. Its first proposal was a staggering $60 million Export-Import bank loan to Finland as a "victim of Russian aggression." He prophetically believed that taking a stand now was "the most concrete step we can take to prevent the spread of war to other Scandinavian countries." His prophecy came true within a month as Germany invaded Denmark and Norway for their precious iron-ore supply. Elliott also proposed a $200 million allocation of American gold for stockpiling "strategically essential minerals that we now lack" in case of American rearmament. He also requested State Department control of materials such as scrap iron to prevent American materials from being exported for foreign armaments. As he dourly noted, all of the Axis powers, including Russia, were still party to reciprocal Trade Agreements with the U.S. as a "neutral."[41]

In 1940 Elliott was rewarded for his astute warnings, which had begun in 1935, for America to stockpile its resources in order to meet a coming imperial war. He was appointed Director of Stockpiling for the Office of Production Management, with particular attention paid to advising on raw material procurement. By this point the British and French had been duped by

Hitler, with Germany overrunning France in June, leaving Britain isolated from the Continent.[42] Britain desperately needed American support and in September 1940, fifty American destroyers were transferred to the British in exchange for leases on Britain's Western hemisphere bases; although this deal may not have involved Elliott, he had previously proposed in February that the French war debts be paid by the transfer of their hemispheric bases, indicating that this idea of bases-for-aid was already circulating.

By early 1941, "lend-lease" of American military equipment had become a standardized practice to solve Britain's inability to pay in cash for American arms and munitions. That autumn, Elliott expressed to Secretary of State Cordell Hull the American public's fear that, as with World War I, America was being "'taken for a ride' by the British again in the matter of debts." Yet Elliott saw in this an opportunity for America and England to finally establish a "joint international holding company" on raw materials. He proposed that loans to England's Commonwealth be granted on the condition that the recipient countries' raw materials be pooled, to "set up for the first time in history a really sensible international control of the world's major raw materials, with a view to their proper development from the point of view of long-run *conservation and planned production*" (emphasis added).[43] This proposal demonstrated Elliott's hope for a supranational control of resources under a socialistic project for planning and distribution.

Although America still appeared isolated and passive in 1941, Elliott did not expect that non-intervention would preclude America from taking an active role in determining the future course of the world economic order. Elliott explained that fall that "we must take hostages, and soon, to see that the resources of the empires of the British, French, Dutch, and Belgians, saved by our aid, are opened to the world. We will have the right to demand that assets be put on the table. Then we can claim a senior partner's share in their redistribution."[44] Whereas America was a resource-rich country, it still depended on goods like rubber, tin, graphite, cobalt ore, and mica from Asia and Africa to support its military-industrial power. While America had traditionally been able to trade with the British and French empires, should their colonies now be seized by the Germans and Japanese, this international economic permeability might be constrained. Germany and Japan "would have control of the principal sources of chrome and manganese for the steel making on which our whole defense efforts now rest. They would be in control of rubber, tin, mica, graphite, manila fiber, many of the tropical fats and oils from which explosives like nitroglycerine have to be made.... *That* is why we must stop Hitler."[45]

Instead, it was Japan's search for raw materials like rubber and oil that precipitated America's entry into World War II. America provoked the attack in a "Machiavellian" manner reminiscent of what Elliott had advocated three years prior,[46] by cutting off American exports to Japan in July 1941 (as a response to Japan's advance into Indochina), thus threatening Japan's industrial productivity and military flexibility. The Japanese retaliated in December by pre-emptively invading British Malaysia, and the American colony of the Philippines and bombing the territory of Hawaii.

Elliott understood that the world order that would emerge from this epochal imperial struggle would have to submit to more international regulations and arbitrations than had been constructed during the previous twenty years. Three weeks before the Japanese attack on Pearl Harbor, Elliott presciently wrote a letter to A.D. Marris[47] at the British Embassy expressing the hope that "shortly," America would be able to lend more support to Britain, including "doing the fighting." At this time, Elliott was also complaining to Marris that America's extension of Lend-Lease aid to all the British Commonwealth "will do quite possibly irreparable harm to such export interests as we have in those areas." Essentially, Elliott's proposal to pool the natural resources of those colonies in exchange for aid had gone unheeded, and instead, President Roosevelt was generously offering the aid to the detriment of international controls on raw materials. Elliott cryptically asserted the Round Table Movement's theme to Marris, complaining that "it looks as if we are going to be dealing with a *government-run* world for some time in the future – a thing which neither one of us looks forward to with particular relish"[48](emphasis added).[49]

Soon enough, America's entry into the war proved that America would no longer have to pool the allied Empires' natural resources in order to have an active role in determining the order of the post-war world. Echoing CFR President Norman Davis' prediction in 1942 that "the British Empire as it existed in the past will never reappear and the United States may have to take its place,"[50] Elliott was delighted that the creation of the future "world system" would now belong to America, finally "committed to a destiny of world leadership."[51] This was because "only the U.S. economy enjoyed the export potential to displace Britain and other European rivals," thus fueling an argument for "the ideal of laissez-faire [as] synonymous with the worldwide extension of U.S. national power."[52] On the other hand, American economic leadership still depended on the allegiance of Britain, with its vast imperial resources.

In 1943 Elliott, then the Vice-Chairman of Civilian Requirements for the War Production Board, explained the power politics of the "world's real wealth" not being found in sterling balances but in "raw materials and productive population." Thanks to the war, the British Empire "will retain and I daresay enlarge, her control over her precious colonial territories and *spheres of influence*." The "spheres of influence" concept predicted the balance of power relationships that would define the Cold War era, when nominally independent nations were expected to choose ideological allegiance to an economic system, or bloc. Elliott inaccurately predicted the British Empire's greatest extension of its "sphere of influence" into South America during the war, when in fact it would be the Rockefeller interests, with whom Elliott consorted,[53] that would most extend the American dollar zone, centered around mining, grazing and oil.[54] Regardless, Elliott remained unconcerned by Great Britain's territorial predominance in the world; so long as the British Commonwealth controlled two-thirds of the world's oil reserves, and most of its tin, chrome, manganese, and other minerals, he still hoped for a "joint trusteeship" between America and England as the major shareholders in the so-called "international" control of raw materials following the war.[55]

It must be noted that such a policy of controlling the raw materials of the planet for American industrial production seems to have been in contrast to President Roosevelt's vision for the post-war world. While the British Empire had predicated its system of trusteeship on a pretense of preserving native welfare while emphasizing its own "free trade" policies, Roosevelt's ideas of trusteeship on a path to decolonization incorporated ideas of investing and developing the nations previously under imperial control with infrastructure projects like irrigation. According to FDR's son Elliott, the President reportedly said,

> Imperialists don't realize what they can do, what they can create! They've robbed this continent [Africa] of billions, and all because they were too short-sighted to understand that their billions were pennies, compared to the possibilities! Possibilities that *must* include a better life for the people who inhabit this land.[56]

Roosevelt's sympathy for the impoverished of the earth, living in a pre-industrial era, was emphasized in other conversations where he was "concerned about the brown people in the East" who were "ruled by a handful of whites and they resent it. Our goal must be to help them achieve independence."[57] In fact, Roosevelt's concern for the colonial peoples may have run so deep that he in fact "believe[d] in the danger of British power, as did many of his military and political advisers."[58] If there were any doubt that Roosevelt was committed to the cause of national independence, he proceeded with plans to grant the Philippines independence from the United States, which occurred the year after his death in 1946.

Thus, in order to assure self-determination and rising standards of living for the post-colonial world, President Roosevelt pursued the idea of a United Nations, under the military leadership of the Big Four [America, Britain, the Soviet Union and China], as a forum to hold trusteeship over the islands and territories newly freed from colonial occupation, until functioning nation-states could be formed. Roosevelt also envisioned the International Monetary Fund and World Bank as instruments to reconstruct the war-ravaged countries and to provide assistance to these new nations that would be forming from the vestiges of Empire. Part of FDR's motivation might be found in his words, as recounted by his son Elliott, regarding "British bankers and German bankers [who] have had world trade pretty well sewn up in their pockets for a long time," thus preventing American access to trade in many international markets.[59]

The implementation of Roosevelt's plan for decolonization, utilizing these supranational organizations to assist in the development of infrastructure and national sovereignty for the post-colonial peoples, will never be known for sure, as his untimely death on the eve of victory in World War II left his vision for peace unfulfilled. But if FDR's words to his son Elliott mean anything, then the President was certainly leery of "the British Empire and British ability to get other countries to combine in some sort of bloc against the Soviet Union" after the war.[60]

1945 found a physically decimated Eurasia, from Western Europe and Russia to China and Japan in the East, leaving America as the only nation in a position to reconstruct the world's economic super-structures. The creation of the International Monetary Fund in 1944, followed by the General Agreement on Tariffs and Trade in 1947, was officially intended to insure a standardized world economy, providing "no interference with trade or international commercial payments, except for non-discriminatory tariffs."[61] In fact, with Roosevelt in office, the original intention had been to incorporate the Soviet Union into the Bretton Woods system, including bilateral loans and aid for reconstruction purposes. However, as member governments in the IMF were forced to commit to collective oversight from the supranational union, including "'exacting investigations' of Soviet gold production, gold and foreign exchange holdings, spending of borrowed funds, and so on – all of which the USSR 'customarily kept secret'," the Soviet Union ultimately declined to be involved in the new fund.[62]

Given the Soviet Union's control of Eastern Europe, and potential influence in a post-colonial world, "Russia, so the thinking ran, would seek to capture selected U.S. satellites by dominating their foreign trade, so foreclosing key portions of the world economy to American access."[63] The CFR's War and Peace Studies Group on Economic and Financial affairs had already pre-determined in October 1940 that America needed to organize a "Grand Area," consisting of the Western Hemisphere, England and its Commonwealth, China and Japan, as "an important stabilizing factor in the world's economy." The development of this area would have to take place regionally, so as to first integrate the separate economies through trading blocs and customs unions.[64]

Thus, Western Europe became an immediate priority for American trade by first revitalizing the European consumer economy, beginning with the European Recovery Program (a.k.a. the Marshall Plan) in 1948, which was designed to extend aid to Europe based on the premise of Europe's consent to cooperate internally. The Marshall Plan itself was culminated from the work of Congressman Christian Herter's Select Committee on Foreign Aid in 1947-'48, for which Elliott acted as staff director.[65] The committee was assisted largely by future CIA Director Allen Dulles, then a director of the CFR.

The Marshall Plan's design for Western European integration soon led to the evolution of one such supranational authority in the European Coal and Steel Community, bringing the coal, iron, and steel industries of six countries under a single High Authority. In 1948 Western Europe created the Organization for European Economic Cooperation (OEEC), which in time developed the 1957 Treaty of Rome, establishing the subsequent European Economic Community (a.k.a. the Common Market) with common tariffs and centralized financial structures. The governmental structures of a European Parliament and European Court of Justice, adopted in tandem with the Common Market, reflected *The City of Man*'s 1940 appeal for a Universal Parliament.[66]

The world was slowly being transformed toward regional economic and defensive blocs, with the creation of the Atlantic Community through the North Atlantic Treaty Organization (NATO) in 1948, which committed America to the defense of Western Europe, and with the Southeast Asian Treaty Organization (SEATO) of 1954, which engendered a concept of collective security against Chinese "communist" imperialism in Southeast Asia. This process of "'regional' groupings among 'like-minded' countries" had been strongly advocated by a Woodrow Wilson Study Group in 1955, chaired by W.Y. Elliott, which consisted of Richard Bissell (a deputy director of the CIA and former staff director for the "Harriman" Presidential Committee on foreign aid which developed the Marshall Plan), Frank Altschul (Vice President of the CFR), and Don K. Price[67] (Vice President of the instrumental Ford Foundation[68]).[69]

The group's book on *The Political Economy of American Foreign Policy* (1955) suggested that America and Canada be added to the European Economic Community to strengthen the cross-Atlantic ties. This ultimately occurred in 1961 when the OEEC transformed into the Organization for Economic Cooperation and Development (OECD), with America and Canada as members. The Study Group also encouraged America to imperialistically utilize its "freedom of action" to extend the West's material goals in the world, for "the progressive unification of the Western Community will depend upon the progressive extension of American influence, power and responsibility within and on *behalf of the Atlantic Community*" (emphasis added).[70]

Essentially, regionalism was but a step toward establishing worldwide economic and political unity, and only America had the strength and vision to accomplish this new world order. Yet, in the terms of co-organic organization asserted by Elliott, imbued from the British Commonwealth model, the study group advocated regional groupings, based on the principle that "effective economic cooperation among fully sovereign national governments, no less than the willingness to subordinate important elements of national economic policies to supranational authorities, require not simply the absence of deep conflicts of interest but also a positive sense of moral and historical community among the countries concerned. *The requisite similarity of culture and social values and consistency of political and economic capabilities and needs do not now exist in the non-Soviet world as a whole and are not likely to be soon attained on a regional basis*" (emphasis added).[71] Consequently, America's chief role upon entering a Cold War with the USSR would be to foster this spiritual sense of constitutional communities amongst the non-Soviet states in an effort to align those nations into pacts and treaties as part of an increasingly legalistic and internationally-oriented superstructure.

Endnotes

1. Elliott, et al. *The Political Economy of American Foreign Policy: Its Concepts, Strategy, and Limits. Report of a Study Group Sponsored by the Woodrow Wilson Foundation and the National Planning Association.* New York: Henry Holt and Co., 1955. p. 30.

2. Ibid. p. 31, 10.

3. Quoted in Chaitkin, Anton. *Treason in America*. p. 292-3.

4. While England, France, and Russia were allied against Turkey in the Russo-Turkish War of 1827-'29, England made sure that Russia did not gain access to any warm water ports after the victory. England and France then aided Turkey against Russia in the 1853-'56 Crimean War. In Germany's conquest of France, deposing Napoleon III in 1870-'71, England supported Germany, whereas by the end of the century England had taken Egypt and the Suez Canal from France, leading to the 1904 Entente Cordiale between the two. Russia was added to the Alliance in 1907, completing the encirclement of Germany, thus helping to precipitate war in 1914.

5. Engdahl, William. *A Century of War: Anglo-American Oil Politics and the New World Order*. London: Pluto Press, 2004. p. 9-10.

6. Davis & Huttenback in *Mammon and the Pursuit of Empire*. Quoted in David C. Korten. *When Corporations Rule the World.*

7. Engdahl. p. 35.

8. Elliott, W.Y. *The New British Empire*. p. 69.

9. Curtis reportedly stated that "public opinion must be led along the right path." (Smith; p. 194).

10. Shoup & Minter. *Imperial Brain Trust*. New York: Authors Choice Press, 2004. P. 22-3.

11. Elliott, W.Y. *The New British Empire*. p. 71.

12. Ibid. p.160-1.

13. Ibid. p. 160.
14. Ibid. p. 34.
15. Ibid. p. 102.
16. Ibid. p. 166.
17. Elliott, W.Y. *The Need for Constitutional Reform*. p. 89.
18. Ibid. p. 9.
19. Ibid. p. 96.
20. Elliott, W.Y., Ed. *International Control in the Non-Ferrous Metals*. New York: The Macmillan Company, 1937. p. 51.
21. Ibid. p. 18.
22. Ibid. p. 17-18.
23. Elliott, W.Y. *Peace or War?* Ed. Harold S. Quigley. Minnesota: The University of Minnesota Press, 1937. p. 20.
24. Ibid. p. 11.
25. WYE to Lord Lothian; March 24, 1937; Box 162, Hoover Institute Archives, Stanford.
26. Elliott, W.Y. "A Joint Policy for Britain and the U.S.A." *The Political Quarterly*. Vol. 9, Iss. 2. April 1938. p. 175-6.
27. Before the 2nd World War, Elliott tried fruitlessly to revitalize the repayment of war debts, which had fallen into a moratorium during the Great Depression. In February 1939 he urged that England's Commonwealth still held the reins on the imperial nations' drive to war and so should repay its debts to America "with tin, manganese, tungsten and chromium. If we take these raw materials and keep them off the market, we will make it difficult for the dictator powers to continue their armament race." (Wallace, Richard. "A Peaceful Way to Silence Guns." *The Press-Scimitar.* Memphis, Tennessee. Feb. 1, 1939).
28. The British government seems to have been more interested in cultivating financial ties with the dictator powers than precipitating a war against Germany and Japan by taking raw materials off the market. As the long-time CFR member Herbert Feis, an International Economic Affairs advisor to the State Department, had explained to Elliott in July 1938, the British government had "never responded" to American proposals for using raw materials to pay off the war debt. "In fact, we have no sign whatsoever that the British Government is disposed *to pay anything on the debts*." (*emphasis added*) (Herbert Feis to WYE; July 7, 1938; Box 160, Hoover Institute Archives, Stanford).
29. "A Joint Policy for Britain and the U.S.A." *The Political Quarterly*. Vol. 9, Iss. 2. April 1938. p. 181
30. Elliott, W.Y. "A Joint Policy for Britain and the U.S.A." p. 179.
31. Davis to WYE; Feb. 14, 1938; William Y. Elliott Papers; Box 160, Hoover Institute, Stanford.
32. Dr. Ernst Feilchenfeld to WYE; January 3, 1939; Box 136, Hoover Institute Archives, Stanford.
33. While the Nazi Party-backer Fritz Thyssen was represented financially in the U.S. by the Anglo-American banking house of Brown Brothers Harriman, the Swiss Banking Act of 1933 allowed the premier Wall Street banks like Morgan and Rockefeller to "secretly own[] the stocks of the Swiss Banks, which owned the stocks of the German banks, which owned the stocks of the German companies." (Loftus, John. *America's Nazi Secret*. p. 18).
34. Engdahl. p. 73, 84.
35. Preparata. *Conjuring Hitler.* p. 224.
36. WYE to Heinrich Bruening; May 10, 1939; William Y. Elliott Papers; Box 136, Hoover Institute Archives, Stanford.
37. Quigley, Carroll. *Tragedy and Hope*. p. 643-5.
38. (Bruening to WYE; June 16, 1939; William Y. Elliott Papers; Box 136, Hoover Institute Archives, Stanford).

39. WYE to Congresswoman Edith Nourse Rogers; Sept. 19, 1939; Box 136, Hoover Institute Archives, Stanford.

40. Quigley, Carroll. *Tragedy and Hope*. p. 681-2.

41. Elliott, W.Y. "Program for Action to be Urged on the Pres. And the Congress of the USA." In a letter from William Lockwood to Princeton Institute of Advanced Studies' Professor Edward Mead Earle; March 27, 1940; Edward Mead Earle Archives; Box 3, Mudd Library Archives, Princeton University.

42. The motivation for Hitler's westward attack on his benefactors may have boiled down to a megalomaniacal delusion of imperial grandeur, but one curious theory holds that Hitler "promised to restore [pro-Nazi King Edward VII] to the throne of England as its first fascist King. As his part of the bargain, it was said, Edward successfully betrayed the entire plan of the Maginot line [defending France] to the Third Reich." (Loftus. *America's Nazi Secret*. P. 9).

43. WYE to Secretary of State Cordell Hull; Re: "Control of Raw Materials through Joint Holding Companies." Sept. 29, 1941; William Y. Elliott Papers, Harvard University Archives.

44. Summary" of WYE's address, "America's Place in the Future World Order"; Nov. 13, 1941; Woman's National Democracy Club, Harvard University; from William Y. Elliott Archives, Harvard University.

45. WYE speech on *National Defense: Policy and Performance*; Nov. 27, 1941; Conference on Public Discussion Methods; from William Y. Elliott Archives, Harvard University.

46. In March 1938 the World Peace Foundation, whose Trustees included American Rhodes Trust Secretary Frank Aydelotte, Elliott's former patron at Harvard A. Lawrence Lowell, and his cousin Harvey Bundy (the father of Elliott's future students McGeorge and William), hosted a round-table discussion concerning a Far Eastern Policy against the threat of Japan, which had invaded China in 1937. Elliott proposed a "Machiavellian" tactic, knowing that much of Japan's tin, rubber, and oil came from the British Commonwealth of Malaya, to create "a non-provocative type of cooperation" with the British Imperial Defense Committee in buying up those supplies to get the stocks off the market, "thus crippling Japan." (From the minutes of the World Peace Foundation conference on Far Eastern Policy; March 2, 1938; William Y. Elliott Papers; Box 161, Hoover Institute Archives, Stanford).

47. The son of William Marris, one of Milner's "Kindergarten" in South Africa and a founder of the Round Table Movement; A.D. Marris became a lifelong member of the merchant bank Lazard Brothers thanks to the Round Table Group's Lord Robert Brand, a Lazard partner and director of Lloyd's Bank. (See Quigley. *The Anglo American Establishment*. p. 80-1).

48. It is difficult to ascertain exactly what the post-government run world would look like, except to say that it would involve the demise of traditional nation-state sovereignty over resources, politics and laws. Supranational organizations, controls and treaties would seem to usurp the role of national agendas, as Elliott had previously advocated for "the only league of nations that has worked – Britain's self-governing dominions. Racial ties, nor blood streams bind these dominions. Economics do." (March 2, 1938; World Peace Foundation Round Table Discussion on Far Eastern Policy; March 2, 1938; William Y. Elliott Papers; Box 161, Hoover Institute Archives, Stanford).

49. WYE to A.D. Marris; November 17, 1941; William Y. Elliott Archives, Harvard University

50. Quoted in Shoup & Minter. *Imperial Brain Trust*. p. 164.

51. From WYE's paper, "Control of Strategic Materials in War and Peace"; for the Institute of Public Affairs; July 7, 1942; William Y. Elliott Papers; Harvard University Archives.

52. Hudson, Michael. *Superimperialism*. New Edition. London: Pluto Press, 2003. p. 10.

53. Elliott's mentee Henry Kissinger was adopted by the Rockefeller Brothers' Foundation after graduating from Harvard.

54. "During World War II, as U.S. Coordinator of Inter-American Affairs, [Nelson Rockefeller] had waged relentless economic and psychological warfare across the hemisphere against striking Indian

workers and Nazi sympathizers with seemingly equal zeal. Then, as Franklin Roosevelt's assistant secretary of state for Latin America, he had launched the Cold War before it had even been declared, fusing hemispheric unity against the Soviets at the Pan American Conference in 1945 and that year's founding conference of the United Nations." (Colby, Gerald. *Thy Will Be Done*. P. 5).

55. WYE to Charles Denby, Office of Lend-Lease Administration; August 27, 1943; William Y. Elliott Archives, Harvard University.

56. Quoting Elliott Roosevelt in Louis, Wm. Roger. *Imperialism at Bay*. New York: Oxford University Press, 1978. P. 227.

57. Quoting Charles Taussig in Louis, Wm. Roger. *Imperialism at Bay*. P. 486.

58. Louis, Wm. Roger. *Imperialism at Bay*. P. 21.

59. Roosevelt, Elliott. *As He Saw It*. New York: Sloan and Pearce, 1946. p. 24.

60. Ibid. p. 228.

61. Elliott, W.Y., et al. *The Political Economy of American Foreign Policy: Its Concepts, Strategy, and Limits*. p. 206.

62. Peet, Richard. *Unholy Trinity*. London: Zed Books, 2003. p. 46.

63. Hudson, Michael. P. 174.

64. Quoted in Shoup & Minter. *Imperial Brain Trust*. 136-7.

65. Richard Nixon was a freshman Congressman on the Herter Committee. Later, as a consultant to Secretary of State Christian Herter, Elliott would become a chief consultant to Vice President Nixon from 1959-'60 during his first Presidential campaign. And of course, Elliott's disciple Kissinger became President Nixon's National Security Advisor and Secretary of State.

66. In fact, the Treaty of Rome "was nurtured at these meetings" of the "Bilderberg" group (founded in 1954), whose members included Nelson Rockefeller's brother David (also founder of the Trilateral Commission in 1973) and Elliott's colleagues Dean Rusk (head of the Rockefeller Foundation), George McGhee (State Department official), and C.D. Jackson (who organized the group's American membership on behalf of former CIA Director Walter Bedell Smith). (Quote by George McGhee in Thompson, Peter. "Bilderberg and the West." *Trilateralism*. p. 165-70).

67. Price was himself a former Rhodes Scholar and became a Principal Trustee of the Rhodes Trust from 1968-'78.

68. At the time, John J. McCloy was Chairman of both the Ford Foundation and Council on Foreign Relations. As will be explored in Chapter 7, McCloy played an interesting role in helping young Henry Kissinger's career in the 1950s.

69. Gordon, Lincoln. "The Political Economy of American Foreign Policy: Its Concepts, and Strategy, and Limits." *The Review of Economics and Statistics*; Vol. 38, No. 1. February 1956. p. 109.

70. Elliott, W.Y., et al. *The Political Economy of American Foreign Policy: Its Concepts, Strategy, and Limits*. p. 322-3.

71. Ibid. p. 11.

William Yandell Elliott, a formal portrait from the 1960s.

Courtesy Elliott family

Chapter VII

Order out of Chaos – Initiating the Cold War

We have about 50% of the world's wealth but only 6.3% of its population... Our real task in the coming period is to devise a pattern of relationships which will permit us to maintain this position of disparity without positive detriment to our national security. To do so, we will have to dispense with all sentimentality and day-dreaming; and our attention will have to be concentrated everywhere on our immediate national objectives. We need not deceive ourselves that we can afford today the luxury of altruism and world-benefaction.

– George Kennan, "Review of Current Trends, U.S. Foreign Policy." February 28, 1948. Policy Planning Staff, PPS No. 23. Top Secret. Included in the U.S. Department of State, Foreign Relations of the United States, 1948, volume 1, part 2 (Washington DC Government Printing Office, 1976).

As far back as 1931, fifteen years before the Cold War, W.Y. Elliott viewed the chief disturbance to the security of international order as coming from Russia. "Russia is potentially threatening to the structure of that capitalist world economy in which the City in London shares with New York the ruling position. As long as capitalist nations avoid war the threat is slight."[1] Yet the capitalist nations did not avoid war, and in 1945 Western Europe was left in shambles, with the Russian military stretched from Germany to Yugoslavia. Meanwhile, the United States demobilized half its army by the end of 1945, while there were still hopes that Russia would agree to the Yalta agreements and permit free elections in Poland and other East European countries.

Instead, the defeat of the Communist Parties in Austria and Hungary in 1945 proved to the Soviets that these neighbors could not be both friendly to Russia and democratic at the same time. Between 1945 and 1948, when Czechoslovakia's government was overthrown by the Communist Party, the Soviets consolidated an autocratic Eastern bloc from East Germany to Bulgaria, Romania, Poland, and Hungary. When the anti-monarchist communist guerrillas began revolutionary activity in Greece in 1946, they sought sanctuary in Soviet-allied Albania. In neighboring Turkey, Russia had already rekindled its aspirations for warm-water ports, demanding northeastern territory from Turkey in a 1945 treaty of alliance.

When the British threatened to withdraw their troops entirely from Greece and Turkey in early 1947, they forced America to take their place, precipitating the "Truman Doctrine" of March 12, which enunciated a pro-active American policy of "containment" and maintaining the status quo by "support[ing] free peoples who are resisting attempted subjugation by armed minorities or by *outside pressures*" (emphasis added). The Truman Doctrine led to immediate Congressional budgetary approval of military aid to both Greece and Turkey.

Samuel P. Huntington, a political analyst and former student of Elliott, commented in a 1981 discussion, when reflecting upon the "lessons of Vietnam," about "an additional problem" for decision-makers who want "to intervene or take some action." He noted, "you may have to sell it in such a way as to create the *misimpression* that it is the Soviet Union that you are fighting.... That is what the United States has been doing ever since the Truman Doctrine" (emphasis added).[2]

The Cold War truly began in this period, especially once the Soviets rejected the extension of Marshall Plan aid that summer, denying American capitalism a hand in the development, and probably the reshaping, of the closed Soviet economic system. With the loss of Eastern Europe, America and England were now limited in their world order to the British Commonwealth and Western Europe. This was codified in 1949. Canada, France, Italy and seven other European nations signed the North Atlantic Treaty Organization as a mutual defense, or collective security, corollary to the League of Nations, promising "to safeguard the freedom, common heritage, and civilization of their peoples, founded on the principles of democracy, individual liberty, and the rule of law."[3] In effect, the Cold War was a battle to ensure that the Anglo-American world order would extend this model of international obligations and law internationally.

The "Cold War" presents an image of a bifurcated world, but its origins lie in the imperial conflicts of the nineteenth century. In fact, despite American official horror at the Soviet Union's annexation of Eastern Europe, Stalin's moves seem to have mostly been conferred by a secret meeting he held with Prime Minister Winston Churchill in Moscow in late 1944, when Churchill had conceded Soviet control of Romania and Bulgaria, with the British maintaining their historical influence over Greece. Yugoslavia would somehow be split 50-50 between the two powers, and indeed, Yugoslavia's Cold War President Josip Tito, while a self-proclaimed Communist, was allowed by the Soviets to remain neutral. For in the 20th Century, instead of the Russian and English Empires in contention for physical territory across the Eurasian "heartland," the renovated empires of the Soviet Union and the

English Commonwealth plus America, were now contending for ideological, and thus financial influence, across the world.

In contrast to the totalitarian system of Soviet governance, the British preferred to present themselves as guarantors of the political rights of their subjects in an on-going process towards nominal independence and self-governance. The United States had begun to merge with the British system by continuing this promise to develop constitutional rights and duties of allied nations, beginning with Western Europe's economic recovery in 1948. Like the British Empire in the nineteenth century, America's hostility to the Soviet system, which sought national independence from Western political and financial controls, manifested as a system of alliances constructed to contain the Soviet sphere of economic interest. The world in turn became a geopolitical chessboard, wherein any newly-formed nation presented potential economic assets to the American-led economic alliance. But in order to establish these ties, America first needed a political and spiritual (or moral) basis to attract foreign nations to its international system.

At the outbreak of World War II, internationalists like Elliott's mentor A.D. Lindsay portended that a stronger international body should replace the corrupted League of Nations system of conferences with enforceable powers of governance. In January of 1940, while Britain remained complacent in the face of Poland's dissolution, Lindsay declared at Oxford the need for another "War to End War." In contrast to the Chamberlain government's fear of German gas attacks and the German military's ability to decimate London in a day, Lindsay argued for war, despite the failure of the First World War to "end war."

In words reminiscent of The Round Table,[4] Lindsay proposed that this new generation could end war entirely by realizing "the necessity of extending to a world society the principles of law which we have learnt to maintain within the State."[5] By normalizing a system of law and applied government action on an international rather than national scale, Lindsay believed that the nations could learn to see themselves as cohesively unified enough to deem all wars as "civil wars," a concept which had become anathema to modern nations. Of course, Lindsay expected that smaller states could "retain their cultural independence" but in order to avoid the struggle for economic self-sufficiency between the "world powers" as was then taking place in nationalist Germany and Japan, the nations would have to join "a world economy," which necessitated "world law." Resorting to his old arguments for fighting World War I, Lindsay affirmed that nations would have to maintain "a constant readiness to make war upon war" for the sake of this international law. Yet, in place of a League of Nations, Lindsay argued that a super-state organization should be created with real advantages for membership, and even the threat of being expelled from such an organization would offer real consequences for violating international standards.[6]

Although this international order might ultimately be deemed a world government, in the meantime the "supra-national order, and sovereignty of mankind" was still obstructed by the concept of the nation-state. The means for achieving this superstructure were enumerated by *The City of Man*'s authors in 1940 as "constitutional order, ethico-religious purpose, and economic justice inside the single communities that must build it."[7] This endeavor would thus require the cultivation of the communities, or nations, toward agreement.

In order to mask the coercion necessary to cultivate a consensus amongst the international community, the Council on Foreign Relations' leaders realized by 1942 that America could "avoid the onus of big-power imperialism in its implementation of the Grand Area [i.e. the British Commonwealth, the U.S., China and Japan] and creation of one open-door world" by creating a "power international in character through a United Nations body." The CFR President Norman Davis, along with five other CFR members,[8] served as the core of Secretary Cordell Hull's "secret steering committee" from January 1943 in formulating the United Nations Charter.[9] On the other hand, Elliott clearly discerned the trouble with the United Nations Organization by early 1946, for simply put, it could not work as the instrument for world government. As an organization, it was made up of states, which were neither democratic nor ideologically purposive in their designs for the world's future.[10]

Elliott understood that World War II had not encouraged "a feeling that all men are brothers," and even worse, the United Nations' Charter had acceded to national sovereignty, undermining the prospects for a global community. The major threat to the UN's power, according to Elliott, came from the veto power of the permanent Security Council member states (U.S., U.S.S.R., Britain, France, and China). By permitting any one of these nations to block legitimate action, the UN suffered a similar flaw to the goal of collective security as had the League of Nations' requirements for unanimous consent for action.

Of course, the one state most jeopardizing Anglo-American security resolutions at the UN after World War II was Russia, whose government system Elliott described as centralized and monopolistic, which ignored "the rights of other systems on equal terms" while reserving the "absolute rightness of its [own] objectives."[11] In the spring of 1946, even before former PM Churchill had denounced the "Iron Curtain" in front of new President Truman, Elliott wrote an article asking if it was in fact "A Time for Peace?" Elliott's response was negative, in spite of the predominating demand to "bring the troops home," because he believed that the international system was still jeopardized by the ideological dissonance of the Soviet system of government.

In Elliott's analysis, "the completely hierarchical" Soviet government was diametrically opposed to the co-organic individualism of Western democracies, and in fact, he predicted that the Soviets would seek to consolidate their hegemony because that was the inherent nature of absolutist systems. No appeasement could be afforded Russia because in its latent czarist imperial tendencies lay the new demands for the retrocession of Turkish provinces and equal apportionments with Britain of Iran's economic concessions, namely oil. Accordingly, Russia would have to be treated as "a power system" in the sense of balance-of-power politics, whereby extensions of Russia's power or influence would be looked upon as dis-balancing the status quo. Thus, by proclaiming the British Empire as the status quo, Russia was inevitably the rebel state in Anglo-American eyes, and in treating with the Russians, "settlements by *rules of an international order will be insisted upon at all costs*" (emphasis added).[12] In this axiomatic statement lay the precept that A.D. Lindsay had proffered as far back as World War I that an order based on international laws should supersede national sovereignty.[13]

Even if the international order now depended upon a balance of power structure of politics between the Soviets and the West, the ideal of international law was still the long-term goal. As Elliott predicted in 1946, "it is hardly a matter of dispute that a future world order will succeed nationalism either by being imposed on reluctant national sovereignties, as nationalism was itself imposed on feudalism, or by being worked out through revision of the United Nation's Charter, dropping the veto power of the Great Five and putting sanctions, including universal inspection and control of armaments, in the hands of the world organization [the UN]."[14]

The reason that international arms control and inspection was of such prime importance was the invention of the nuclear bomb the previous year, which had radically altered the geography and scale of warfare. The dropping of the atom bomb on Japan had "shattered in one apocalyptic blast all previous conceptions of strategy," for there was no defense against such total destruction. At the time, America enjoyed a monopoly of the atom bomb and its scientific "know-how," but Elliott contended that the very possibility of its invention necessitated international controls, for "the need of security might be urged as sanctioning any world order, no matter how imposed." On the other hand, the Soviet Union was uncooperative with such an international inspections program, and Elliott depicted the closed Soviet bloc in a similar fashion to Churchill's image of an "Iron Curtain," shielding the East from Western oversight.[15]

Russia's totalitarian secretive political dictatorship indicated to Elliott that the Soviet Union would be uncooperative in the creation of any international order. In 1945 and '46, America's military was not yet geared toward fighting another war, having not positioned itself for an immediate continuation of hostilities.[16] On the other hand, Elliott was one official within the government who began raising the alert that Russia, though America's war-time ally, was in fact America's enemy. Elliott's evidence for his claim was that Russia was trying to compete with American nuclear pre-eminence by building its own nuclear bomb.

As an economic advisor to the House of Representative's Post-War Planning Committee in 1945, Elliott had actually toured Europe, including Russia, to determine Europe's aid requirements. He believed that Stalin's plans for industrial development, as part of Russia's Five-Year Plan drafted in 1946, was not intended "for improved living standards" in the satellite states, but instead the industrial and scientific investments were intended "for harnessing atomic energy to war." Elliott, acting as an alarmist, spoke of "five years" as the time available to find "a livable solution" between America and Russia before an atomic "Armageddon."[17]

The idea that Russia and America could live peacefully with atomic weapons was never broached because Elliott believed the Soviet and American systems were inherently antagonistic. Accordingly, just as Elliott had called for the international control of resources before World War II to check the rearmament of imperialists in Europe, he now extended this vision of international oversight to include atomic energy, theoretically to prevent Russia from developing nuclear weapons to start "an armament race."[18]

When the Russians detonated their first nuclear bomb in 1949, an arms race did indeed ensue, and would last for the next forty years. Elliott foresaw the necessity of this arms race in 1946 because if international controls could not regulate Soviet armaments, then America would have to maintain its nuclear arsenal for retaliatory purposes. The idea of deterring Soviet nuclear threats with a preponderant nuclear capacity became official policy in the 1950s by Secretary of State John Foster Dulles' doctrine of "massive retaliation."

Elliott, then on President Eisenhower's National Security Council Planning Board, continued to argue through the late 1950s for international inspection of nuclear weapons as a way of probing behind the Iron Curtain. While he admitted that a "really unlimited" inspection would also give America "difficulties," he felt that the Soviet Union would be even more disadvantaged, since the Iron Curtain was so opaque to the West. As the threat of total destruction mounted through the 1950s, with the development of thousands of nuclear missiles (along with the new Intercontinental Ballistic Missiles which could dispatch the nukes directly between Russia and America), Russia proposed a moratorium on further nuclear testing in 1958. Elliott, then a special consultant to the new Secretary of State Christian Herter, adamantly opposed such a moratorium, charging that the Soviets were simply trying "to escape the necessity for having any kind of inspection system, or a system of international control." Alleging that the Soviets would develop nuclear weapons discreetly behind the Iron Curtain, Elliott urged that America needed to continue testing in order to develop "cleaner" nuclear weapons, which could be used "to fight limited wars" and to "reduce the threat of human destruction *to liveable and bearable proportions*" (emphasis added).[19]

Elliott's advocacy for threatening nuclear warfare with "liveable and bearable" destructive capacities found reinforcement in the paradigm shift toward "limited warfare" taking place between 1957 and 1960. At that time, the United States had not directly engaged in war with the Soviet bloc since the Korean War (1950-'53), although America could have directly engaged, for example, during the Hungarian uprising in 1956. Instead, Secretary Dulles had pursued a policy of alliances to surround Russia with regional allies through SEATO (1954) and the Central Treaty Organization in the Near and Middle East (CENTO; 1955).

At a Harvard Summer School Conference in 1958, W.Y. Elliott expressed the need for such alliances to preserve Anglo-American regional allies from falling to communist nationalist forces, as for example, "the danger of the loss of [British] Malaya this afternoon, or the potential loss of it, and what that means to the future of the Pacific."[20] Despite his rhetoric about the British Empire's interest in educating the natives, the truth of the matter was that Malaysia was rich in natural resources and remained a strategic asset to America so long as it remained under Britain "trusteeship." Yet the doctrine of "massive retaliation" would prove ineffectual against indigenous nationalist movements, with sponsorship from the Soviets or Chinese. "Massive retaliation" had not only failed to protect Hungary from Soviet takeover in 1956, but Elliott argued that the policy had even failed during the Korean War when President Truman had not permitted General Douglas MacArthur to use nuclear weapons against a non-nuclear China.

America's lack of resolve in overthrowing the North Korea communist dictatorship, and potentially China as well, was ascribed by Elliott to President Truman's "fear of acting beyond the Yalu [River] and so, he professed to believe, of unleashing a third world war at that time (when *we possessed what amounted to a nuclear monopoly that could be brought to bear before there was any possibility of Russian delivery of such weapons on the Continental United States*), as one of the most unworthy actions that an American leader has ever shown in the face of direct aggression. To it we owe the subsequent collapse of Asia." To Elliott, a pre-emptive war was the only means of averting China's expanding communist influence across Asia, due to China's territorial and historical hegemony over the region.

In order to prevent further "falling dominos" of communism in Asia, America would have to commit herself to the English Commonwealth's policy of collective security because of the region's rich substantive resources of food and raw materials. Since 1949 China's promotion of revolutionary communism throughout Asia threatened America's regional power and intended "to do to us [i.e. America] exactly what we fought Japan to prevent – throw us out of eastern and Southeast Asia and to exert military measures that would bring it all, through puppets or directly, under Communist control."[21] Accordingly, in order to avoid any more shifts in the balance of power toward Russian or Chinese imperialism, Elliott advocated "limited wars" in 1958, noting that his student Henry Kissinger "has also stressed limited wars" as an attractive means of altering the scales of power toward the "free world" incrementally.[22]

Kissinger's advocacy of limited wars had begun with his 1955-'57 work for the CFR culminating in *Nuclear Weapons and Foreign Policy,* wherein he predicted the Vietnam War by arguing that America should not refrain from fighting limited wars out of fear "that any limited war must automatically lead to all-out war." At the time, Kissinger "argued for a strategy placing reliance on early use of tactical nuclear weapons"[23] (a theory he would tactfully amend in 1960 to the early use of "conventional" weapons), but the philosophy of note was the "willingness to fight," which Kissinger and Elliott felt America needed to demonstrate.

The invasion of Cuba with a small expeditionary force of ex-patriots at the Bay of Pigs in 1961 was one such example of limited warfare, as was the build-up of American military and CIA "advisors" in South Vietnam and Laos since the mid-1950s. Yet, this strategy of limited warfare was negated by Fidel Castro's Cuban government, which played the Soviet Union against America until the threat of full-scale nuclear war came to a head during the Cuban Missile Crisis of October 1962. Rather than face a direct conflict with Russia, cooler heads prevailed as President Kennedy and Khrushchev agreed to take the Russian warheads out of Cuba in exchange for American ICBM's from Turkey.

Elliott had long been an advocate of bringing America into a war environment against the threat of communism, and his endorsement of revitalizing military spending to face the Soviet challenge in 1946 was heeded quickly after the end of the second world war, as the Russians detonated their nuclear bomb in 1949. That winter "NSC 68" was drafted by Paul Nitze, head of the Policy Planning Staff at the State Department, calling for an extensive arms build-up. Elliott was a consultant to Nitze at the time, and it seems likely that he would have helped formulate the plan. The policy was blocked by the Budget Bureau but only until the outbreak of the Korean War in the summer of 1950.

Ten years later, after nearly a decade of Eisenhower's military cut-backs predicated on a massive nuclear arsenal for "massive retaliation," Elliott's colleagues at the Foreign Policy Research Institute (FPRI), of which he and Kissinger were both members since its founding in 1955, portentously advised altering the American psyche from believing that the Cold War was a struggle to contain communism to believing that it was in fact a "total war" to defeat the communist systems of power throughout the world.

The 1950s had demonstrated to the FPRI that America was engaged in a "protracted conflict" with communism.[24] In the FPRI's nightmarish scenario of *Protracted Conflict* (1959), the study group (whose report was discussed with and critiqued by its associates, including Kissinger and Elliott) determined that peace did not actually exist but was merely a continuation of the "power struggle" through "nonviolent means." Consequently, "the current struggle for the mastery of the globe has been waged for five decades, albeit by diverse contenders," and even if the Soviets and Americans made peace, the agreement would not cease the ideological hostilities to establish a global order.[25]

In *Protracted Conflict* the FPRI, reminiscent of *The City of Man*'s authors, emphasized that America was the inevitable power to herald "a new world order" based on the ideal of "the Good Society." The international order did not depend upon a federally-united "world state," but it did require "the rule of liberty under law" for "the great majority of mankind," the ultimate effort of which would lead to "the prevention of war" after centuries of revolutionary conflict within and between states.[26] The strategy of achieving this world order would depend on America adopting both a military and economic program to be launched against communism, as well as a more psycho-political propaganda affront on nationalistic communism.

Thus, FPRI's 1961 book, *A Forward Strategy for America,* recalled NSC-68 of the Korean War by calling for bigger government spending, which would include an increase in federal spending from 33 to 50% GNP by 1964, "to double our rate of international development assistance and to improve the national performance in the psycho-political fields. We deem a "Korean War" level of effort necessary during the sixties, even though this may entail credit and price controls, rationing, materials allocation and deficit financing until the revenue problem is reduced as a result of augmented GNP."[27]

This forecast for socialistic government spending, as well as military-industrial complex welfare, proved remarkably accurate during the 1960s Vietnam War and Great Society programs. As for the FPRI's proposal for "international development assistance," this proposal was not purely philanthropic, for it was targeted at the post-colonial and non-aligned nations as part of a "psycho-political" effort, which would be undertaken domestically as well.

After the publication of the FPRI's other book of 1961, *American Study for the Nuclear Age*, the *The Bulletin of Atomic Scientists* published a book review in March, only two months after President Eisenhower's farewell address brought public attention to the dangers of "the military-industrial complex." The *Bulletin*'s book review questioned the interlocking of the Richardson Foundation, the FPRI, and the Institute for American Strategy (IAS),[28] which was itself a creation of the 1958 National Military-Industrial Conference and host of "National Strategy Seminars."[29] The allegations led The *New York Times* to discover that in 1958 the National Security Council (on whose planning board sat Elliott) had issued a policy directive that "the military be used to reinforce the cold war effort," which led to the presence of military officers at these IAS Seminars.[30]

The allegations led to a memo in July by the Senate on Foreign Relations Committee Chairman William Fulbright citing growing "Right-Wing radicalism" amongst military officers engaged in educating soldiers and civilians as part of the IAS and FPRI conferences at the National War College, "at variance with established goals and policies of the Government." In its defense, FPRI director (and co-author of *Protracted Conflict*) James E. Dougherty acknowledged the Institute's ties to IAS, the Richardson Foundation, the National War College, and the Joint Chiefs of Staff, but he denied any charges of "right-wing radicalism." Instead, Dougherty called attention to FPRI's speakers at its 1959 and '60 summer seminars at the National War College; the speakers included CIA Director Allen Dulles, Paul Nitze, Henry Kissinger, Hans Morgenthau, Herman Kahn, and W.Y. Elliott, all of whom could certainly be labeled as right-wingers, though far more establishment figures than radicals.[31]

In fact, FPRI was extremely legitimate, though it was connected to militarist components in government. For example, Col. William Kintner, a founding member of FPRI, was a planning officer at the CIA who also joined IAS in 1961. As for its ties to the financial world, in 1956 Nelson Rockefeller hosted Frank Barnett, Robert Strausz-Hupe, Kintner, Elliott (as well as Profs. Walt Rostow and Max Millikan) to discuss "What Can be Done by Private Institutions?" in regards to U.S. Foreign Policy.[32]

Much of the propaganda work that Elliott was involved with at this time, aside from teaching at Harvard, was carried out through the private Foundations like Ford, Mellon, Rockefeller, and Richardson. In a 1955 letter to Frank Barnett at the Richardson Foundation, Elliott admitted "working with the Central Intelligence Agency and with Nelson Rockefeller in this general area of development of experience in dealing with Communism."[33] It would seem that Elliott was working within the realm of the Congress on Cultural Freedom's attempts, using CIA financing, "to build up the reputation of artists in the West whose work could in some way be viewed as supportive or at least uncritical of American foreign policy and free trade, and to show Western Europe as somewhere where the arts were both supported and allowed to flourish uninhibited by the ruling elite." The CIA conducted financing through private foundations like that of the Rockefeller Foundation.[34]

Having worked with the private Mellon, Richardson, Rockefeller, and Ford Foundations, as well as the Rhodes Trust, Elliott indubitably understood the necessity of private funds in strategically organizing and influencing policies without having to negotiate with government bureaucracy and oversight. In 1966 Elliott edited a book on U.S. Foreign Aid, wherein he advocated that America become "the 'school' for the free world" by educating and assisting the leaders of the ex-colonial countries. Post-World War II strategy had emphasized the economic development of these countries while overlooking the training of their civil servants, technicians, and political leaders in the spiritual concept of free institutions, particularly "independence from outside control," i.e. Moscow's or Beijing's.

Yet, with the U.S. government's congressional subcommittees scrutinizing allocations toward educational purposes, Elliott proposed a non-government organization (NGO) be established with "university and business representation as well as government representation." It would "have on its board of directors representatives of the large foundations that are engaged in international development," i.e. Ford Foundation's Education and World Affairs Foundation. Such an NGO would be supplemented by "an international advisory economic council under the aegis, say, of the International Bank." Out of this educational process, the leaders of the third world would be expected to adopt democratic institutions and become "responsible" to their peoples, rather than being "agents of Soviet imperialism."[35]

If such a strategy seemed reminiscent of Cecil Rhodes' vision for inculcating the Anglo-Saxon traditions across the British Empire through the Rhodes Scholarship, Elliott was even more clear in a speech at the War College defense seminar in July 1960, extrapolating on the psychological aspects of foreign intervention as part of the doctrine of protracted conflict in the post-colonial world:

> We must help find and train people to run a country before they can develop a country, before they can do anything really. But, above all, they must have this sense of an ethos, of the deep roots of political community, – I would call it a Platonic mythos if I weren't afraid of being misunderstood. It doesn't mean "myth" in our sense of something that is not a reality. It means a basic system of beliefs and values by which people live, and by which they are conditioned.[36]

This statement implicates Elliott's ambition, in the tradition of the British Round Table, to educate people toward strategically constructed myths in order to create the so-called "co-organic" state, with a common purpose and morality.

At the end of World War II, aside from the pressing need for international controls on atomic energy, natural resources, and arms control, Elliott had also argued that an international order would prevail "through persuasion and through finding a voluntary basis for voluntary consent to the powers of such an order over the nations."[37] The United Nations failed in his sense of a "co-organic" organization because "its powers cannot be used coercively with success - an organic factor; and this fact, in turn, rests on the absence of the elements of a truly shared common set of moral values for law," i.e. the co-factor.[38] Taking a line from Rousseau, Elliott argued that America would need to be a vehicle for coercing people's obligations into duties in order to form within "a true community, a shared sense of moral values strong enough to make men accept the coercion of a world organization and break down the finality of national sovereignty."

Instead of the UN, Elliott believed that America could initiate the task of creating a consensus for respecting international laws and duties; yet the endeavor could not rest content with the creation of democracies, for the rise of fascism in democratic parliaments like Germany and Italy in the 1920s and '30s had proved that "democracy, too, can become perverted and evil." Therefore, in 1948 Elliott reiterated his political philosophy of 1928 about the utility of pragmatism, *within* constitutional limitations, by claiming that democracy meant the "testing of ideas," except for "*the absolute value of freedom*," which must be preserved.

On the other hand, Elliott understood that absolute individual freedom would lead to anarchy, even in a constitutional society, so the only preservation of individual freedom would be through an unspoken limitation on that freedom by the "common morality." Quoting the British liberal imperialist and ally of the Milner Round Table Group Arthur Balfour, Elliott emphasized that international organization depended upon an "agreement on fundamentals." Elliott's efforts throughout his life were to inspire a local, national, and international base of fundamentals for the "common morality" that would pave the way for acceptance of the international normalization of economic and political standards.[39]

Elliott never openly advocated governmental coercion of a democratic population against its will, but he did stress the importance of the government directing and even manipulating the democratic dialogue. As a manipulator of cultural morality, Elliott was perfectly placed while serving as a Professor Emeritus at Harvard. In one telling insight on the professor's influence over his students' futures in academia and beyond, Alfred G. Myer wrote in his autobiography *My Life as a Fish*,

> Professor Elliott welcomed me as his student and encouraged me to write a doctoral dissertation about the founding father of communism,

> V. I. Lenin. Unfortunately, my thesis did not turn into the anti-Communist indictment he obviously had expected, and he therefore did not promote my career any further. I found that academia in the U. S. functioned very much like an old boys' network in which senior people make the crucial decisions affecting their disciple's careers. In the end, Bill Elliott found a student who was much more in tune with him politically, and whom he had spotted when the student was still an undergraduate. I once met this young man when Elliott called me into his office, saying, "Al, I want you to meet Henry. He is very bright and will be going places." Henry Kissinger indeed owed the rocket-like start of his career to this professor.[40]

The clubby nature of academic institutions also lent them to infiltration by government intelligence agencies. Elliott was a CIA officer (furnished with an office at the CIA) since at least 1949, and a consultant to Frank Wisner (then its deputy director for plans). In 1951 Elliott had to accept "inactive status" at the CIA (with his consultation now given "gratis") due to his work with the new Office of Development Management, and he simultaneously requested from Wisner "an inactive consultant status similar to my own, but one that could be changed at need, for Mr. Henry Kissinger."

If his request was granted, then Kissinger was working for CIA since at least 1951, and possibly earlier, given that he was appointed as a lieutenant in military intelligence for the Army Reserves between 1948 and 1959. Similarly during the 1950s, Kissinger (under Elliott's supervision) was informing for the FBI on his colleagues visiting from abroad during the annual Harvard Summer Seminars, of which Elliott was director. Kissinger's activities included opening his colleagues' mail to discern if they were communist sympathizers.[41] As for Elliott, though on inactive status, he continued to pass on information to his contacts in the CIA, particularly to deputy director Robert Amory, Jr. after 1953.[42]

In 1950, Elliott, on behalf of the Office of Production Management, drew up for the Senate a proposal for defense requirements for the coming decade, arguing for and against "peacetime psychological warfare." The favorable argument posited that America "had better take more of the defense or welfare billions and put a few more millions into a counter psychological and economic warfare offensive" against the Soviets.[43] In the report, Elliott defined "economic warfare programs" as being synonymous with "economic aid" like the Marshall Plan to Europe, while "psychological warfare" consisted of activities like "The Voice of America" program abroad and other "'information programs' carried on in connection with the military assistance programs" at home.

As for Elliott's focus on teaching "anti-communism" to Americans through educational outlets in the media and the newly expanding television market, he was one of the founding trustees of the American Committee for Liberation in 1951, which launched "Radio Liberation" (Radio Liberty) the following year as a CIA propaganda front. Then, in 1955 Elliott was working with Paul Mellon of the Mellon Foundation toward "making a few small grants to the development of programming experiments on educational television." The principal question they faced was "how to organize the total programming resources, especially those of films of the Nation, so that educational television stations will have something that will hold audiences and still be worthy to be called education."[44] The meaning of "education," of course, depended on the praxis of the educators.

As a Harvard professor of government, Elliott understood the importance of educating a population to have effective democracy, but more critically, as a CIA officer and government employee, he knew that a government must represent itself well for the sake of public approval. By 1953, "McCarthyism" was waning, but Senator Joe McCarthy's radical anti-communist denunciations of government officials and ultimate over-reaching had polarized the citizenry toward "McCarthyism" or "toward the sort of Civil Liberties Union attitude" of full protection of communist speech and ideas.

Elliott, still part of the Office of Defense Mobilization, wrote a memo to C.D. Jackson in April, before Jackson became psychological warfare advisor to President Eisenhower in September 1953. Elliott's memo regarded the "Organization of Psychological Defense Measures at Home," for C.D. Jackson was no stranger to propaganda.[45] Not only was he Henry Luce's deputy as managing-editor of *Time-Life* since the 1930s, he became Deputy Chief of the Psychological Warfare Branch at Allied Forces Headquarters in 1943, remaining in a similar position at Supreme Headquarters throughout World War II.[46] Elliott's advice to Jackson on propaganda in 1953 was to cease relying on "the survival of ideas in a free market and in open competition" to communicate the government's intentions against communism.[47] Elliott knew from his experiences at Harvard that McCarthy's raving anti-communism was losing the battle to win the intellectuals of the country, who would in turn instruct the youth.

According to Elliott, the State Department would have to be more open in calling intellectuals to "consultative groups" where they could be "educated and often converted to the Department's point of view." At a "grass roots" level, Elliott echoed the British imperialists like Arnold Toynbee at the turn of the century who espoused worker education associations, only this time broadening the tactic in "cultivating" the opinions of "women's clubs," "churches," and "academic professional groups" through the use of speakers favorable to government policies; Elliott was one such frequent speaker at these types of organizations. Yet Elliott's main point was clear: "We are going to have more and more unpleasant types of security operations," and these unspecified "security operations" (obviously referring to some type of warfare against communism) required better handling of "public relations," i.e. propaganda. Though the American democratic system could not abandon its commitment to free speech, Elliott certainly hoped that the government and its agents in organizations like the "restricted and elite" Council on Foreign Relations would do a better job in shaping the discourse.[48]

The principle means by which Elliott would strive to realize the co-organic community was through his idea for "A Round Table for the Republic," a national prototype for an internationally organized "Round Table for Freedom." Elliott claimed that his model was a "dinner-and-discussion club" called "The Round Table" back in Nashville, Tennessee, where the communities' "leading citizens" would meet to discuss "metapolitical" issues concerning "fundamental values."[49]

As a member of the Council on Foreign Relations between 1934 and 1942, Elliott would have known that the CFR was already developing localized discussion groups of international policies. Elliott's Round Table was certainly no more egalitarian than the elite CFR group, for his Round Table conception also excluded the common man, preferring the "leading citizens" like Supreme Court Justices, University Deans and Chancellors, Presidents of Societies, etc. who could then influence their own circles based on their shared ideas. The main difference from the CFR, then, was that Elliott's Round Table was not only interested in international affairs, but all aspects of social life.

Yet Elliott's intention for the Round Table also had a purposive aspect of spreading certain values, in the tradition of the English Round Table's movement to encourage a shared purpose in the Commonwealth. "The Round Table in England for many years brought together a devoted group of people with common purpose from the Commonwealth and made an indelible imprint to some aspects of the surviving bonds in the British Commonwealth. The magazine of the name [*The Round Table*] played a large part in this effort. I would hope that we could do better."[50] Elliott offered his idea for a national Round Table to everyone from Nelson Rockefeller in 1955 to National Security advisor McGeorge Bundy in 1964,[51] though it is surprising that Elliott did not recognize the "Bilderberg Group," which had been meeting since 1954, as such a Round Table.

The Bilderberg Group gathered annually over 100 members of the political, corporate, academic and financial elite, largely from Europe and North America, to discuss socio-political and economic ideas and strategies for the future. Along these lines, Elliott idealized his own Round Table to be composed in the United States from the "leaders who symbolize our best traditions" to serve as unelected Wise Men for presidential and congressional policy planning. This idea was an extension of his conceptions for constitutional reform from the 1930s, to create permanent civil servants (as in the English government, where the Round Table Group members constantly served in unelected government posts between the turn of the century and the 1950s).

Perhaps the pre-existence of the Council on Foreign Relations, with its members incestuously linked to government posts of both Democratic and Republican administrations, explains why Elliott never managed to launch his Round Table idea (from 1955 when he first petitioned his fellow Rhodes Scholar and friend Frank Barnett for $500,000 from the Richardson Foundation, until 1969 when he retired from academic life entirely to pursue the Round Table idea). Ultimately, the closest Elliott ever came to realizing the Round Table was his creation, as Director of the Harvard Summer School's Arts and Sciences program in the 1950s, of the Harvard International Summer Seminar, "with Henry Kissinger as the prime guide for it through most its life."[52]

In 1951, Elliott and his graduate student Henry Kissinger were concerned with the preservation of the bonds between the Western European members of NATO and America. When Kissinger proposed the summer seminar in 1951, he acknowledged that its maximum objectives were to bring together international students of a post-World War II generation verging toward "cynicism and indeed nihilism," in an attempt "to create nuclei of understanding of the true values of a democracy and of spiritual resistance to Communism." Much as Rhodes had wanted to inculcate the spirit of the British tradition into young men of the British Empire, Elliott and Kissinger understood that the younger demographic seemed "more promising. Their greater plasticity would outweigh the possible superiority of their older brethren in terms of scholarly achievement. Their influence, of course, would take longer to make itself felt." Nonetheless, they hoped that in time these future leaders would warrant the investment.[53]

If the Harvard International Seminar could be comparable to a Rhodes scholarship,[54] then *Confluence* magazine was comparable to *The Round Table*. In truth, it was not so cohesive an organ of a single voice as was *The Round Table*, for *Confluence* represented a symposium for debate (of the non-communist persuasion), but its mission was to discover if there were "any really common values that underlie the civilization of the West" as a purposive community. Confluence: An International Forum, founded in March 1952 with Elliott as Director and Kissinger as Editor, intended to continue the "experiment" of the Summer Seminars by fostering the discussion until there would emerge "common answers and faiths" for Western society to recognize and teach to other cultures. From the "streams of national cultures," an international confluence was hoped to form through "a sufficiently common channel."[55] *Confluence* was founded with Rockefeller Foundation money, but by 1953 John J. McCloy, the Chairman of Rockefeller's Chase Manhattan Bank, the CFR, and the Ford Foundation, arranged for the Ford Foundation grant that "assured" the magazine's survival.[56]

Amongst the magazine's advisory board (and contributors) was the former Fugitive poet/Agrarian leader John Crowe Ransom. When he left the board in 1956, he was replaced by his Agrarian counterpart Allen Tate. There were two other future national leaders on the Advisory Board from the beginning: McGeorge Bundy (future National Security advisor under President Kennedy) and Arthur Schlesinger, Jr. (also a Kennedy cabinet advisor). Schlesinger, then an associate professor of history, had worked with Elliott on the 1950-'51 Woodrow Wilson Foundation report on *United States Foreign Policy*. Bundy, who was appointed dean of Harvard's Faculty of Arts and Sciences the following year, had adopted Elliott as "his patron" when he arrived at Harvard in 1949 as a lecturer in the government department;[57] Bundy's having "never taken a class in government was not a problem for Elliott."[58] Bundy's biographer Kai Bird claimed that *Confluence*'s "sole purpose seemed to be to introduce influential men to its editor [Kissinger]."[59] Elliott, in truth, would have appreciated the magazine's worth as a point of confluence for scholars to interact and discuss transcendental values in an effort at codifying a common Western value system.

In this context, *Confluence* allowed Elliott to expound his case that ideas are products of their "cultural context" and hold no inherent "truth" beyond their empirical, or pragmatic, testability.[60] This understanding of ideological flexibility could be translated to the Cold War, as being a conflict between the free, empirical systems of the Western democracies, and the ideological monolith of communism. In Western Europe, disintegration of state-oriented fascism, the Marshall Plan's reconstruction aid, the extension of NATO as far as Turkey, and the birth of a European Economic Community, had all proved to Elliott the viability of the democratic process in the current cultural context. Yet if the proof-test of political affinity could be found in economic policies, then democratic capitalism's weakness lay in its timidity "to force the pace of savings and capital investment in backward societies which have cut off the international flow of capital by an exacerbated nationalism, often produced as a reaction against colonialism.... [T]he free systems of the West must find some more effective measure of control over the economic area of the world which is still available to them before the complete disintegration of colonialism."[61] American pragmatism would have to use all its resources to contend with doctrinaire communist and nationalist ideologies to capture the allegiance of the post-colonial nations.

Despite Prime Minister Churchill's opposition to colonial independence at the end of World War II, the anti-colonial movements of the 1950s and '60s struck a fatal blow to the implementation of natural resource controls. In the 1950s, from Indochina and Malaysia to Egypt and the Congo, national independence movements threatened the Western economic superpowers by modeling themselves on the Soviet "ideology" of nationalism, sometimes to the point of attempting to nationalize resources like oil in Iran and arable land in Guatemala. The prospect of nationalizing domestic resources terrified Western financiers and governments holding long-term contracts on colonial property and cheap labor, prompting CIA-sponsored coup d'etats in both countries, with Iran's Prime Minister Mohammad Mosaddegh deposed in 1953 and Guatemala's President Jacobo Árbenz.

The Foreign Policy Research Institute (FPRI) was formed at the University of Pennsylvania in 1955, the year that "non-aligned" nations, including the former British colonies Egypt, Indonesia and the crown jewel India, convened the Bandung Conference in Indonesia to espouse their neutrality in the Cold War. Elliott and Kissinger joined FPRI as founding members, and both served on the Editorial Advisory Board for *Orbis*, FPRI's quarterly journal after 1957.[62] That year, *Orbis*' editors announced their disappointment with America's "containment" strategy of massive retaliation for failing "to galvanize the West into an effective counterforce" against communist influence. For example, NATO's "shield" for Western Europe lacked far enough "geopolitical range," as demonstrated by the Suez Crisis of 1956. The hawkish FPRI intentionally misconstrued Egyptian President Nasser's nationalization of the Suez Canal as communist-inspired, and thus deserving of the subsequent invasion by England, France and Israel.[63] President Eisenhower broke with Truman's previous pro-British policies by not only condemning the British invasion but ultimately working with the Soviet Union to force the invaders' withdrawal.

Seventy-five years earlier, England had been powerful enough to occupy Egypt to protect the Suez Canal, despite the colony then belonging to the French Empire. Elliott would later conjecture to Harvard professor of British History Samuel Beer that the British had lost their resolve "to carry their part of the load of the world" when Eisenhower "gave a sort of coup de grace" to England. Elliott lamented this fact, having been trained by the British philosophy of property-rights belonging to the common wealth rather than the nation; thus, in British eyes, Egypt's nationalization of the Suez Canal, though in Egyptian territory, was an act "of aggression on the part of [President] Nasser rather than on the part of Israel."[64]

The following year the FPRI formalized its outlook on the demise of imperialism in *The Idea of Colonialism* (1958), which featured an article by Elliott about the necessity of national "responsibility" for newly independent nations. Elliott's conception of responsibility was steeped in his moral philosophy that the new nations be committed to constitutional governance as evidence that they were capable of "governing themselves." Responsibility also implied their commitment to "the protection of development of the resources in the areas where they [i.e. the natives] happen through *accidents of history* to dwell."

Alas, if they could renounce nationalism for the sake of internationalism, through an allegiance to the Western bloc, they would be considered "responsible members of the international community." Elliott adopted much of his argument for self-governance from J.S. Mill, the nineteenth century political philosopher who had opposed native self-government.[65] Now, in the twentieth century, Elliott speculated that any weakness in self-government could lead to the seizure of that nation by communist influence, which could take the form of nationalization of private property by the state.

But the world had enlarged since the height of imperialism, thanks to the formation of new nation-states, particularly in Africa and Asia. Elliott and his ilk hoped to limit this expanding world through the creation of federations amongst states. For example, he advocated (to no avail) that France not cede independence to Algeria unless it formed a federation with its neighbors, Tunisia and Morocco, in order to avoid Soviet economic influences. This federation model was probably derived from the British, who had created the Central African Federation in 1953, though the federation lasted less than ten years.

Elliott believed that federalism could deter the nationalist impulses of post-colonial states while also making small states more internationally-minded. A critical part of this international "responsibility" meant keeping their natural resources open to the international industrial community, i.e. Western Europe and particularly America. In Elliott's proof, should the "tribal nomads" of the Near East have claimed true territorial sovereignty over their land, and thus the world's oil reserves, the industrial countries would be at their mercy. Yet Elliott contended that these were "resources of which the value and use would be negligible without the needs of the highly developed industrialism of the outside world." In this sense, the underdeveloped nations depended upon the industrial and economic investments of the Western powers to utilize the resources of their pre-industrial societies.[66]

Elliott argued that just as Western jurisprudence recognized the right of governments to seize property for the public interest, so too should the "international community" be guaranteed the right to vital raw materials at the expense of national interests. Envisioning the world as a true commonwealth, Elliott argued that the colonial nations were purely fabrications of the European imperialists, and hence they lacked fundamental claims to national sovereignty.[67] As Elliott clarified in a note to his friend Vice President Richard

Nixon, "the right of national (truly national) self-determination" depends on a country genuinely becoming "a true state," meaning that it can be "prepared to support the responsibilities of modern statehood, with all its international obligations, before we can accept the liquidations of either trusteeship or the remaining colonialism which operates more and more in that way."[68]

"International obligations" included the submission of new nations to property contracts and titles, as well as a commitment to the United Nations and any international rules of law. Knowing that American policies might appear self-interested to foreign opinion or native peoples of the former colonies, Elliott cautioned the Editors of *Life* Magazine in 1961 not "to over-estimate our need for courting favorable reactions from that mythical construct: 'the opinion of mankind.'" To do so would be tantamount to "selling" American policy to people who have "never achieved high cultures" or have "lost them" and so could not be "morally" trusted.[69]

In order to end the era of "trusteeship" of the empires over the colonies, Elliott knew, as Cecil Rhodes had before him, that the West should train the economic and political leaders of the colonial countries to mold their socio-political worldview. The Round Table Movement ideologue Lionel Curtis had written after World War I that "the idea that the principle of the Commonwealth implies universal suffrage betrays an ignorance of its real nature... the task of preparing for freedom the races which cannot as yet govern themselves is the supreme duty of those who can. It is the *spiritual end* for which the Commonwealth exists, and material order is nothing except as a means to it."[70]

During the 1950s, however, England was squeezed between the fiscal burden of the empire, the local anti-colonial movements and the international liberal criticism of the Western hypocrisy (when faced with Soviet imperialism) to ultimately concede increasing sovereignty to those same Commonwealth nations in Africa and Asia which had been deemed incapable of self-governance only a few years before. Yet, due to the Cold War's emphasis on preventing the expansion of Soviet influence, just as America was forced to adopt the defense of countries such as Greece and Turkey in England's stead after World War II, so too did the U.S. aid England in educating and training its Commonwealth citizens for self-governance in the post-colonial world.

Elliott believed that his International Harvard Summer Seminar program under Kissinger acted as a prototype for "dealing with a group of highly influential cultural leaders." As he expressed to Under Secretary of State Christian Herter in 1957, America had to pursue similar "cultural exchange" programs, to supplement its "regional institutes and institutes for special studies in the Middle East, in the Far East, Africa, and in other languages and cultures [which] are beginning to serve us with resources for assisting in training institutes abroad."[71]

In the mid-1950s Elliott had co-founded, with Christian Herter, Paul Nitze, and George McGhee,[72] one such school to teach area studies after World War II; the Foreign Service Educational Foundation in Washington D.C. became "the parent organization for the School of Advanced International Studies."[73] Area studies were suddenly indispensable after World War II to teach the relatively uneducated American service officers about foreign affairs, languages, cultures, etc. The concoction of area studies programs was comparable to, if not predominately influenced by, the British educational system's colonial studies departments, utilized to educate the foreign officers and policy experts in managing the Empire. Elliott explained the need to study the decolonized regions, for "this is the area of decisive combat in the political struggle which is now the main battleground with the Soviets." In order for Americans to be delicate in the process of cultivating non-Western cultures to Western traditions, the area studies and education of natives abroad does "not attempt to ram our civilization down the throats of others but assists them in developing their own civilization in conformity with their own objectives and toward the progress which they uniformly desire."[74]

Yet this assertion that the decolonized countries were being developed toward their own objectives was largely cant, and the progress they so desired was subordinate to the progress intended for them by the West. By the early 1960s, decolonization had become all the more rapid, beginning with the disintegration of the French Empire. In early 1962, Elliott, an official consultant to Secretary of State Dean Rusk, warned his old colleague at the State Department, Under Secretary George McGhee, that "the emergence of new countries which have achieved independent statehood may radically change the terms of trade by increased costs as well as by the prospects of the interruption of development, and prevention by other means of present production of raw material supplies. Africa is an obvious area of such danger, but Southeast Asia, the Middle East and Latin America are also potential danger zones."[75]

The fear of decolonization was clearly based on raw materials, which America and the Western industrial powers had long presupposed to be under international control, i.e. under British control through their Commonwealth property. America had to strategize new ways of securing its access to raw materials. Accordingly, the Office of Emergency Planning, with Elliott's supervision, was soon drafting a report to emphasize that "the preservation of access to basic primary resources... is a justification for the massive U.S. expenditures on foreign aid and arms assistance" to decolonized nations. "The story indicates the crucial nature of not losing substantial parts of the world to *monopolistic state imperialism* of either the Soviet or the Red Chinese systems... Their further success would one day force us into military operations, under grave disadvantages, to recover lost territory, if we were not successful in our existing foreign policies and foreign aid programs; and in stepped up counter measures to meet Sino-Soviet political economic offensives for disruption or takeover."[76]

This cynical attitude toward socialist-style nationalism let to the view of Nasser's Egypt and Ho Chi Minh's North Vietnam as mere puppets of Moscow and Beijing. Elliott had already been advising the State Department since 1960 to dispatch military "advisors" to emerging nations in an effort to coax them to align with the West, a tactic the Soviets had already deployed in Lumumba's Congo and Nasser's Egypt. He even went so far as to recommend "the kind of training of security forces, and perhaps even military forces, capable of a "back up" of the newly emerging regimes in some of these countries," conforming to a policy of dispatching military advisors like U.S. Green Berets, which did indeed mark the build-up to war in Indochina.[77]

Consequently, decolonization played into the protracted conflict narrative of "Soviet" and "Chinese" supported communist nationalism against Anglo-American-led internationalism. In order to win this new struggle for the "uncommitted" and inexperienced emerging nations, a policy of total war would be implemented by America to fight "communist" infiltration in the post-colonial world. This policy found its culmination with the American entry into the Vietnam War from 1965 to '73, though American involvement in the conflict began during World War II when Vietnam was still part of French Indochina. Then President Roosevelt had to navigate the predicament of cultivating French support against the Nazis, and standing by his commitment of decolonization.[78] Following FDR's death, the British backed the French imperial hold in southern Vietnam against the nationalist Viet Minh, who ultimately found support from the communist Chinese and Soviets, turning the conflict into a war over "spheres of influence" lest communism or nationalism challenge the United States policy of regional alliances.

However, during the 1960s, America saw the assassination of three epochal leaders (President John Kennedy and presidential candidate Robert Kennedy, and national civil rights and anti-war activist Martin Luther King, Jr.), along with the deepening quagmire in Vietnam following the Tet Offensive of 1968. The American public's faith in American pre-eminence in the world was suddenly challenged in a way that would be termed the "crisis of democracy" as expressed by Elliott's student Samuel Huntington during the 1970s.

One of those responsible for that crisis of democracy was Henry Kissinger, then entrenched in political power as the Assistant to President Nixon for National Security Affairs since 1969. With Kissinger's policy of engaging the Soviets through détente, the forecast for the progression was to move "from détente to mutual involvement, then to world community, and finally to world society."[79] Nation by nation, the world would fall into an international order based on like-minded economic and legal assumptions under the auspices of supranational organizations like the United Nations (with its powers to sanction and declare war on international violators), GATT (with its powers over national tariffs), and the World Bank & IMF (with their controls on international loans and debt conditions). Thus the Club of Rome could gloat by the end of the 1980s, "smaller countries already have very little control over their own affairs in consequence of decisions taken outside their territories, such as the establishment of commodity policies modified to obtain IMF funding. Erosion of sovereignty may be for most countries a positive move towards the new global system in which the nation-state will, in all probability, have a diminishing significance."[80]

Endnotes

1. Elliott, W.Y. *The New British Empire.* p. 33.

2. Stanley Hoffmann, Samuel Huntington, et. al., "Vietnam Reappraised," *International Security* (Vol. 6, No. 1, Summer 1981), p. 14.

3. Quigley, Carroll. *Tragedy and Hope.* p. 915-6.

4. Lord Lothian published an article anonymously in *The Round Table*'s summer 1939 journal, proposing "a new system of international organization, stronger than the League. It must be strong enough to prevent rearmament and war. It must be empowered to restrain economic nationalism and prevent the undue restriction of emigration. The price of this is that the nations should be willing to surrender some of the unlimited sovereignty they now possess." (See "Grand Alliance Against Aggression." *The Round Table*; June 1939. p. 456).

5. Lindsay, A.D. "War to End War." *Background and Issues of the War.* Oxford: Clarendon Press, 1940. p. 32.

6. Ibid. p. 34-5.

7. Elliott, W.Y. et al. *The City of Man.* p. 93-4.

8. One of whom was the new Undersecretary of State in 1943, Edward Stettinius, Jr. (also a CFR member); his father was a former partner of J.P. Morgan Bank and a friend of W.Y. Elliott's (and of Elliott's uncle, Princeton Professor and banker Edward Elliott) who had served with WYE on the Business Advisory Council to FDR in the late 1930s.

9. Shoup & Minter. *Imperial Brain Trust.* p. 169-70.

10. This problem would be exacerbated over the next twenty years until the Foreign Policy Research Institute (FPRI) published a book on *The United States and the United Nations* (1964) bemoaning the doubling of the UN's size to include newly decolonized states; according to Elliott, "every Communist society and many of the new countries that have been promoted into statehood from little more than tribal systems have an authoritarian character entirely different from our own political system. *The fact is that our ethics is acceptable only to advanced cultures and peoples.*" ("Applied Ethics: The United Nations and the United States." Gross, Franz B., Ed. p. 322).

11. Elliott, W.Y. "A Time for Peace?" *The Virginia Quarterly Review.* Vol. 22, No. 2. Spring 1946. p. 173.

12.Ibid. p. 174-6.

13. It is of little surprise that Elliott's diagram of international relations beginning in 1946 would be restated by his protégé Henry Kissinger ten years later in his doctoral thesis, which became *A World Restored* (1957), dedicated to his advisor Elliott, "to whom I owe more, both intellectually and humanely, than I can ever repay." Kissinger was looking toward the post-Napoleonic formation of the Concert

of Europe as a model for the post-World War II era. Kissinger explained that "stability" depended on international "legitimacy," "not to be confused with justice. It means no more than an international agreement about the nature of workable arrangements and about the permissible aims and methods of foreign policy." In this case, Russia played the role of Napoleonic France as the "revolutionary" power which felt so threatened by the international order that "only absolute security – the neutralization of the opponent" could reassure it. In such circumstances, diplomacy becomes unproductive, while the powers self-consciously stress "principles" and the threat of force to attain their ends. (Kissinger; 1957; p. 1-4).

14. Ibid. p. 166.

15. Ibid. p. 165-7.

16. Elliott's disciple and friend Samuel Huntington, in his book *The Soldier and the State* (1957), described the sea-change between pre-World War II (Sept. 11, 1941) military planning for the "prevention of the disruption of the British Empire… [including the] eventual establishment in Europe and Asia of balances of power which will most nearly ensure political stability in those regions…" and the May 1944 view of the Joint Chiefs of Staff (JCS), echoing the "idealistic" Atlantic Charter, that military priority should be given to the defeat of the Axis powers and maintenance of "the solidarity of the three great powers [Russia, Britain, U.S.A.]… to establish conditions calculated to assure a long period of peace." Huntington concluded by characterizing the civilian role of President Roosevelt and the JCS, with their Atlantic Charter idealism, as having obstructed the military from "formulating postwar goals before the conflict ended" and "directing policy toward the achievement of a world-wide balance of power" by situating American soldiers in the Balkans and preparing for the Russian threat to Europe. (Huntington, p. 330-344.)

17. Such heavy-handed rhetoric was not limited to conservatives as even the "liberal" imperialist Bertrand Russell, who had sparred with H.G. Wells and the Round Table Group over the means of achieving world government, argued in 1948 that "If America were more imperialistic (…) it would be possible for Americans to use their position of temporary superiority to insist upon disarmament, not only in Germany and in Japan, but everywhere except in the United States, or at any rate in every country not prepared to enter into a close military alliance with the United States, involving compulsory sharing of military secrets. During the next few years this policy could be enforced; if one or two wars were necessary, they would be brief, and would soon end in decisive American victory. In this way a new League of Nations could be formed under American leadership, and the peace of the world could surely be established." (Quoted in Carlos Escudé. *Bertrand Russell's Advocacy of Preemptive War, 1945-1949*. 2006.)

18. Blair, William M. "Declares Russia Plans Atomic War: Prof. Elliott of Harvard Says Loans and Scientific Data Should Be Denied to Soviet." *The New York Times*. June 15, 1946.

19. Memo from WYE to the Under Secretary (Robert Thayer). "The Trap Concealed in Proposals to Cease all Further Nuclear Testing by Accepting the Soviet Proposal at this Time." May 23, 1958. The Dwight D. Eisenhower Library (online). p. 3, 5.

20. W.Y. Elliott. Address on "A Balanced Policy Toward 'Uncommitted' Areas." Harvard Summer School Conference on National Security Policy. p. 3. July 15, 1958. William Y. Elliott Papers; Box 36, Hoover Institute Archives, Stanford.

21. WYE to Frank Altschul; Nov. 24, 1958; William Y. Elliott Papers; Box 93, Hoover Institute Archives, Stanford.

22. Elliott, W.Y. "A Balanced Policy Toward 'Uncommitted' Areas." p. 7. July 15, 1958.

23. Bird, Kai. *The Chairman: John J. McCloy: The Making of the American Establishment*. New York: Simon & Schuster, 1992. p. 463.

24. Taking a line from Kissinger's A World Restored, the group determined that "protracted conflicts" arise from the search for "a new equilibrium." The FPRI described "the doctrine of protracted conflict" as "a strategy for annihilating the opponent over a period of time…" This strategy is synonymous with

total warfare because "any one conflict undertaking in one geographical-cultural area is correlated with any other conflict undertaking in the same environment. Thus, for example, a propaganda campaign in the Middle East is geared to the economic, political, and military penetration of the region." (Strausz-Hupe, et al. *Protracted Conflict*; p. 1-3).

25. Strauz-Hupe, Robert, et al. *Protracted Conflict.* New York: Harper Colophon Books, 1959. p. 3-4.

26. Ibid. p. 148-50.

27. Dougherty, James E. From a Draft "Letter to the Editor" of *The New York Times.* July 28, 1961. William Y. Elliott Papers; Box 100, Hoover Institute Archives, Stanford.

28. The interlock point seems to have been Frank Barnett, director of research at the Richardson Foundation, which financially launched the FPRI between 1955 and 1959; Barnett was also a program director for the IAS, which co-sponsored FPRI"s *A Forward Strategy for America.* Barnett was an Elliott confidante throughout the 1950s and '60s, and Barnett's idea of "political warfare" fit perfectly with FPRI's, including fomenting "strikes and riots, economic sanctions, subsidies for guerrillas or proxy warfare…" (Quoted in Bellant, Russ. *Old Nazis.* p. 37).

29. Lyons, Gene M. and Louis Morton. From a Copy of "School for Strategy." *Bulletin of the Atomic Scientists.* March 1961. William Y. Elliott Papers; Box 100, Hoover Institute Archives, Stanford.

30. Bellant, Russ. *Old Nazis, the New Right, and the Republican Party.* Boston: South End Press, 1991. p. 36-7.

31. Dougherty, James E. From a Draft "Letter to the Editor" of The New York Times. July 28, 1961. William Y. Elliott Papers; Box 100, Hoover Institute Archives, Stanford.

32. Nelson Rockefeller to WYE; May 24, 1956; William Y. Elliott Papers; Box 91, Hoover Institute Archives, Stanford.

33. WYE to Frank Barnett; July 22, 1955; William Y. Elliott Papers. Box 14, Hoover Institute Archives, Stanford.

34. Harman, Mike. "The cultural Cold War: corporate and state intervention in the arts." Libcom.org (online). September 11, 2006.

35. *Education and Training in the Developing Countries: The Role of U.S. Foreign Aid.* Ed. William Y. Elliott. New York: Frederick A. Praeger, Publishers, 1966. p. 4-17.

36. W.Y. Elliott. "Objectives and Vital Interests of the United States," p. 15. Address to the National War College; *Defense Strategy Seminar,* Washington, D.C.; July 12, 1960.

37. Elliott, W.Y. "A Time for Peace?" p. 161-2.

38. Elliott, W.Y. "The Co-organic Concept of Community Applied to Legal Analysis: Constitutional and Totalitarian Systems Compared." From the Appendix to *The Pragmatic Revolt in Politics.* (1968) p. 529.

39. Elliott, W.Y. and McDonald. *Western Political Heritage.* P. 952-3.

40. Meyer, Alfred G. *My Life as a Fish.* (online) http://www.ritchieboys.com/DL/fish205.pdf. Self Published. 2000. Chapter 5, p. 2.

41. Diamond, Sigmund. *Compromised Campus.* New York: Oxford University Press, 1992. p. 138-50.

42. Amory's assistant happened to be Skull & Bonesman William Bundy, brother of Elliott's student McGeorge, and one of the main architects of CIA involvement in South Vietnam, culminating with the outbreak of war a decade later.

43. Elliott, W.Y. *Mobilization Planning and the National Security (1950-1960): Problems and Issues.* Washington D.C.: Government Printing Office, 1950. p. 35-40.

44. WYE to Frank Barnett; July 22, 1955; William Y. Elliott Papers. Box 14, Hoover Institute Archives, Stanford.

45. Jackson was also director of the Free Europe Committee, Elliott's American Committee for Liberation's European branch, which ran Radio Free Europe. Jackson and Elliott's connections actually went back to at least 1940, when they were both directors of the National Council for Democracy (with

such men as Henry Luce, W. Averell Harriman, and Nelson Rockefeller on the board). According to Elliott, the Council's mission was "to inculcate a deeper understanding of, and devotion to, the democratic way of life, and to rebuff at every level attack upon that way of life." Elliott hoped that the central Council in New York would allow for "regional" and eventually local councils to organize patriotic activities, public games, Boy Scouts, etc. Elliott believed that the grass-roots of American life needed to be cultivated and educated in a co-organic fashion to ensure that the citizenry felt an essential tie to the preservation of America "in the battle for unity." (W.Y. Elliott. "Proposed Program for submission to Mr. Nelson Rockefeller." Sept. 1940. William Y. Elliott Papers. Box 147, Hoover Institute, Stanford.) Although Elliott ultimately resigned in 1941, finding the Council's attitude unreliable, his relationship with Jackson and Rockefeller continued through the 1950s, as Elliott continued his efforts for propaganda programs.

46. Levenda, Peter. *Sinister Forces – A Grimoire of American Political Witchcraft: The Nine.* Oregon: TrineDay Press, 2005. p. 123.

47. Memo from WYE to C.D. Jackson. "Organization of Psychological Defense Measures at Home." April 24, 1953. Jackson, C.D.: Records, 1953-1966. The Dwight D. Eisenhower Library (online). p. 1.

48. Ibid. p. 6-8.

49. Elliott, W.Y. "Public Aspects of Private Associations." *The Pragmatic Revolt in Politics.* 1968. p. 563-5.

50. WYE to Frank Barnett; March 28, 1956; William Y. Elliott Papers; Box 4, Hoover Institute Archives, Stanford.

51. Rockefeller deferred the idea, while Bundy responded tersely, noting that "advice is not what we are short of at the moment." (Bundy to WYE; Dec. 15, 1964; William Y. Elliott Papers; Box 14, Hoover Institute Archives, Stanford.)

52. Elliott, W.Y. "Public Aspects of Private Associations." *The Pragmatic Revolt in Politics.* 1968. p. 563-5.

53. Henry Kissinger to WYE. "Informal Memorandum for Prof. Elliott"; 1951. William Y. Elliott Papers. Box 2, Hoover Institute Archives, Stanford.

54. Fellow Rhodes Scholar (and future Dean of Harvard's school of public affairs) Don K. Price was Vice President of the Ford Foundation, which underwrote most of the budget for the Seminars through the 1950s.

55. Elliott, W.Y. "Foreword." *Confluence.* Vol. I, No. 1. Harvard University Printing Office, 1952. p. 1-2.

56. Bird, Kai. *The Color of Truth: McGeorge Bundy and William Bundy: Brothers in Arms.* New York: Simon & Schuster, 1998. p. 462 .

57. It is unclear whether Elliott and "Mac" had previously met, for Bundy had worked with Richard Bissell on the Senate bill for the Marshall Plan in 1947-'48, while Elliott was staffing the House's Herter Committee on European Recovery. Either way, Elliott knew Mac's father, Harvey Bundy, a staple of the East Coast Establishment.

58. Ibid. p. 107.

59. Ibid. p. 142.

60. Elliott, W.Y. "Ideas and Ideology." *Confluence.* Vol II, No. 3 Harvard University Printing Office. p. 131.

61. Ibid. p. 138.

62. Kissinger officially ended his role on *Orbis*' Editorial Board in 1958 but continued his relationship with FPRI as an associate for a few years thereafter.

63. "Reflections on the Quarter." *Orbis.* Vol. I, No. 1. April 1957.

64. WYE to Samuel Beer; August 25, 1961; William Y. Elliott Papers; Box 77, Hoover Institute Archives, Stanford.

65. Mill's father, James, had directed the British East India Company's intelligence division since 1830; J.S. Mill succeeded his father in 1856 and thus superintended the brutal repression of the Indian rebellion in 1857. (See Chaitkin, Anton. *Treason in America.* p. 283-4).

66. Elliott, William Y. "Colonialism: Freedom and Responsibility." *The Idea of Colonialism*. Ed. Robert Strausz-Hupe and Harry W. Hazard. NY: Frederick A. Praeger, Inc., 1958. p. 435-450

67. Ibid. p. 444.

68. WYE to Vice President Richard Nixon; Sept. 11, 1958; William Y. Elliott Papers; Box 166, Hoover Institute Archives, Stanford.

69. WYE to the Editors of *Life* Magazine; August 24, 1961; William Y. Elliott Papers; Box 112, Hoover Institute Archives, Stanford.

70. Quoted in Quigley, Carroll. *Tragedy and Hope*. p. 147.

71. Memo for Under Secretary of State Christian Herter. "Some Suggested Areas for the Development of Policy Planning in the Department of State, in Response to your Suggestions in our Past Conversations." p. 4. June 10, 1957; William Y. Elliott Papers; Box 93, Hoover Institute Archives, Stanford.

72. Former Rhodes Scholar McGhee was a founding member of the Bilderberg Group.

73. WYE to Wilma Hutchinson Smith; Sept. 24, 1952; William Y. Elliott Papers; Box 3, Hoover Institute Archives, Stanford.

74. Memo for Under Secretary of State Christian Herter. "Some Suggested Areas for the Development of Policy Planning in the Department of State, in Response to your Suggestions in our Past Conversations." p. 5.

75. WYE memo for George McGhee. Re: "Assignment to think out in some detail the terms of reference and the type of committee or commission, including personnel suggestions, which would carry out the general responsibilities suggested in my memorandum of January 5 to the Secretary on 'setting up a new Paley Commission.'" Jan. 26, 1962; William Y. Elliott Papers; Box 112, Hoover Institute Archives, Stanford.

76. "Outline for Report from the Office of Emergency Planning to the President Recommending the Need for Updating Governmental Policies with Respect to Increasing Security of Free World Access to Basic Raw Materials." p. 6. August 17, 1962; William Y. Elliott Papers; Box 112, Hoover Institute Archives, Stanford.

77. WYE to Under Secretary Robert Thayer; June 10, 1960; William Y. Elliott Papers; Box 112, Hoover Institute Archives, Stanford.

78. At the Cairo Conference of 1943, FDR conferred heavily with the Chinese about the future of Indochina, at which point, per his son Elliott, he concluded that "the French would have no right, after the war, simply to walk back into Indo-China and reclaim that rich land for no reason other than it had once been their colony." (see Louis, Wm. Rogers. *Imperialism at Bay*. p. 279).

79. Nutter, G. Warren. *Kissinger's Grand Design*. Washington D.C.: American Enterprise Institute for Public Policy Research, 1975. p. 13.

80. King, Alexander and Bertrand Schneider. *The First Global Revolution*. A report by the Council of the Club of Rome. New York: Pantheon Books, 1991. p. 16.

Elliott's protégé Kissinger became an important advisor for presidents.

Chapter VIII

Kissinger's Understanding of History – The End of the Cold War

It was therefore a rude awakening when in the 1960s and '70s the United States became conscious of the limits of even its resources. Now with a little over a fifth of the world's GNP, America was powerful but no longer dominant. Vietnam was the trauma and the catharsis but the recognition was bound to come in any event. Starting in the '70s, for the first time, the United States has had to conduct a foreign policy in the sense with which Europeans have always been familiar: as one country among many, unable either to dominate the world or escape from it, with the necessity of accommodation, maneuver, a sensitivity to marginal shifts in the balance of power, an awareness of continuity and of the interconnections between events.

– Henry Kissinger, Speech to the Royal Institute of International Affairs (1982)[1]

In 1982, Henry Kissinger, having dominated American foreign policy from 1969 as National Security advisor then Secretary of State (1973-1977), delivered a speech at Chatham House before the British Royal Institute of International Affairs (RIIA), which had been founded in 1919 by Lionel Curtis using Sir Abe Bailey's financing[2] as "nothing but the Milner Group 'writ large.'"[3] William Yandell Elliott had passed away in 1979, but H.G. Wells' "open conspiracy" was ongoing when Kissinger described the American historical philosophy as fundamentally flawed. To Kissinger, the paradigmatic conflict between the British and American world-views had been evinced during World War II, when Churchill had hoped to prepare an imperial "balance of power" to check Russia immediately after the cessation of hostilities with Germany, while Roosevelt "toyed with the idea of non-alignment between a balance-of-power oriented colonialist Britain and an ideologically obstreperous Soviet Union." Essentially, Roosevelt hoped to continue the American tradition of independence of action to avoid the chicanery of English balance-of-power politics, which had played one ally-enemy against another throughout the 19th century. To Kissinger, the post-Concert of Europe from 1815 to 1914 was "peace for 99 years without a major war."[4] If a century of lesser wars and revolutions can be described as peaceful, it indicates a great deal about Kissinger's understanding of the nature of peace.

While an undergraduate at Harvard writing his Senior Thesis in 1951 for Elliott, Kissinger chose to explore "The Meaning of History" by comparing Oswald Spengler's *The Decline of the West*, with A.J. Toynbee's *A Study of History*, and Immanuel Kant's philosophical writings, including *A Critique of Pure Reason* and "Perpetual Peace." Kissinger, like Elliott, felt most comfortable with Kant as a guide to navigate the individual's desire for freedom "in a world of causal laws."[5] Kant's answer had been the Categorical Imperative, for the individual to act as though one's actions were bound to universal imitation. This foundation for morality legitimized the constitutional state, according to both Elliott and Kissinger, because the legislation would be derived with the consent of, and in response to, the people, in accordance with their sense of morality and justice.

In order for nations to subordinate their individual interests to the will of the international order, Kant supposed that the nations involved would have to be republican (i.e. constitutional) in order to understand the concept of legislative authority, and in order to act responsibly on behalf of their citizens. In 1795, Kant had sketched a proposal for "Perpetual Peace" by beginning with a Hobbesian premise, which inspired the notion of British balance-of-power politics, that "the natural state is a one of war." Consequently, in order for peace to reign between nations, there would need to be "established" a lasting legal grounding for cooperation.[6] The republican states would then form a "league of peace" to advance international law and trade. Kant was careful to distinguish the "league" as a federation of republican states, as opposed to a democratic Empire merging all peoples into a single body, because "the idea of the right of nations" still predominated at a time when the supremacy of kingship and nation-states had yet to be challenged.[7]

From Kant's essay, Kissinger extrapolated that while a constitutional government could only emerge from physical conflicts and ideological struggles *within* civil society, so too did the international constitutional order need to be molded by continuous wars between states. The result of these wars for perpetual peace would end with "a just civil constitution, *which will forever banish war and begin the harmony among mankind, [and] therefore constitutes the purpose of history*."[8] Kissinger had, via Elliott's tutorship, rearticulated the goal of Cecil Rhodes, with all his various wills from 1877 to the time of his death in 1902, to establish a universal British Empire "to hereafter render wars impossible and to promote the best interests of humanity."[9]

As Assistant to the President on National Security, perhaps Henry Kissinger was striving toward this end, by allowing the war in Vietnam to drag on, dispiriting the nation until 1973, when US military forces left South Vietnam with the same status quo governments as when the American military had commenced its "police action" eight years prior. In the meantime, Kissinger and Nixon had extended bombing campaigns into Cambodia and North Vietnam in a fruitless and unconstitutional effort[10] that Kissinger would ultimately describe as "America's first experience with limits in foreign policy, and it was something painful to accept."[11] Yet while American militarism could not claim victory over the "communist" guerrillas in South Vietnam, technically the military presence had achieved its initial aim of preserving a pro-American government in South Vietnam until 1975. By that time, Kissinger had worked out, in a true balance of power shift, a "détente" with the Soviet Union and China.

At the onset of the American war in Indochina in 1965, American politicians and intellectuals predicated intervention on the fear of "falling dominoes" as Asian countries would fall to communist-nationalist impulses, backed by Chinese or Soviet arms and trade. Yet in the early 1970s Kissinger was actively steering an opening to the Soviet Union, which involved corporate trade and banking credits, via the U.S.-U.S.S.R. Trade and Economic Council, with old Soviet allies like Armand Hammer, plus Chase Manhattan Chairman David Rockefeller, along with many other corporate luminaries on the board. [12]Such an economic opening to Soviet Russia, headed by some of the nation's largest corporations, came on the heels of an era when American corporations had become increasingly transnational by using the dollar-based Bretton Woods system to take over foreign industries, particularly in Western Europe. "By running persistent and large capital-account deficits in its balance of international payments, the United States effectively forced foreign central banks to buy excess dollars with their own currencies in order to decrease the supply of dollars in circulation. This provided American investors with the francs, marks, and other European currencies necessary to buy assets in France, Germany, and elsewhere. Thus, at the price of international stability, foreign central banks were put in the awkward position of financing the takeovers of their own countries' industry."[13] Though still technically American, these corporations often ended up importing goods for the United States consumer market, helping catalyze the overall trade deficit that was sinking the value of the dollar.

By the early 1970s, it could be remarked that "the rise of the global corporation over the U.S. economy has thus occurred simultaneously with the accelerating concentration of power in the hands of the 500 biggest U.S. corporations. Virtually all of these corporations are global – in the location of their assets, the source of their profits, and their production and marketing outlook."[14] The U.S. trade deficit, coupled with massive U.S. government expenditures on a war economy, created a crisis whereby a mass conversion of gold to dollars would have drained the U.S. gold supply or forced a massive devaluation of the value of the dollar. Instead, Nixon simply ended the Bretton Woods regime by suspending dollar convertibility to gold, so the US could continue "to flood the world with dollars without constraint as it has appropriated foreign resources and companies, goods and services for nothing in return except Treasury IOUs of questionable (and certainly shrinking) value."[15]

In this climate, American corporations and investors looked to Soviet trade as one potentially large market, as well as Red China, where Kissinger managed to open diplomatic relations. Formalization of ties would play a significant role by the 1980s, when China became a net exporter to the United States, leading it to a position of creditor, able to purchase billions of dollars' worth of U.S. Treasury Bonds. But in the process of opening markets for investment and trade, the U.S. became an import-based, debtor nation with investments moving in search of cheaper currencies and labor; for as Lord Milner had warned in 1925, financiers would inevitably sacrifice the domestic industry for the sake of foreign investments based on the policy of "free trade."

Milner, then head of the Round Table Group, had known the power of the international bankers, which he called the "Moneyed Interest," for his ties to the J.P. Morgan Bank were so close that in 1901 he was offered a role as partner of Morgan's London House. Thus, near the end of his life, Milner wrote that "it does not much matter to the Moneyed Interest if home production falls off ... they have all the world to invest in and are, for the most part, naturally quite indifferent where, or in what they invest, being simply guided by the consideration of *the return*." Forecasting the future with supreme accuracy, Milner proclaimed that if free trade became the policy of international economics, then "the ultimate destiny of this country is to become predominantly... a money owning and money lending country, the mortgagee of a great part of the rest of the world."[16]

By the end of the 1970s, it appeared that America had followed the British lead to play the part of global banker, utilizing such Machiavellian power politics as described by John Perkins, a self-proclaimed "economic hitman" when he reflected on his career with the strategic-consulting firm Chas T. Main, which advised the World Bank, United Nations, IMF, U.S. Treasury Department, Fortune 500 corporations, and select countries from the post-colonial world in Africa, Asia, and the Middle East:

> First, I was to justify huge international loans that would funnel money back to MAIN and other US companies (such as Bech-

> tel, Halliburton, Stone & Webster, and Brown & Root) through massive engineering and construction projects. Second, I would work to bankrupt the countries that received those loans (after they had paid MAIN and the other US contractors, of course), so that they would be forever beholden to their creditors and would present easy targets when we needed favors, such as military bases, UN votes, or access to oil and other natural resources.[17]

The international financiers were working hand-in-glove with international corporations, seeking to lay claim to natural resources from the former British Commonwealth and other former colonies, predicating their claims on the notion of international trade and expanding markets. In the meantime, American post-war productivity was declining as the average American suffered the consequences of economic stagnation following the oil embargo of 1973 that sent the price of oil up 400 percent, affecting commodities accordingly. In the words of one labor spokesman, the outsourcing of production overseas at a cheaper cost was turning the United States into "a nation of hamburger stands ... a country stripped of industrial capacity and meaningful work... a service economy."[18]

Kissinger accurately described America's demoralized condition in 1982 as having come to recognize "the tragic."[19] And yet, his belief was unshaken that the destiny of man was to continue to overcome the restraints of the nation-state by creating a supranational world order. Kissinger thus gloated in his speech before the RIIA that America had been forced in the years after World War II to accept that it could no longer enjoy its uniquely independent position in world affairs but was in fact subject to rules of international balance of power and the constraints of supranational order. For Kissinger, America needed to understand what he had come to learn while writing his Thesis under the tutelage of Elliott, that individuals must "accept constraints on their freedom for the sake of establishing a stable political community," and so, too, did nation-states.[20] This idea was a continuation of the antipathy felt for the nation-state by the Anglophile elites like Elliott who did not believe that self-interested governments could ever compromise to plan the constitutional and economic designs for the *theoretical* benefit of the world commonwealth.[21]

This ideology found voice in the conservation movements burgeoning around the private sector like the Rockefeller Brothers Fund, where Henry Kissinger sat on the board. In 1977 the Fund issued a Malthusian book, *The Unfinished Agenda,* expounding upon Kissinger's National Security Study Memo 200, which deemed population growth a threat to

U.S. national security and thus advocated population control measures in at least 13 foreign countries. The Fund's book likewise recommended for America a "reduction of legal and illegal immigration; promotion of contraception, abortion and sterilization in the U.S. and abroad; promotion of non-marriage and childlessness.... Logically, it also contained recommendations to reduce energy use..."[22] While the recommendations may have been scientifically valid, it is important to understand that the world-view prompting the shift toward environmentalism was steeped in an agenda of abrogating the rights of national sovereignty.

Beginning in 1968, many of the global elite, even of the CFR, who had previously supported the Vietnam War, began to comprehend that global governance would not be achieved by America imposing its will upon nationalist movements, which could then look to the Soviet Union for military support.[23] The Vietnam War was doing for the American elite what the unpopular Boer War had done for the British Round Table Group, by inspiring a reevaluation of how to maintain the Anglo-American Empire without heavy commitments of ground troops in war.

Simultaneously, 1968 saw the promulgation of a new "limits to growth" ideology beginning with Stanford Professor Paul Ehrlich's *The Population Bomb*, and the founding of the Club of Rome, whose membership included European oligarchs like Aurelio Peccei and Princess Beatrix of the Netherlands (whose father Prince Bernhard organized the first Bilderberg meetings and served as Chairman of the Steering Committee); in Canada, Prime Minister Pierre Trudeau, who had been Elliott's student while at Harvard, promoted the Club. In the words of the Club's founder Alexander King, "in searching for a new enemy to unite us, we came up with the idea that pollution, the threat of global warming, water shortages, famine and the like would fit the bill. In their totality and in their interactions these phenomena do constitute a common threat which demands the solidarity of all peoples."[24]

Elliott and his co-thinkers had previously promulgated the imperial war against the nation-state, by advocating for international controls on resources, often through the instrument of conservation movements. It was thus not surprising to find Elliott's cohorts in the "City of Man" project, Giuseppe Borgese and Robert M. Hutchins (Vice President of the Ford Foundation), who had formally advocated for world government, were integral to the origins of the environmental movement by helping to form the Aspen Institute in 1949. Not only did Aspen promote the early education seminars on environmentalism, "Aspen also played a role in developing and advocating a post-industrial strategy for the U.S. economy, i.e., a shift from an industrial, energy intensive economy to one based more on services or, for some, information processing."[25]

Decisions to shift the economy from the industrial productivity of the World War II era into the post-industrial economy worked in tandem with the financier and merchant-based economy that found profit from moving production in search of cheaper labor. Of course, the merchant mentality had formed the basis of the British Empire against which the American colonies revolted, though the United States also had a merchant class, centered amongst the Anglophile Boston Brahmins and Bluebloods of the Northeast. While it is historically true that "international companies have traditionally taken a relaxed view of patriotism" to the degree that "the great oil and chemical companies that had cartel agreements with German firms at the outbreak of the Second World War were actively opposed to fighting Hitler," and "[Assistant Secretary of State] Adolf Berle describe[d] the difficulties the State Department had on the eve of the war in getting U.S. companies to stop cooperating with the Germans in Latin America," the era enshrined by Kissinger saw the economic takeover of American foreign and domestic policy by the heads of the major transnational corporations, with their partner banks.[26]

By 1966, Professor Quigley, a supporter of the Round Table Group's ambitions for world governance,[27] had summarized the coming incarnation of "economic pluralism" as an evolution "concerned with the allotment of resources" to private and public sectors of the economy in accord with "rationalist and scientific methods" for decentralized "planning." In the process of this quantified social planning, there would appear to be a "gradual reduction of numerous personal freedoms of the past accompanied by the gradual increase of other fundamental freedoms, especially intellectual" (i.e. intellectual property rights and patents).[28]

This mentality had been articulated by Elliott's former student Samuel Huntington, on behalf of the Trilateral Commission, in the wake of the resignation of President Nixon over the cover-up of a burglary at the Watergate Hotel. Huntington would argue that society could not be left to the absolute whims of the democratic process, for "*the vitality of democracy in the United States in the 1960s produced a substantial increase in governmental activity and a substantial decrease in governmental authority*."[29] In order to counter the democratic "distemper" created by the anti-war movement, along with newly-enfranchised and organized African-American voters, Huntington cautioned that "the effective operation of a democratic political system usually requires some measure of apathy and noninvolvement on the part of some individuals and groups... We have come to recognize that there are potentially *desirable limits to economic growth*. There are also potentially desirable limits to the indefinite extension of political democracy" (emphasis added).[30]

Thus, if it was no longer the citizens within the democracy whom the government represented, then it must have been the intellectuals like Elliott and Huntington, with their protégés in the political establishment like Henry Kissinger, and their allies in the international business and finance community like the Rockefellers, who would be left to determine the international consensus for planning and directing policy. Such internationalist organizations like the Council on Foreign Relations (where Kissinger began his career in 1955 by drafting a CFR study group policy for his *Nuclear Weapons and Foreign Policy*), the "Bilderberg" Group (of which Kissinger was a steering committee member), and its spawn the Trilateral Commission (of which Kissinger became director in 1977), certainly typified the think-tanks that could draft workable ideas to check the democratic processes of nation-states.[31]

The Trilateral Commission, for example, was a brain-child of David Rockefeller (founder of the Bilderberg Group in 1954) and Zbigniew Brzezinski, who articulated the idea in *Between Two Ages* (1970) of "setting up a high-level consultative council for global cooperation, regularly bringing together the heads of governments of the developed world to discuss their common political-security, educational-scientific, and economic-technological problems...perhaps initially linking only the United States, Japan, and Western Europe."[32] In 1972, Rockefeller, after having discussed the matter with Henry Kissinger (who later joined the International Chief Advisory Committee on Rockefeller's Chase Bank in 1977), met with Brzezinski, Robert Bowie (a former Harvard professor who had worked with W.Y. Elliott in the 1950s on the NSC planning board), and McGeorge Bundy (now head of the Ford Foundation), among others, to discuss the inclusion of individuals from the private sector, "from the academic communities, labor and religious groups, as well as businesses" to "consider neglected longer-term issues and to translate their conclusions into practical policy recommendations."[33]

This meeting produced the Trilateral Commission in 1973, which drew political, financial, and business elites from Western Europe, Japan and North America for yearly meetings to discuss plans of action to combat economic protectionism, political isolationism, and to generally help their countries accept "the age of global interdependence."[34] Hence "Kissinger's habit, which by 1975 had become marked in his public speeches, of referring to the 'fact' or the 'reality' of 'interdependence'...'the big problem is to bring the nations of the world together in recognition of the fact of interdependence.'"[35]

Brzezinski and Rockefeller's initial vision for a Trilateral Commission may not have been inspired by W.Y. Elliott's idea from 1955 for a "Round Table for Freedom"; nonetheless, the intellectual resonance of Elliott's idea may have at some point reached Brzezinski, even peripherally, since Brzezinski had known Elliott since the 1950s when Brzezinski was at Harvard's Center for International Affairs and had participated in some of Elliott and Kissinger's International Summer Seminars. When Elliott made his "Proposal for a North Atlantic Round Table for Freedom" (1958) in FPRI's *Orbis* magazine, his call for "epic leadership" from the democratic communities of Europe, led by an Arthurian Round Table, was perhaps prophetic. Its intellectual origins lay in the ideal of the Round Table Group, inspired by the ideals of Cecil Rhodes, to bring together leaders from the legal and moral community of the British Empire to continue that legacy.[36] Like the later Trilateral Commission, Elliott's parameters for the Round Table included the selection of 45-50 members from the North Atlantic Community to convene annually "to study and report with recommendations for appropriate policies and actions on the power and responsibilities of big business, big labour, and big government." The Round Table would be constituted by an Institute with ten "Knights" to devote one-quarter of the year for cooperative research (like an All Souls College at Oxford or an Institute of Advanced Study at Princeton). Elliott suggested England as the base for the Institute as "geographically and perhaps culturally between the two Atlantic shores."[37]

By 1968, two years before Brzezinski's proposal, Elliott expounded further on the Round Table idea, this time suggesting that the Atlantic community should ultimately "bring in Japan and those nations of the Far East and other continents that have a sense of honor and decency and courage, and are willing to join us in protecting the free world."[38] In many ways, these ideals were met by the Trilateral Commission, with its study groups and reports issued annually for its "epic" leaders from Japan, Western Europe, and America, like Kissinger and Brzezinski (Trilateral Director, 1973-'77). As though the Round Table Group had merely broadened its membership base, the Trilateral Commission seemed to be a working continuation of the project, likewise publishing a quarterly journal to encourage interdependence, and holding annual meetings at various locations.

In words reminiscent of the post-World War I deliberations of the Round Table Group on the benefits of an English-based world federation versus a world commonwealth emanating from the English-speaking world, Brzezinski explained in 1970 that "though the objective of shaping a community of the developed nations is less ambitious than the goal of world government, it is more attainable.... Though cognizant of present divisions between communist and non-communist nations, it [i.e. the Trilateral Commission] attempts to create a new framework for international affairs not by exploiting these divisions but rather by striving to preserve and create openings for eventual reconciliation."[39]

By offering the idea of finding moral, political and economic common ground between the communists and the West, Brzezinski presaged Kissinger's mission of détente. By 1972 Kissinger had worked out an accord with the Soviet Union that simultaneously limited America's own Anti-Ballistic Missile defenses, as well as offensive arms, thus working to establish the international arms controls and supervision that had been advocated by Elliott at the end of the last world war. Kissinger also initiated that crucial step beyond the United Nations' Human Rights Accord, toward a legitimating international morality, by signing the Helsinki Accords (1975) with the Soviets, who finally made public commitments to moral standards. By moving to officially recognize Eastern Europe under communist governments, and by moving toward restrictive arms controls with the Strategic Arms Limitation Treaty of 1972, Kissinger expounded that "détente" was an effort to "insist on responsible international behavior by the Soviet Union and use it as the primary index of our relationship."[40]

As H.G. Wells had written in 1929, "the Open Conspiracy is not necessarily antagonistic to any existing government.... It does not want to destroy existing controls and forms of human association, but either to supersede or amalgamate them into a common world directorate."[41] What Kissinger ultimately seems to have been driving towards was an insinuation that America was simply another nation within an international power system. Kissinger expected America, as a descendant of the British tradition, to accept its responsibility to the world constitutional community, not as a nation-state but as a power broker. It was irrelevant that America had historically arrogated a geo-politically independent role from Europe's problems, for in the new world order, America was but a system whose power was based on the influence and vitality of its international commitments. As Kissinger understood it, America, as a nation-state, could be compromised in order to accommodate the emerging international consensus.

By the time Kissinger was finishing his tenure as American Secretary of State in 1976, his former Harvard colleague and *Confluence* board member Arthur Schlesinger, Jr. could easily issue a proclamation against American exceptionalism under the new regime of "globalization": "Surely... it is time for Americans to abandon the childish delusion that the Almighty appointed the United States of America to redeem a sinful world.... No nation is sacred or unique, the United States or any other. America, like every other country, has interests real and factitious; concerns, generous and selfish; motives, honorable and squalid. *We too are part of history's seamless web*."[42]

Along with Kissinger's détente with the Soviets and the increasing debtor status of the government, the 1970s seemed to pronounce the end of America as the world's pre-eminent nation-state, ushering in the new order under the auspices of the Trilateral Commission and a semblance of a legitimate order. Yet the semblance of legitimacy was all that mattered, as Kissinger had written in his doctoral thesis under Elliott, for legitimacy did not pretend to mean the end of war; "a legitimate order does not make conflicts impossible, but it limits their scope. Wars may occur, but they will be fought *in the name of* the existing structure and the peace which follows will be justified as a better expression of the "legitimate," general consensus" (*emphasis added*).[43] The only question that remained, as to who controls the consensus in the international system of power, had been answered by Rousseau two hundred years before as "the strongest," i.e. those who rule.

Rulership seemed to be passing more and more into the hands of what Kissinger's fellow Trilateralist Brzezinski termed "*transnational elites*," like financiers, businessmen, and politicians, who were responsible for "establishing frameworks of rules, standards, and procedures" for governments to follow, like managers making "operating decisions."[44] The fact that the managers originally came from Western Europe, America, and Japan did not preclude the eventual involvement of leaders from other nations, which had accepted the moral prescriptions of constitutionalism and a respect for the world order.

Toward that end, the Trilateral Commission, like the Bilderbergs and CFR before it, advocated to establish the annual G-7 summit of the advanced democracies' central bankers and finance ministers, not to assume the power of world government on behalf of the nation-states, but simply as another vehicle by which the world community would be established under common laws and economic standards.

Thus, the Anglo-American empire's notion of the common morality underlying the commonwealth has perhaps been replaced by the "democracy" of the corporation, where the consumer "votes" with his or her wallet. In the process of the transnational corporations' growth, the largest corporations out-produce most countries after the first decade of the 21st Century.[45] Nevertheless, the expansion of such corporate wealth could not have occurred without the conditions created by the international agreements accorded by the IMF, World Bank, World Trade Organization and other such transnational agreements traditionally backed by the "Washington Consensus" of trade liberalization, privatization and currency deregulation. Yet the most recent extension of international regulation of trade through the Trans-Pacific Partnership between the United States and the Pacific Rim countries surrounding China will create even more stark advantages for corporate power vis-à-vis the nation-state.

Former Chief Economist of the World Bank Joseph E. Stiglitz critiqued the grave pro-corporate dangers of the TPP's investor-state arbitration terms, for

> ...the obligation to compensate investors for losses of expected profits can and has been applied even where rules are nondiscriminatory and profits are made from causing public harm... Imagine what would have happened if these provisions had been in place when the lethal effects of asbestos were discovered. Rather than shutting down manufacturers and forcing them to compensate those who had been harmed, under ISDS [investor-state dispute settlements], governments would have had to pay the manufacturers not to kill their citizens.[46]

As the TPP and other such transnational agreements seek to normalize property and intellectual property rights globally, often times in favor of the transnational corporations' financial interests, the aim clearly remains world government, though the question remains whether it will be achieved through the means of governments working through accords to justify laws for the socio-economic elite minority, or whether it one day might find form in a globalized corporate state under the pretense of democracy through "choice" of produce.

Either way, the Anglo-American empire's war on the nation-state continues in the 21st Century, as evidenced by its wars in the Middle East, as had been prophesied by W.Y. Elliott's dismissal of the post-colonial realms' attempts to lay sovereign claim to their land, and the resources therein. By the time his ideological protégés Kissinger and Brzezinski had introduced the world to the corporate internationalism of the 1970s, the writing was on the wall that though "the Cold War was largely symbolic, the conflict shaping up today between the industrialized world and the Arab states, on the one hand, and among the industrialized states, on the other, is not... In purely economic terms, as we shall see, the advantages all lie with the oil-producing states. Thus the temptation to introduce military power to shift that balance will obviously increase as the Arabs continue to demonstrate their bargaining power."[47]

Endnotes

1. Kissinger, Henry. Speech to the Royal Institute of International Affairs. "Reflections on a Partnership: British and American Attitudes to Postwar Foreign Policy." May 10, 1982. Reprinted in Executive Intelligence Review (online). Jan. 11, 2002.

2. Bailey had also initially financed Milner's Round Table Group, as well as his "Closer Union" movement in South Africa in 1907. (See Carroll Quigley. *Anglo American Establishment*. p. 182).

3. Quigley, Carroll. *The Anglo-American Establishment*. p. 182

4. Kissinger, Henry. Speech to the Royal Institute of International Affairs. "Reflections on a Partnership: British and American Attitudes to Postwar Foreign Policy."

5. Kissinger, Henry. "The Meaning of History." (unpublished undergraduate Thesis for Harvard University) p. 260.

6. Kant, Immanuel. *Perpetual Peace and Other Essays*. Trans. Ted Humphrey. Indianapolis: Hackett Publishing Co., 1983. p. 111.

7. Ibid. p. 112 - 117.

8. Kissinger, Henry. "The Meaning of History." p. 304.

9. Quoted in Quigley, Carroll. *The Anglo-American Establishment*. p. 33.

10. In 1970, the Nixon Administration invaded Cambodia to target the North Vietnamese supply line along the border. At the time, the objection was that a neutral country's sovereignty could now be violated "by anyone else in the world as a precedent for invading another country, in order, for example, to clear out terrorists." This, in fact, did become the precedent for such U.S. military operations in Afghanistan, Somalia, Yemen and Pakistan post-2001. Of course, all such incursions derived from the new world order conception that nation-states are no longer sovereign. (See Greg Grandin. *Kissinger's Shadow*. p. 3.

11. Quoted in Grandin, Greg. *Kissinger's Shadow*. New York: Metropolitan Books, 2015. p. 76.

12. The board included 25 of the most powerful businessmen in America, such as the chief executives of General Electric, American Express, Xerox Corporation, IBM, Du Pont, Caterpillar Tractor, et al. (See Joseph Finder. *Red Carpet*. p. 255).

13. Bluestone, Barry and Benntt Harrison. *The Deindustrialization of America*. New York: Basic Books, Inc., Publishers, 1982. p. 113.

14. Barnet, Richard J. and Ronald E. Mueller. *Global Reach*. New York: Simon and Schuster, 1974. p. 229-230.

15. Hudson, Michael. *Superimperialism*. p. 386.

16. Milner, Viscount Alfred. "Notes Written During 1923-24." Questions of the Hour. p. 208-9.

17. Perkins, John. *The New Confessions of an Economic Hitman*. California: Berrett-Koehler Publishers, Inc., 2016. p. 27.

18. Quoted in Barnet & Mueller. p. 305-306.

19. Kissinger was fascinated by the idea of "the tragic," which he derived from Spengler's understanding of history as the inexorable demise of civilizations. He blamed the nineteenth century's "long interval of peace" as having desensitized Europeans to "the sense of the tragic… it was forgotten that states could die, that upheavals could be irretrievable, that fear could become the means of social cohesion." (See Henry Kissinger. *A World Restored*. p. 6).

20. Dickson, Peter W. *Kissinger and the Meaning of History*. Cambridge: Cambridge University Press, 1978. p. 97.

21. It seems hardly coincidental that Kissinger would also admit to the RIIA that as Sec. of State, "the British played a seminal part in certain American bilateral negotiations with the Soviet Union – indeed they helped draft the key document. In my White House incarnation then, I kept the British Foreign Office better informed and more closely engaged than I did the Ameri-

can State Department." (See Henry Kissinger. "Reflections on a Partnership.").

22. Gibson, Donald. *Environmentalism: Ideology and Power*. New York: Nova Science Publishers, 2004. p. 83.

23. The "Wise Men" around President Lyndon Johnson, 12 of 14 of whom were CFR members, had promoted the war until they concluded "the war was unwinnable, that the opposition to it within the United States would continue to grow, that it was economically damaging, and that it was hurting the country's reputation around the world." (See Donald Gibson. *Wealth, Power, and the Crisis of Laissez Faire Capitalism*. p. 149-150).

24. King and Schneider. *The First Global Revolution*. p. 115.

25. Gibson, Donald. *Environmentalism*. p. 64.

26. Barnet & Muller. *Global Reach*. p. 77.

27. In *Tragedy and Hope*, Quigley states, "I have no aversion to it or to most of its aims and have, for much of my life, been close to it and to many of its instruments... in general my chief difference of opinion is that it wishes to remain unknown." (p. 950).

28. Quigley, Carroll. *Tragedy and Hope*. p. 552-3.

29. Huntington, Samuel P. "The United States." *The Crisis of Democracy*. Report on the Governability of Democracies to the Trilateral Commission. New York: New York University Press, 1975. p. 64.

30. Ibid. 114-115.

31. There is a great deal of linkage between these three groups, as the founding American members of Bilderberg, including its American head David Rockefeller, were CFR members, including George Ball and Dean Rusk. Arthur Dean, a CFR director, replaced W.Y. Elliott's friend Dean Rusk as U.S. co-chairman for the Bilderberg Group in 1957. As for the Trilateral Commission, it was coordinated by David Rockefeller and former CFR Director George Franklin. Both the CFR and Trilateral Commission were in turn financed by the Ford Foundation, where Elliott's disciple McGeorge Bundy was then head.

32. Brzezinski, Zbigniew. *Between Two Ages: America's Role in the Technetronic Age*. New York: The Viking Press, 1970. p. 297.

33. "Meeting on Proposed Trilateral Commission; Pocantico, N.Y., July 23-24, 1972." From *The Trilateral Commission at 25*. (1998) Ed: François Sauzey. p. 7.

34. Ibid. p. 12.

35. Quoted in Gardin, Greg. P. *Kissinger's Shadow*. 170-171.

36. Curiously, David Ormsby Gore, the son of Round Table Group founding member William Ormsby Gore, was a founding member of the Trilateral Commission.

37. Elliott, W.Y. "Proposal for a North Atlantic Round Table for Freedom." Orbis. Vol. II, No. 2. Summer 1958. p. 222-8.

38. Elliott, W.Y. "Public Aspects of Private Associations: The Nature of Groups as they Bear on Political Action in Free Systems." From the Appendix to *The Pragmatic Revolt in Politics*. (1968) p. 565.

39. Brzezinski, Zbigniew. p. 208.

40. From his Statement to the Senate Foreign Relations Committee, 1974. Quoted in Nutter, G. Warren. *Kissinger's Grand Design*.

41. Wells, H.G. *The Open Conspiracy*. p. 43.

42. Quoted in Dickson, Peter W. *Kissinger and the Meaning of History*. p. 84.

43. Kissinger, Henry. *A World Restored*. United States: Echo Point Books & Media, 2013. p. 1-2.

44. Sklar, Holly. "Trilateralism: Managing Dependence and Democracy – an Overview." *Trilateralism*. Ed. Holly Sklar. South End Press, 1999. p. 22.

45. The merchant Walmart would be the 25th largest country; oil giants Exxon Mobil, Chevron and ConocoPhillips would rank in the top 50 countries; financial service companies Bank of America, Wells Fargo and Morgan Stanley would rank in the top 82. (See Vincent Trivett. "25 US Mega Corporations: Where They Rank If They Were Countries." *Business Insider*. Online. June 27, 2011.)

46. Stiglitz, Joseph E. & Adam S. Hersh. "Opinion: The Trans-Pacific Partnership charade: TPP isn't about 'free' trade at all." *MarketWatch*. October 5, 2015.

47. Barnet & Muller. *Global Reach*. p. 100.

Sir Halford Mackinder, Director of the London School of Economics and creator of the geopolitical strategy known as the Heartland Theory.

Epilogue

The Clash of Civilizations

The conception of Euro-Asia to which we thus attain is that of a continuous land.... According to physical conformation, these regions are four in number, and it is not a little remarkable that in a general way they respectively coincide with the spheres of the four great religions – Buddhism, Brahaminism, Mahometanism, and Christianity ... Britain, Canada, the United States, South Africa, Australia, and Japan are now a ring of outer and insular bases for sea-power and commerce, inaccessible to the land-power of Europe.... The spaces within the Russian empire and Mongolia are so vast, and their potentialities in population, wheat, cotton, fuel, and metals so incalculably great, that it is inevitable that a vast economic world, more or less apart, will develop inaccessible to oceanic commerce.

– Sir Halford Mackinder[1]

A dozen years before the rise of rigid state capitalism, a.k.a. communism, in the Soviet Union, the Coefficients Club, organized by Fabian Socialists Sidney and Beatrice Webb, but also including Lord Milner, L.S. Amery, Lord Balfour and others from the Round Table Group, held meetings to discuss the nature of the coming world government. Amongst the Coefficients was a brilliant geographer and Director of the London School of Economics, Sir Halford Mackinder, who had come to believe that Russia, thanks to its geographic position at the center of the Eurasian continent, was the "pivot state" upon which world history could turn.

> In the world at large she [Russia] occupies the central strategic position held by Germany in Europe. She can strike on all sides and be struck on all sides, save the north.... The oversetting of the balance of power in favour of the pivot state, resulting in its expansion over the marginal lands of Euro-Asia, would permit of the use of vast continental resources for fleet-building, and the empire of the world would then be in sight. This might happen if Germany were to ally herself with Russia.[2]

The same month that Mackinder's paper was published, the British government adopted the policy of the "Entente Cordiale," forming an alliance with France and Russia that set the stage for the First World War's bloodletting. During that conflict, Russia found itself unable to defend against German industrialized militarism, thus immiserating the population to the point that a coup d'état could occur against the Russian imperial family. As we have seen, the Bolsheviks who ultimately prevailed in the conflict had found financial support from the J.P. Morgan Bank on Wall Street.[3] While the new Soviet Union then served as an "enemy" which the Round Table Group's Cliveden Set could take advantage of by fomenting conflict between the Eurasian neighbors Germany and Russia, the plan appeared to backfire when Adolf Hitler turned his army west after initiating a peace agreement with the newly-industrialized Soviet Union. A Second World War ensued, during which time the United States proved its industrial capacity was strong enough to replace British influence in the Commonwealth. Despite the intention of President Roosevelt to continue the war-time alliance with the Soviet Union and check the imperial politics of the British Empire, Roosevelt's death ultimately saw the adoption by American statesmen of the British anti-Russian Empire policy. This effort harked back to the 19th Century "Great Game" for political control in the "heartland" of Eurasia, from the Suez Canal, Greece and Turkey on the Mediterranean, to Afghanistan and British-created Pakistan along the Arabian Sea. In fact, President Truman's first initiative to check Soviet "imperialism" after World War II was centered on aid to Greece and Turkey, in an attempt to block Soviet naval expansion from the Black Sea into the waters of the Mediterranean, and the world beyond.

As we have seen, the United States' commitment to the Cold War had much to do with checking Russian, then Chinese, economic and military influence on the countries created by the disintegration of the British and French Empires. By the early 1970s, an overall balance of power seems to have been achieved, wherein economic cooperation would begin between the United States and the U.S.S.R. Yet this strategy took a decidedly hard-line turn with the insistence upon increasing the power and influence of transnational corporations, beginning in the mid-1970s when the establishment Council on Foreign Relations embraced "neo-liberal" economics. CFR analyst Laurence H. Shoup cites Nixon and Kissinger's war on socialist President Salvador Allende in Chile from 1970 to 1973, leading to a violent military coup by General Augusto Pinochet, as the ideological launching pad for neo-liberal policies of privatization via deregulation of formerly state-run industries.[4] After all, Pinochet's economic advisors were disciples of "free market" ideologue Milton Friedman at the Rockefeller-founded University of Chicago who was committed to the principles that "governments must remove all rules and regulations standing in the way of the accumulation of profits. Second, they should sell off any assets they own that corporations could be running for a profit. And third, they should dramatically cut back funding of social programs... In short, and quite unabashedly, he was calling for the breaking of the New Deal."[5] Indeed, in contrast to FDR's vision for using government powers to industrialize the developing world, author Naomi Klein described such a "shock doctrine" as the ideological launching point for the marriage of neo-liberal economics with neo-conservative politics to overthrow sovereign nation-states in an effort to force markets to be free.

Following the Pinochet coup, the CFR's Albert Fishlow had surmised by the mid-1970s, "in short, a truly interdependent new order must rely on symmetrically freer market forces, not on immediate national advantage." If privatization and deregulation were on the agenda for the CFR's "1980s Project", which predicted the Reagan revolution, it would be a top-down, forced freeing of markets. It was in this period during the mid-70s that Kissinger's co-thinker from Harvard and at the Trilateral Commission, Zbigniew Brzezinski, began to formulate a way of shattering the Soviet Union's borders, along the lines described by the CFR's war on nation states to "engage all nations within a freer market."[6]

Brzezinski, having taken Kissinger's place as the National Security Advisor to the new incumbent Jimmy Carter, spoke in 1978 of "an arc of crisis [that] stretches along the shores of the Indian Ocean, with fragile social and political structures in a region of vital importance to us threatened with fragmentation. The resulting political chaos could well be filled by elements hostile to our values and sympathetic to our adversaries."[7] Of course, this arc stretched along the underbelly of the Soviet Union, which the British imperialists perceived as the pivot position on the Eurasian heartland. In Brzezinski's nightmare, Russian influence could extend southward into Pakistan, Iran and ultimately to Egypt, to not only allow Soviet access to the Indian Ocean, but to control access to the world's energy supply of oil centered under Iran and Saudi Arabia.

Following his speech, Brzezinski actively took a role in encouraging the Soviets into a trap in Afghanistan, which would serve as their own version of Vietnam, fighting a costly and futile war against mountainous tribes reinforced by Muslim mujahedeen "jihadists" gathered by Jordanian, Saudi and Pakistani intelligence, under the guidance of the U.S. and Britain. Brzezinski even bragged of the covert operation years later, stating that in the official version, "CIA aid to the Mujahadeen began during 1980, that is to say, after the Soviet army invaded Afghanistan, 24 Dec 1979. But the reality, secretly guarded until now, is completely otherwise. Indeed, it was July 3, 1979 that President Carter signed the first directive for secret aid to the opponents of the pro-Soviet regime in Kabul. And that very day, I wrote a note to the president in which I explained to him that in my opinion this aid was going to induce a Soviet military intervention."[8]

The degree of the Afghan War's effect on the Soviet Union's collapse is debatable, as factors such as the cheap price of oil maintained by OPEC through the '80s may have done more to hurt Russia's economy by limiting the value of its major export. Regardless, by 1991 the Russian Empire was fracturing into new nations, much as had occurred during the transformation of the British Empire into the Commonwealth. And while President Bush heralded the inevitable "new world order," the intellectual disciples of Elliott were determining the best trajectory for achieving that order.

With the emergence of a new map across Central and Eastern Europe in the early '90s, Francis Fukuyama, who had studied under Elliott's student Samuel Huntington in earning his political science doctorate at Harvard, seemed to have been vindicated in his theory that the world had reached "the end of history as such: that is, the end point of mankind's ideological evolution and the universalization of Western liberal democracy as the final form of human government."[9] The rhetoric spoke of human freedom; yet as the economic "shock doctrine" moved to liberalize Russia, its economy and resources were gobbled up by oligarchs, often with financing from the west. By the end of the decade, "more than 80 percent of Russian farms had gone bankrupt, and roughly seventy thousand state factories had closed, creating an epidemic of unemployment.... By the time the shock therapists had administered their "bitter medicine" in the mid-nineties, 74 million Russians were living below the poverty line, according to the World Bank."[10]

Meanwhile, as Russia was subjected to the looting of "free market" economics gone to excess, Fukuyama's mentor at Harvard, Samuel Huntington, was determining the coming conflict that would replace the axiomatic feud between democratic and autocratic states as spelled out by his mentor Elliott at the end of the Second World War. While denying that these wars might be "primarily ideological or primarily economic," Huntington asserted in the CFR's *Foreign Affairs* magazine, "the great divisions among humankind and the dominating source of conflict will be cultural."[11] Taking the term "clash of civilizations" from former British Intelligence officer Bernard Lewis,[12] Huntington gave priority to the British imperial policy of alliances predicated on language, culture and religion. After all, this had been the basis for the assumed Anglo-American empire conceived by Cecil Rhodes and formalized by "the special relationship" that took shape during the Cold War.

Now, Huntington was advancing the notion of civilizational conflicts to further undermine the notion that nation-states could have sovereign political and economic interests. Instead, geographical "fault-line" conflicts would be proclaimed around the civil war in Bosnia, where Orthodox Serbs fought Catholic Croats and Bosnian Muslims, or George H.W. Bush's war against Saddam Hussein's Iraq over the invasion of Kuwait. Huntington intentionally ignored the economic motivations of opening or preserving markets in his analysis, because the civilizational differences might excuse American culpability as the lone superpower driving the global economic order; "through the IMF and other international economic institutions, the West promotes its economic interests and imposes the economic policies it thinks appropriate," in a fashion that might seem as though "what is universalism to the West is imperialism to the rest."[13]

The argument against a civilizational clash could be found by looking at the transnational corporations and financiers that were rapidly entrenching in the emerging markets of the formerly Soviet realm, as well as the oil-rich Gulf States and still-communist China. As markets expanded in the post-cold war economic boom of the 1990s, "McWorld" seemed to be the actual driving engine of U.S. foreign policy, with the creation of the North American Free Trade Agreement and the World Trade Organization.[14] In the process of breaking frontiers for production, marketing, and retail, the global corporations were creating a curious dichotomy based on commerce, where "Iranian zealots keep one ear tuned to the mullahs urging holy war and the other cocked to Rupert Murdoch's Star television ... Chinese entrepreneurs vie for the attention of party cadres in Beijing and simultaneously pursue KFC franchises.... The Russian Orthodox church, even as it struggles to renew the ancient faith, has entered a joint venture with California businessmen to bottle and sell natural waters," and the list goes on.[15]

Consequently, a culture clash was ensuing; yet it was largely driven by a corporate drive for profit under the guise of "free markets." Such a dichotomy could, of course, create tension in countries that wished to maintain a semblance of national identity and economic integrity, while the world was being recreated such that "our only choices are the secular universalism of the cosmopolitan market and the everyday particularism of the fractious tribe."[16] This simplified dichotomy was noted by Benjamin Barber, who had studied for his political science Doctorate at Harvard with Zbigniew Brzezinski's chief mentor Carl Friedrich.

Barber's analysis of the economic reality of McWorld led him to conclude that jihad, or fundamentalist moral and religious attitudes, would replace the formerly anti-colonial strife in the "third world". This analysis was similar to the determination by the oligarchic Club of Rome that "the ending of the cold war has led to the awakening of numerous expressions of nationalism that had been stifled under the lid of East-West tension and will inevitably produce conflicts of varying degrees. It confirms the tension which will continue to grow between the rich countries and the poor countries, between the North and the South, while the injustice and humiliation it breeds is found especially and increasingly unbearable by the Arab-Muslim countries."[17] Whether such intellectual observations of a coming conflict with the Muslim world were prophetic or strategic, there was certainly a utility to the "arc of crisis" centered along the predominantly Muslim underbelly of Russia and China.

Using religion as "a central defining characteristic of civilizations," Samuel Huntington had inevitably confirmed, as Halford Mackinder had at the beginning of the century, that the major civilizations were centered in the heartland of Eurasia.[18] Thus, any fault-line wars would ultimately occur around the Middle East, from Bosnia and Turkey in the West, to Pakistan and Western China in the East. While Huntington laid the groundwork for defining the conflict that would emerge in the coming century as civilizational, rather than economic or political, the actual strategy for American policy was asserted by his former colleague from Harvard, Brzezinski, who proclaimed, "for America, the chief geopolitical prize is Eurasia."[19] Accordingly, he urged America to "prevent collusion and maintain security dependence among the vassals, to keep tributaries pliant and protected, and to keep the barbarians from coming together."[20]

The Western relationship to the heartland of Eurasia had not changed since Brzezinski's warnings about controlling access to the region's oil, in spite of the collapse of the Soviet Union. In fact, in the neo-conservative world-view, Russia still posed a threat to the expanding role of the United States in the new world order. Not only was Russia still the geographical pivot of Eurasia, but it also wielded a nuclear capability that could challenge the United States, even if its conventional military could not compare.

Thus, in strategizing for access to the region's oil, along with the new discovery of over 160 billion barrels of oil under the Caspian Sea, the U.S. Army War College issued a document in 2000 entitled "U.S. Military Engagement with Transcaucasia and Central Asia." The document alleged that given the importance of the energy resources in Caspian Sea region, "Russia could sabotage many if not all of the forthcoming energy projects by relatively simple and tested means and there is not much we could do absent a strong and lasting regional commitment.... Therefore, for a win-win situation to come about, some external factor must be permanently engaged and willing to commit even military forces, if need be, to ensure stability and peace."[21] Such a military factor became viable after September 11, 2001, when a terrorist attack on New York City and Washington D.C. created the necessary pressure and fear for the George W. Bush Administration to launch a retaliatory war against Afghanistan for safe-havening the alleged mastermind of the terror plot, Osama bin Laden. The continued U.S. military and economic commitment to Afghanistan would seem to ensure the necessary presence to prevent external forces from building pipelines to the Caspian Sea that might contend with a U.S.-approved one.

Of course, the Army War College document was not the first to speak of America's interests in committing to the Middle East, as Brzezinski,'s sentence in the Carter Doctrine of 1980 concluded that any attack on "the Persian Gulf region will be regarded as an assault on the vital interests of the United States." Such a position was rearticulated by the neo-conservative's Defense Planning Guidance document for 1992, drafted by CFR members Paul Wolfowitz and I. Lewis Libby. The document called for the United States to "endeavor to prevent any hostile power from dominating a region whose resources would, under consolidated control, be sufficient to generate global power." Toward this end, the United States' objective in the Middle East would be to remain "the predominant outside power in the region and preserve U.S. and Western access to the region's oil."[22] Ten years later, Wolfowitz and Libby would be integral to the Second Bush Administration's preparation for war in Iraq,[23] which would lead to the American recreation of the Iraqi government and economy, along with the largest embassy ever built by the U.S.

Thus, in the wake of the September 11th catalyst for war, jihad had served to revitalize McWorld's access to the Middle East under the semblance of defending the U.S., much as the sinking of the Lusitania and the attack on Pearl Harbor had previously catapulted the U.S.A. into global affairs. But as the *San Francisco Chronicle* pointed out, "The map of terrorist sanctuaries and targets in the Middle East and Central Asia is also, to an extraordinary degree, a map of the world's principal energy sources in the 21st century. The defense of these energy resources – rather than a simple confrontation between Islam and the West – will be the primary flash point of global conflict for decades to come." Further, it stated: "It is inevitable that the war against terrorism will be seen by many as a war on behalf of America's Chevron, ExxonMobil and Arco; France's TotalFinaElf; British Petroleum; Royal Dutch Shell and other multinational giants, which have hundreds of billions of dollars of investment in the region."[24] So long as McWorld could profit from oil as an energy source, it would need to maintain its presence in the Middle East, if not to overthrow regimes that might restrict foreign corporate access, then to prevent economic rivals such as Russia and China from locking the West out of this vast market.

By the mid-2000s, Brzezinski's "Arc of Crisis" had been rebranded by the Bush II administration as the "Arc of Instability." "It involves at least 97 countries, across the bulk of the global south, much of it coinciding with the oil heartlands of the planet."[25] Such continuous warfare across most of the planet has mandated a corollary explosion in militarization not only from America, but globally. In the process, a new type of Cold War seems to be re-emerging, with the U.S. and Russia dominating the arms export business with over $110 billion and $30 billion, respectively, sold by each to the developing world between 2008 and 2011. Saudi Arabia, despite its right-wing Islamic government, enjoyed the lion's share of those sales from the U.S.[26] The various powers have found themselves at odds over the fate of Syria, whose President Bashar al-Assad has been supported by Iran and Russia, against the U.S. and Saudi-backed rebel groups attempting to overthrow him since 2011. In the process of this civil war, the Islamic State arose on the Syria-Iraq border.

According to a Defense Intelligence Agency report from 2012, Army intelligence recognized at the outset of the civil war, "there is the possibility of establishing a declared or undeclared Salafist [fundamentalist Sunni] principality in Eastern Syria, and this is exactly what the supporting powers to the opposition [the United States, Saudi Arabia, et al.] want, in order to isolate the Syrian regime." Essentially, the U.S. support for rebel groups against the Syrian dictator Bashar al-Assad, whose family alliance with Russia dated back to the Cold War, created the conditions for the radical Islamic State to proclaim a Sunni caliphate over the border region of Syria and Iraq. The former Director of the Defense Intelligence Agency, upon revelation of the report, confirmed his belief that it was "a willful decision" on the part of the Obama Administration to "support an insurgency [in Syria] that had Salafists, Al Qaeda, and the Muslim Brotherhood."[27] Such a strategy of tension would ultimately serve the "clash of civilizations" agenda that had replaced the anti-communism dialectic utilized by the West. Syria would also serve as an ideal demonstration for a fault-line conflict, in Huntington's formulation, where civilizations from North America to Russia would vie for influence between secular and denominational Islamic cultures. It is possible that the Syrian conflict may formulate the future of national sovereignty, as the Syrian nation may splinter if the vying sects and armies cannot find an ultimate peace.

The Syrian civil war may, in fact, serve the intention outlined by Joseph Biden (before becoming Vice President to Obama) and Council on Foreign Relations President Leslie Gelb, who jointly called for the practical "Balkanization" of Iraq in 2006. "The idea, as in Bosnia, is to maintain a united Iraq by decentralizing it, giving each ethno-religious group – Kurd, Sunni Arab and Shiite Arab – room to run its own affairs, while leaving the central government in charge of common interests." Such a structure recalls the discussions of achieving order through federal governance, which was already provided in the Iraqi Constitution, drafted during the American occupation, and "provides for a federal structure and a procedure for provinces to combine into regional governments."[28] The policy of Balkanization, or "Lebanonization," was originally inspired by Huntington's co-thinker on the clash of civilizations, Bernard Lewis.

As early as 1979, Bernard Lewis "presented the secret Bilderberg group with a plan for redrawing the borders of the larger Middle East into a mosaic of competing mini-states, thereby weakening the power of the existing republics and kingdoms."[29] While Lewis may have been the actual progenitor of Brzezinski's "arc of crisis," he also seems to have articulated some of the reasons for the neo-con war on Iraq. Following Bush's successful expulsion of Iraq from Kuwait, Lewis wrote an article in *Foreign Affairs*, "Rethinking the Middle East." In this article, Lewis raised the prospect of a policy, "which could even be precipitated by fundamentalism, is what has of late become fashionable to call 'Lebanonization.' Most of the states of the Middle East – Egypt is an obvious exception – are of recent and artificial construction and are vulnerable to such a process. If the central power is sufficiently weakened, there is no real civil society to hold the polity together, no real sense of common national identity or overriding allegiance to the nation-state. The state then disintegrates – as happened in Lebanon – into a chaos of squabbling, feuding, fighting sects, tribes, regions and parties."[30] All of this language is reminiscent of Elliott and the Council on Europe's proposal for regionalism in the 1930s, under a mixture of centralized global authority with decentralized regions of cultural autonomy.

In the build-up to the invasion of Iraq, Bernard Lewis advocated for the overthrow of Saddam Hussein's government on the pretext that America could thus seed the roots of democracy in the region, despite the "hazards of regime change."[31] What Lewis and others left out of their analysis, upon the fall of the ruling government in Iraq, was the potential for "Lebanonization" to occur along ethnic and sectarian divides. But perhaps behind the strategy for the Iraq war, in the very heart of the Middle East, was another intention all along: to reformulate the borders created by the Anglo-French Empires. Even the Iraqi Prime Minister Tariq Aziz had warned, "This is not regime change but regional change."[32] Surely, a dozen years later, his warning had proven prescient when the former CIA and NSA Director Michael Hayden could announce, "we're certainly seeing a melting down of the borders drawn at the time of Versailles: Sykes-Picot… Iraq no longer exists. Syria no longer exists. They aren't coming back. Lebanon is teetering. And Libya is long gone."[33]

While Bernard Lewis had helped concoct the notion of Lebanonization, Samuel Huntington's clash of civilizations elaborated upon it, to normalize the "economic modernization" that was serving to "weaken the nation state as a source of identity."[34] Huntington saw civilizational concepts of religion, culture, and language filling the void created by the economic warfare waged by the "free market" ideologues against nation states. Thus, Huntington's civilizational model was essentially reminiscent of the Committee on Europe's proposal for regional groupings and agreements working to stabilize the various sectors of the world, until an overarching superstructure could be achieved. Further, as the new economy of "information technology" becomes the basis for communication and jobs, nation-states will be seen as increasingly replaceable by cities, regions, and/or corporations.

According to Walter Wriston, longtime chief executive of the Rockefeller's Citicorp Bank and officer of the Council on Foreign Relations through the 1980s, "the information technology, which carries the news of freedom, is rapidly creating a situation that might be described as the twilight of sovereignty… this does not mean the nation-state will disappear; indeed, we will see more countries formed."[35] Thus, through a process of centralized authority across borders, and weakening of national sovereignty, the new world order will continue its quest for supranational authority in the 21st Century.

Benjamin Barber, reflecting on the 1990s, asked if "what Jihad and McWorld have in common is anarchy, the absence of common will and conscious and collective human control under the guidance of law we call democracy?"[36] Yet it could also be argued that jihad and McWorld are, unfortunately, expressions of democracy itself, flaunting the fatal flaw of democracy, much as fascism had proved it in the previous century. Democracy, as a pure expression of the will of the people, does not pretend to guarantee or protect the rights of the minority, nor a system of checks and balances, as a constitutional republic might. In the case of corporate dominance, the corporation predicates its power on wealth earned by its consumers. The corporation, just as in an election process, lays claim to the general will of the people. So too does jihad depend upon the will of vehemently angry, and often unemployed, people in search of a non-secular meaning. Both corporatism and jihad depend upon propaganda and marketing to convince people to "buy" the world-views and brands, or religious doctrine, they are selling.

As Henry Kissinger points out in his most recent work *World Order,* "the international economic system has become global, while the political structure of the world has remained based on the nation-state."[37] Kissinger's commitment to balance of power politics leads him to believe that "world order will require a coherent strategy to establish a concept of order *within* the various regions, and to relate these regional orders to one another."[38] While such regional power structures will inevitably lean to regional, or civilizational, clashes, he conceives of a future global culture, perhaps designed by the mold of economic globalization.

And yet the greatest protection against such radical formations of monopolistic corporatism as McWorld, or its nihilistic antithesis in jihad, neither of which is tethered to a singular country, may be found in the nation-state. The United States, as the prime model for a constitutional republic, formed by the various states and their citizens, allowed for the 10th Amendment to guarantee that laws not granted to the federal corporation are reserved for the people themselves. Thus, there is a notion, within the constituted republic, of checks and balances to inhibit the power of transnational corporations, and other international groupings, from overwhelming the sovereign realm of the nation. As the center of power shifts further from the people's range into regional and global bodies, so does the feeling of disempowerment shape radical responses. After all, people, no matter their ethnicity, nationality, religion, or race, desire a sense of social contract, in the Rousseauian sense, with their governing bodies. But in the theoretical realm of Kant, Elliott, Kissinger and other globalists, citizens are expected to surrender their national sovereignty for the supposed betterment of all. In fact, it is the very essential concept of a sovereign corpus of citizens, influencing and shaping the decisions of its government, that can best know and protect the best interests of the people in an era of global agreements and alliances.

Endnotes

1. Mackinder, Halford J. "The Geographical Pivot of History." *The Geographical Journal*, Vol. 23, No. 4. April 1904. p. 431.

2. Ibid. 436.

3. Aside from Sutton's *Wall Street and the Bolshevik Revolution*, former White Army pilot Arsene de Goulevitch alleges that "there existed in America before the First World War a veritable syndicate of Jewish bankers, formed for the purpose of supplying funds for Russian revolutionary propaganda, while in the spring of 1917, Jacob Schiff [the head of Kuhn, Loeb & Co. investment bank] openly boasted of having been instrumental in overthrowing the Czarist regime by his financial support of the revolution," presumably as revenge against the Russian Empires' acquisition of largely Jewish territories in the 19th Century, leading to anti-Jewish policies and violent pogroms. (See Arsene de Goulevitch. *Czarism and Revolution*. p. 224).

4. Shoup, Lawrence H. *Wall Street's Think Tank*. p. 168-170.

5. Klein, Naomi. *The Shock Doctrine*. New York: Metropolitan Books, 2007. p. 56-57.

6. Shoup, Lawrence H. *Wall Street's Think Tank*. p 171.

7. Quoted in "Iran: The Crescent of Crisis." *Time* magazine. January 15, 1979.

8. Interview with Zbigniew Brzezinski. *Le Nouvel Observateur*. Paris. 15-21 January 1998. Translated and reprinted in *Global Research* (online). "The CIA's Intervention in Afghanistan." October 15, 2001.

9. Fukuyama, Francis. "The End of History?" *The National Interest*. Summer 1989.

10. Klein. p. 237-238.

11. Huntington, Samuel P. "The Clash of Civilizations?" *Foreign Affairs*. Vol. 72, No. 3. Summer 1993.

12. Huntington quoted Lewis: "This is no less than a clash of civilizations – the perhaps irrational but surely historical reaction of an ancient rival against our Judeo-Christian heritage, our secular present, and the world-wide expansion of both." Bernard Lewis, perhaps hoping to incite the clash of which he speaks, intentionally pitted Islam as alien to an imagined Judeo-Christian religion, even though Islam's teachings are predicated on the same Judeo-Christian lineage; meanwhile, the notion of Judeo-Christian solidarity discounts thousands of years of Jewish persecution by Christians, leading to the creation of Israel as a Jewish "home" to protect them against Christians in Europe. (See Bernard Lewis. "The Roots of Muslim Rage." *The Atlantic Monthly*. Vol. 266. September 1990.)

13. Huntington, Samuel P. *The Clash of Civilizations and the Remaking of World Order*. London: Touchstone Books, 1996. p. 184.

14. Curiously, such "agreements" by-pass the Constitution's Treaty Clause which demands a 2/3 Senate approval; instead, these agreements only needed to receive a majority decision in Congress.

15. Barber, Benjamin R. *Jihad vs. McWorld*. New York: Ballantine Books, 1996. p. 5.

16. Ibid. p. 7.

17. King and Schnieder. *The First Global Revolution*. p. xx-xi.

18. Ibid. p. 47.

19. Brzezinski. *The Grand Chessboard*. p. 30.

20. Ibid. p. 40.

21. Blank, Stephen J. "U.S. Military Engagement with Transcaucasia and Central Asia." Strategic Studies Institute. June 2000. p. 26.

22. Shoup. p. 203.

23. Wolfowitz was Deputy Secretary of Defense, while Lewis Libby was Assistant to the Vice President for National Security Affairs, during the preparation and implementation of the invasion.

24. Quoted in Marshall, Andrew G. "Creating an "Arc of Crisis": The Destabilization of the Middles East and Central Asia." *Global Research* (online). December 7, 2008.

25. Turse, Nick. *The Changing Face of Empire*. United States: Haymarket Books, 2012. p. 79.

26. "Conventional Arms Sales to Developing Nations, 2004-2011." Congressional Research Service Report for Congress. August 24, 2012.

27. Hoff, Brad. "Former DIA Chief Michael Flynn Says Rise of Islamic State was "a willful decision" and Defends Accuracy of 2012 Memo." *Levant Report* (online). August 6, 2015.

28. Biden Jr., Joseph R. and Gelb, Leslie H. "Unity through Autonomy in Iraq." *The New York Times*. May 1, 2006.

29. Bonney, Richard. False Prophets. England: Peter Lang Ltd, 2008. p. 56.

30. Quoted in Marshall, Andrew G. "Creating an 'Arc of Crisis': The Destabilization of the Middles East and Central Asia." *Global Research* (online). December 7, 2008.

31. Bonney, Richard. p. 55-56.

32. Afroz, Sultana. "The Yinon Plan and the Role of ISIS." *The Daily Star* (online). March 8, 2015.

33. Interview with Michael Hayden. "Former CIA Director: Iraq, Syria 'no longer exist'." CNN (online). http://www.cnn.com/videos/world/2016/02/25/michael-hayden-syria-isis-bts-

holmes.cnn. February 25, 2016.

34. Huntington, Sam. *The Clash of Civilizations*. p. 26.

35. Wriston, Walter B. *The Twilight of Sovereignty*. New York: Charles Scribner's Sons, 1992. xii-xiii

36. Barber, Benjamin R. p. 5.

37. Kissinger, Henry. *World Order*. p. 368.

38. Ibid. p. 371.

Sir Cecil Rhodes, 1853 – 1902

Afterword

The Ghibelline Globalists of the Techno-Structure:

On the Current Destinies of Empire and Church

For the past fifty years, the definitive establishment of the great Asian-American-European federation and its unchallenged domination over scattered leftovers of inassimilable barbarousness, in Oceania or in Central Africa, had accustomed all peoples, presently clustered into provinces, to the bliss of a universal, and thenceforth imperturbable, peace. No fewer than one hundred and fifty years of wars were needed to achieve this marvelous development [...]. Contrary to public proclamations, it wasn't a vast democratic republic that emerged from the aggregation. Such an eruption of pride could not but raise a new throne, the highest, the strongest, the most radiant there ever was.

Gabriel Tarde, *Fragment d'histoire future* (1896)[1]

Sean Stone's *New World Order* (NWO) tells the story of a "Deep State," of an extraneous apparatus within the American Federation. This foreign entity, which acts in inconspicuous ways, i.e., through extremely exclusive lodges and clubs, appears to be bent on taking over the wholesome strata of America, her exceptional manpower and resources, and harnessing them to a vast design of centralized, planetary domination. This "extraneous body" is typically an oligarchic mindset of unmistakable British make. Professedly "democratic" and "Liberal," this English drive is, in fact, ferociously elitist and exploitative. To date, it represents the most sophisticated conception of imperial management. Technically, it uses finance and commerce as its consuetudinary instruments of rent- and resource-extraction; politically, it keeps public opinion "in flux" by playing (i.e., scripting) both sides of the electoral spectrum (Left vs. Right) and everything in between with an attentive and solicitous eye to the appetites of the masses; militarily, it exerts control by patrolling, proprietarily, the main sea and air "corridors" of the world; and intellectually, it is ever alert to promote a flurry of "authoritative" charters with which to legitimize its ever-expanding jurisdiction.

The narrative thread of *New World Order* is original in that it details the story of America's British seduction by following the career of a high priest of higher learning, Harvard doyen William Yandell Elliott (1876-1979), who is credibly credited with the feat of having refashioned, almost ex nihilo and single-handedly, America's propagandistic bastion after Britain's imperial image. Throughout the chronicle of Elliott's lengthy office and indefatigable service, we re-encounter some of the familiar faces of America's political discourse and their significant filiations: Henry Kissinger, Samuel P. Huntington and his pupil Francis Fukuyama, to name but a few.

New World Order recounts how this new Anglo-American brethren, fascinated with the occult and far-reaching ways of Jesuitism (p. 9), sought to cement the budding alliance for the establishment of the great Commonwealth by training and indoctrinating America's aspiring recruits at Oxford via the Rhodes Scholarship. In Britain, the Americans were introduced to an advanced study of the physics of domination, which, in the pursuit of optimal flexibility, was developed to include organizational forms best suited to pacify labor, as well as novel designs for federalism and religious worship. By such measures, one could expect that workers and people at large could be pacified and their anarchistic instinct somehow comforted, and neutralized thereby, by the statutory incumbency of ("regionalistic" and "pro-labor") structures purportedly designed to protect them all from the bullying of a central authority (p. 14). No less important in this regard is the role of religion, of credence proper, which, too – like the insubordinate bent – had to be "absorbed" in a league of churches "as part of supranational organizing in the face of burgeoning nationalism" (p. 10). Mentally, therefore, the chief obstacle, the chief notion to negate and thereby *erase* completely from the range of affective sentiments is that of *nation*, nationhood, or national belonging. This, then, was going to be a work of psychological effacement to be perpetrated mostly against *foreigners*, i.e. non Anglo-Saxon subjects. Yet, preliminarily, Americans themselves had to be educated in construing their patriotism as a pillar of the great Commonwealth; they were to see themselves as leaders, *primi inter pares*, of a "flexible family of allied but independent Dominion States, free to pursue their own domestic policies but expected to cooperate with inter-imperial affairs and security" (p. 11). As a variation on the self-same theme, Julian Huxley, e.g., reiterated in 1941 this basic directive clearly enough:

> Looked at from another angle, we may contrast Hitler's plan for a New Order (however badly it has now gone astray) with the type of New Order which we would hope to see established [...]. Any New Order we could think of establishing [...] should be based

> politically, so far as possible, on the principle which we have developed to such an extent in the British Commonwealth; namely, of free and equal units, co-operating on the basis of consent and of agreement on common values *(though some more centralized control will be needed in Europe than in the British Commonwealth).*[2]

A first, partial attempt to extend the British model to a supranational body came, after WWI, with the League of Nations in 1919, which was the precursor, in some fashion, of the Organization of the United Nations. As experimental forerunners of the NWO, neither the League nor the U.N. really "worked," however, and Sean Stone shows how eventually it appeared to Britain's international policy-makers far more fitting to re-think the One-World project by transferring and applying its (organizational) designs to an American board of imperial action under Britain's strategic guidance and tutelage. It was more consequent to do so for "there already existed [in America] an Anglo-Saxon ruling class which shared 'a common language and sentimental and racial ties'" with London's elites (p. 24).

As far as the propagandistic effort was concerned, much intellectual activity was condignly devoted to giving formal, discursive, "authoritative" expression to this plan. The first three chapters of *New World Order* discuss the work of several "panels and committees" of Anglophile intellectuals that were set up in America for the purpose. Of these intellectual "productions," the one that intrigues me the most, for it is very poorly known, and that will afford me the point of attack for this essay, is the 1949 draft for a World Constitution. As told in the book, this project was blessed by Thomas Mann and jointly penned by University of Chicago President Robert M. Hutchins (1899-1977), Lewis Mumford (1895-1990) and Giuseppe Antonio Borgese (1882-1952). Except for Mann, the other three are now virtually obliterated, especially Borgese, who could not even stake a residual claim to (minor) fame through his marriage (the second) to Mann's daughter Elizabeth. More than a visionary force for pedagogy (he was nominated President of the University of Chicago at only twenty-nine), Hutchins seemed to have been mostly an organizer. Mumford, an American Knight of the British Empire (1943), was once the celebrous poetic adversary of "authoritarian, system-centered technology,"[3] and he seemed to have been recruited in this particular team as the token "anarchical romantic," tasked, that is, with commending the pastoral delights of regionalist autonomy versus the noxious encroachments of national(-ist) and technocratic centralization. As for Borgese, it is said that the World Constitution was essentially his; he, for his part, appeared on this peculiar stage in 1938 as the token (Italian) anti-Fascist man-of-letters, critic, and publicist. This group, variously flanked by other collaborators throughout the years of the gestation (1938-1947), gave life to the so-called "Committee on Europe." The objective of this Committee was, pedagogically, to destroy, to "balkanize" (p. 31), again, the notion of nationhood in the name of loftier bonds, such as universal brotherly love. According to the thesis of *New World Order,* the end-goal was thus to draw up a constitution for the world, which was but a discursive cover for the imposition, with American muscle, of the British system on the entire planet. In this sense, the post-1945 Pax Americana should have served as the exordium to a palingenetic *pax humana* and *pax universalis,* and, accordingly, the United States was to function as the grand incubator of the One World archetype in the key of British oligarchism (pp. 29-35). In keeping with the suggestions of a cosmic reverie, the Americans would "carry on" as the legitimate heirs of the (still very much alive) British, who, in turn, had made it sufficiently manifest that their Commonwealth was the legitimate, modern-day heir of Rome's *Imperium* (p. 32). The Committee's output culminated in Borgese's *Preliminary Draft for a World Constitution* (1949), which will be succinctly reviewed hereafter.

Obiter dictum, what is chillingly manifest behind the universalist verbiage of all such pioneering endeavors, is how intimately such writers, as well as their latter-day epigones, have been committed to a general acquiescence in the ways of unbounded violence in order to see their pet-project of One World Government come to life, some day. It is disquieting – and this is an essential theme to which we will return in the conclusive segment of this Afterword – to read these men who lyrically professed at every turn their unshakable allegiance to the highest values of human cooperation and goodness, and yet who wove their abstractions, in more or less conscious deceit, fully confident and satisfied that the devastating fire of the war would have cleared the terrain for a glorious, promising, and irreversibly peaceable rebirth (p. 31).

In the end, propaganda-wise, we come to learn that Borgese's World Constitution turned out to be a fiasco: it completely failed to capture the public eye; and to this day it has scarcely left a trace in the records. Possibly the "Committee on Europe" had misread the mood of the masses; or, possibly, despite its undeniably outdated fixtures, the *Draft* was ahead of its time, especially considering that when it was released, in 1949, the "game" was "stuck" in that grand charade of American "freedom" vs. Soviet "collectivism": in other words, there might not have been congruous space in the collective imagination of the West for the vision of a World Republic at a time when the elites were too consumed in bisecting everything for the sake of keeping power. But now that the game is "unstuck," now that Russia appears to be an enemy for real, the pining architects of the New World Order could be thinking that they might have a pretty good shot after all. It is one of the several merits of Sean's *New World Or-*

der that it also dredges up to the surface forgotten artifacts which hide a variety of critical clues for understanding our epoch.

Speaking, then, of *de-territorialized empires,* when the last vestiges of Eurasian recalcitrance will have been swept away (China is still an unknown, though from the present geopolitical vista, she may be safely expected, in time, to join the western Alliance), the only remaining "force" on earth that Britain's extended Commonwealth will be facing (off) is the Holy See.

In the pages that follow, I will take Borgese's anti-Fascist credentials, specifically the anti-Fascist tract he composed "in exile" in the late thirties, as a stepping-stone to a discussion of the relationship between Empire and Church; the discussion owes its relevance to the fact that the Catholic Church, throughout the late and crucial interval of the One-World oligarchic rally recounted in *New World Order,* has not proven herself a leading protagonist so much as she has shown, rather, that the chief players of the (geopolitical) game – essentially Britain and America – are still at a spiritual/organizational stage at which they do not seem fully capable of reckoning without her. This introductory on Borgese leads into a discussion divided into three segments: the first is a reprise of the classic question of the relationship between secular and spiritual power (Vico and Dante), and especially of its elaboration by so-called "Conservative Revolutionaries," i.e., Fascist/monarchist thinkers such as Carl Schmitt, Julius Evola, and Charles Maurras – which elaboration is, in my view, the most incisive for the problem at hand. It is the most incisive not only for its shameless yet rigorous appreciation of power's violent and cynical anatomy, but also because it foreshadows the late pragmatic approach of American Neoconservatives to dealing with the Catholic Church. The thesis here is that America's Neoconservatives are behaving like the imperial potentates of the middle ages, who sought to co-opt the Church as their charitable and spiritual annex (so-called "Ghibelline" strategy), all the while, the Church, on the other hand, pushed in the opposite direction, endeavoring by subtle means of mimesis and religious/educational indoctrination to gain indirect control of a pious nation's institutions, including the army, and turn them to her own hegemonic advantage (so-called "Guelph" strategy).

A dramatic illustration of this tension is recounted in the third section, which retraces the geo-strategic course navigated by the Vatican in the first half of the twentieth century, between Fascism and Nazism. That story is here retold to explain how the Church came, after WWII, to play a defining role in the developmental beginnings of the NWO by virtue of her privileged association with the United States, and to appraise the legacy of this cumulative experience in the context of the transition from the Cold War to the present juncture, at which time the Roman central of Catholicism is studying how best to position herself vis-à-vis the proliferating structure of Anglo-America's One-World machine.

Finally, Ernst Jünger's 1934 essay *On Pain* will provide the socio-existential key for deciphering the nature of the particular and ongoing transformation of our "system," which is *concomitantly* characterized by oligarchic consolidation and pervasive mechanization. One may designate the entire apparatus as the "Techno-Structure." The Techno-Structure has arisen as the institutional foundation of the NWO. The final contention of this Afterword is that America's Techno-structure has presently deployed its two partisan halves in a carefully choreographed offensive against the Vatican. On one front, the "fanatical atheists" of the Democratic Left work to disaggregate "progressives" from "conservatives" by forcing them to take adversarial sides on issues of sex management. On the other, the "die-hard Christians" of the Republican Right are attempting to amalgamate by osmosis the Vatican and its flock of one plus billion souls by appealing to the patriotic conservatism of a majority of Catholic leaders (both laymen and clergymen). The conclusive impression is that the two incumbent "parties" of the Techno-Structure are equally imperialist, i.e. "Globalist," and that by cooperating to de-potentiate/absorb the Church for the greater glory of Anglo-America's One-World Commonwealth, *both of them* (not just the Neocons) are *de facto* retracing the steps of the Ghibellines of old – i.e. of that medieval faction of imperialist zealots who propounded the Emperor's spiritual superiority over that of the Pope.

G.A. Borgese and the "English-Speaking Idea"

> *No present Catholicism is sufficiently Catholic, no universalism sufficiently universal, to join in spirit the divided nations and make possible our imperative goal: One World.*
>
> Lewis Mumford, *The Conduct of Life*[4]

When the document became available in 1949, Piero Calamandrei, one of Italy's most respected jurists, and an associate of Borgese, presented *A Preliminary Draft of a World Constitution* to the Italian public as a most worthy endeavor for two orders of reasons. The first, as Calamandrei saw it, was the absence, in this World Constitution, of a *deus ex machina*; the second lay in its preemptive, deterring arrangements, which he thought were just the sort of jurisprudential dispositions required to uphold a new world community born under the disquieting sign (and, thenceforward, the perennial menace) of nuclear devastation. But Calamandrei was being untruthful by half. He knew the first statement to be patently false, for a *deus ex machina* there clearly was – Anglo-America's victorious condominium; and he thought fit to qualify the second point, by venting the preoccupation, by apophasis as it were, that "some peoples," in order to ban nuclear bombs altogether and thereupon inaugurate the aeon of peace, might be tempted, verily, to implement the World Federation by bombing all recalcitrants into submission. In partisan fashion, Calamandrei might have been alluding to the Soviets, but in any case it is easy to see by a straightforward attribution of the evil where it properly belongs – in/to "us" westerners, who have fathered the bombs in the first place – that the admonishment was issuing straight from the western core of the Techno-Structure. And such a foreboding also brings home to us the meaning of the most recent shift in international affairs, during which the United States has been busy drafting a raft of highly confidential "trans-global" commercial compacts wherewith to render the vassals ever more resource-dependent on the imperial center, while adding relentlessly to its stockpile of nuclear ammunition.

Borgese's world charter features, to a fault, all the token staples of the One-World gospel. To begin, all iniquity and war are blamed on *national* rivalry. Therefore, the era of nationhood, it is proclaimed, must come to an end. In view of this goal, the American model is to serve as the constitutional blueprint; the World Federation is thereupon entitled to wield a monopoly of violence to repel violence within the confines of the law; and, logically, the Federation is to have its World (central) Bank.

The globe itself will be divided into nine regions: 1) there will be *Europe* on one side, and, neatly *separated* from it, Russia, on the other (the Mackinder clause, as ever); 2) Russia, for her part, will be the core of *Eurasia*, whereas 3) North America will be called *Atlantis*. 4) There will be (sub-Saharan) *Africa*, and 5) *Afrasia*, which will comprise North-Africa and the Near East. 6) *India* will be its own province. 7) China, Korea and Japan, and the sum of their respective archipelagoes will form *Asia Major*, while 8) Indo-China, Indonesia and the Pacific will make up *Austrasia*. 9) The western hemisphere, south of *Atlantis* will be named *Columbia*. (Pakistan has the option of merging either with *India* or *Afrasia*). Britain and her Commonwealth – here is another revealing gem – may choose to be counted either with *Europe* or with *Atlantis*.

A World Assembly will be garnered from the representatives of these nine regions, and the delegates of the Assembly will, in turn, elect a World President, who will find his/her alter-ego in a World Tribune. The function of the "Tribune" is to defend the natural and civil rights of single individuals and groups against the negligence and the eventual abuses of (any of the departments of) the World Government. In its defining outlines, the plan is not without a splash of postmodernism: to round off the institutional architecture, a special House will be devoted to the representation and safeguard of minorities and local autonomy (viz. the token "lifestyle anarchism" of the Universalists).

All weaponry is to be surrendered to the Federal Republic of the World. The control of the Republic's armed forces is thereby entrusted to a House of the Custodians of the Peace, who, along with the auxiliary support of the General Staff and a special-purpose "Institute of Technology," will act under the World President in the guise of Protector of the Peace. Finally (article 39), the chief bodies of the World Government may grant the President extraordinary powers, locally or internationally, to face a State of Emergency. One simply has to wonder, in this hyper-global setup, what the "State of Emergency" could possibly be.[5]

All of this evokes pop scenarios à la *Star Wars* and *The Hunger Games.*

What, then, of Borgese the artist? Leonardo Sciascia, possibly Italy's finest political novelist, thought Borgese, his fellow Sicilian, a "heretic" and "one of the greatest protagonists" of Italian culture in the first half of the twentieth century. Not without a tinct of provincial pride, and mostly to vindicate the name and honor of his compatriot, whom Italy has thoroughly – and to Sciascia, shamefully – forgotten, Sciascia praises the World Constitution to the skies, and acknowledges, moreover, Borgese's anti-Fascist opus, *Goliath, the March of Fascism* as "one of the most rigorous, intelligent, enlightening, and passionately exact books ever written on, and against, Italian Fascism." Sadly, Sciascia observes, *Goliath* attracted no attention outside the United States.[6]

Borgese was no heretic. A second-rate writer/thinker at best, he nonetheless had an extraordinarily lofty opinion of his penmanship, erudition, and sophistication, the sum of which, somehow, had managed to propel him early on into a variety of top-level journalistic, scholarly, and academic positions (including a university chair in German literature). Sciascia recalls, admiringly, how Borgese was one of the dozen or so Italian academics that, in 1931, refused to swear the oath of allegiance to the Fascist regime and had, therefore, to go into voluntary exile in the United States, where he became a citizen, and whence he would return only after the war. For Sciascia, Borgese's name has been expunged from Italy's literary record in a fit of retaliatory envy by all those intellectual gatekeepers who had stayed behind and timorously compromised with Fascism, and who thus felt insufferably shamed by Borgese's heroism and integrity. Be that as it may, Borgese's exile was a golden exile, to be sure, for very few Italians, let alone Italian academics, could, at the time, rely, and at the highest level, on the full support of America's intelligence *réseau* [network], and, thereby, seamlessly land a job, freshly ejected out of Mussolini's Italy, at the University of Chicago. Such, indeed, were/are the perks of being an apparatchik of the Anglophile intelligentsia.

Atrociously written (in English), *Goliath* is an unbearably prolix and pompous tome full of uninsightful bombast (it is scarcely credible and, indeed, there is no evidence whatsoever, that it achieved any success in the United States either). Conceived with a view to tracing the roots of the post-WWI debacle that had begot Fascism and its brigandish leader Mussolini, the work is stacked in the fashion of an Italian epic in prose from the middle-ages to 1937. A brief examination of the book will only serve here to extract therefrom the elements pertinent to the next step of our discussion, which is that of contrasting the "religious" afflatus of the "One-Worlders" with that of the Catholic Church and seeing, in extreme synthesis, how the two have "cohabited" for the past century.

In *Goliath*, Borgese broaches the theme of spiritual vs. temporal power in traditional fashion, i.e., by citing Dante, whose *Divine Comedy* he describes as a labyrinth hosting "not one but two Minotaurs: the twin superstitions of the Roman Empire and of Catholic mythology." Thus, the starting point is typically that of the Liberal, free-thinking (atheistic) Democrat, who auspicates a "peaceful and progressive world-federation," graced by "a *rational religion*, disentangled from all mythological" animism. In this light, the assessment of Italy's weakness is the standard, Anglo-Saxon one: because Italy has remained blindly wedded to barbarous superstitions, she could not but make poor political choices, such as allying herself "unnaturally" with Prussia and the Habsburg Empire, i.e. the German-speaking *enemy* (in the Triple Alliance of 1882). And even after the Great War, i.e., after having betrayed the Central Powers (in May 1915 by joining the conflict on the side of Britain), the Italians still failed to understand the "genius" of U.S. President Woodrow Wilson and his League of Nations – which League, however, ended up effecting little because, most unfortunately, says Borgese, America herself and Russia were not part of it.[7] Be all that as it might have been, out of this postwar morass and the regrettable failures of the epoch, in some inexplicable and twisted fashion, Fascism came into being:

> ...The mind of the nation is crazed: Fascism remains what it is: an outburst of emotionalism and pseudo-intellectualism, thoroughly irrational in its nature. [It is] nothing else than the conditioned reflex of another resurgent pseudo-classicism and the political gesture of a second pseudo-Catholic Counter-Reformation [...]. It had been born in Italy of the perversity of a few and the stupidity of many, without any imperative, economic or social necessity of any sort.[8]

The characterization of Mussolini is just as inane:

> There had never been socialism and there never was nationalism in him. There was consistently the anarchist.[9]

At last, on February 11, 1929, after three years of intense negotiations, the Church and the Fascist regime signed the famous Concordat, the "Lateran Pacts," whereby, in exchange for confessional, financial, and territorial concessions, the Vatican granted Italian Fascism sacral recognition, so to speak; Mussolini had been in power for nearly seven years, and Italy's dictator since 1925. For Borgese, the Church and Fascist Italy were on this occasion "driven mad by a necromantic obsession, by the impossible desire of resurrecting what was dead." From Borgese's standpoint, the incongruence, of course, was that, since Italy had been a political irrelevance for at least five centuries, the Catholic sacral investiture that was thus being bestowed upon Mussolini's Italy by Pope Pius XI in 1929 could be considered "effective only as long as it remained subconscious or, in other words, only as long as Catholicism kept on believing itself identical with Christianity and Universality." Which, in the Anglophile sentiment of Borgese, it most definitely was not: he saw the (hegemonic velleities of the) Church entirely out of sync with the times; to him, history, instead, held in store other, far more enticing plans, which could be divined from a different interpretation of the 1929 Concordat. In other words, Borgese and his fellow One-Worlders were hoping that Roman Fascism and Roman Catholicism would fuse their destinies in "a second Counter-Reformation" and eventually, through some military misstep, come to suffer, *together*, so crushing a defeat as to allow, through their joint demise, the emergence of "a human religion [of love] including the permanent elements of Christianity and embracing all cultivated races and all superior creeds."[10] A universalist creed, in other words, for which God would be "the faint glimmer of a design fully to emerge, a rationality still to be achieved, a justice still to be established, a love still to be fulfilled" (L. Mumford).[11]

In the final analysis, for Borgese, Mumford and their brethren, the glory and the sacrality of universality belongs to the British Commonwealth alone.

Goliath's epilogue, written in January 1937, makes it clear that Borgese was not so deep into the princes' secret as to have been given intelligence of Britain's true strategy toward Nazism (Italian Fascism being quasi-irrelevant in the big picture). In a gush of servile flattery (not unmixed with a dash of smugness), he anxiously put down what he, like the totality of his contemporaries, mistook for a lamentable state of "unpreparedness" in the face of German re-armament and re-militarization to "the angelicalness of the Anglo-American mind." Because "the English and Anglo-Saxon mind is averse [to the idea of all-round villainy], and is thus kindly inclined," toadies Borgese, it often runs the risk of losing touch entirely "with radical evil," and is thus liable to responding and protecting itself inadequately "if the hour of a supreme challenge strikes." Then came the admonishment: "What havoc the nationalistic tumor was making of the disturbed organisms in continental Europe, [Englishmen and Americans] were far even from imagining" – though *he*, Borgese, knew.[12] Yet he did not despair, sensing, anyway, that, when the clash would come, victory would be on his masters' side; England would win, and the League would be resurrected, greater and mightier than ever; that much was understood:

> [England's] movable steadfastness in trying evolutionary courses in India; her craftsmanship in meeting depression, devaluation, unemployment, together with her early successes in reviving prosperity and cheer; her aloofness from both revolutionary mania and involutionary shirt-sleeved pestilence [...]: all these and several others were and seemed admirable performances, *setting a model of some sort for a confederate world to come* [...].[13]

Guelphs vs. Ghibellines

> *[The] conception [of "State religion"] can be realized in forms other than that of a "national" church properly speaking. Of this we have a most striking example in such a regime as the Napoleonic "Concordat," which transformed priests into civil servants – a true monstrosity.*
>
> René Guénon, *Spiritual Authority and Temporal Power*,[14]

> *It is not easy to conceive the way in which a consecration could confer a new legitimacy to new men, who move in the world created by technique and the machine, a world which is by and large de-humanized and spiritually devastated, yet also imbued with elemental force.*
>
> Julius Evola, *"L'idea organica e la crisi del tempo"*[15]

This segment is devoted to a summary exposition of the nature of the tension between secular and religious power, from a few of its classic formulations to the interwar treatment of the issue by so-called "Traditionalist" thinkers. This sets the intellectual background against which is presently unfolding the match between the Anglo-American forces of Globalization and the millennial incumbency of the Roman Catholic

Church. It still appears that the differences that array the ones versus the other bear the traits of the ancient rivalry between papal authority and imperial sovereignty. And to understand, for instance, what motivates the strong interest manifested by the U.S. Republican party, since the days of Ronald Reagan, for the establishment of a privileged rapport between the American Nation and Roman Catholicism (dating from the mid-1980s), the terms and institutional roots of this particular match need to be reviewed. The so-called Neoconservative *rassemblement* [great coalition], which owed its flamboyant ascendancy to the presidency of George W. Bush (2000-2008) and which is a direct outgrowth of Reagan's Neo-Liberal swerve, is presently one of the keenest U.S. interlocutors of the Vatican. And it appears that, intimately, the strategy of the Neocons is, for all intents and purposes, virtually identical to that of all imperialist factions, which, throughout the ages, have striven to bend the Holy See into the ancillary role of a mere consecratory office of the imperial executive.

In *La Scienza Nuova* (The New Science), one of the politological gems of the 18th century, Neapolitan philosopher Giambattista Vico claims that political society, everywhere, "began with religion." When men are wild, wild with war, religion is the only means to bring them to abide by the *laws*, and this explains, long ago, the pervasive presence of priests and religious officers in the armed assemblies of the elders where justice was administered. As the nature of peoples, in time, shed its crudity, the political regime mutated accordingly: when the collective mien turned "severe," men congregated in "aristocratic republics." These republics "of optimates," were extremely loath to engage in war lest habituation to it should sharpen the rebellious aggressiveness of the plebs: fear of plebeian mutiny thus brought the optimates to create "orders" where political business could be transacted, "in secret," away from the scrutiny of the servitude: it is in this context that the expression "*arcana imperii*" came into usage. As men are inclined to escape subjection, desiring equality, they may succeed in changing aristocratic into "democratic republics" (*repubbliche popolari*). In the degraded, "oligarchic," phase of this transition, it so happens that democratic leaders (*i potenti*) manage to bend the public counsel to their own, private ends, and the masses, for their private utility, surrender their freedom to the leaders' ambition, thereupon sundering into parties, engaging in sedition and civil strife, and, through cross-border slaughter, bringing on, eventually, the death of their own nations. The mayhem resulting from this stage of "tyrannous anarchy," which is the extreme debauchment of democratic governments, eventually compels men to seek protection and soothing redress in the *legality of the monarchy.*[16]

Thus, we seem to have, in shifting combinations, three forces in a constant state of play: the regimentation of religion for keeping in check our feral drive, the monarchical bent, which reawakens with a vengeance after the fire, and our progressive, anarchistic instinct.

It is, then, no accident that in many ancient political formations, the monarch was concomitantly high priest and emperor; he was the *pontifex,* the "bridge-builder" between the sacred and the worldly, between the spiritual and the secular. In the case of Christianity, the unity was maintained in the special bipartite arrangement of the *respublica christiana,* which rested on the spiritual See of the Pope (*sacerdotium*) and on the throne of the Emperor (*imperium*). For Carl Schmitt, the fluid that assured the continuity of the Christian Empire was the diffuse perception that such an empire stood as Christendom's "defender" (*Aufhalter*) i.e., as that organized authority possessing deterrent, awesome force against the coming onslaught of the Anti-Christ. This medieval unity of *imperium* and *sacerdotium* – a western creation – never implied the accumulation of all power in the hands of a single man: the assumption of the imperial title was not the exclusive privilege of Germanic kings; other Christian monarchs had been equally consecrated, and the mandates for crusading missions they were concomitantly vouchsafed – for the "legitimate" acquisition of additional territory – did not negate, but rather reinforced the unity of the *respublica christiana* on the basis of assured localizations and legal force. In the 13th century this unity broke down: ever since the Germanic kings established a dynastic authority, and conflated thereby the imperial title in the dynastic line of inheritance, this power ceased to be wielded as that peculiar sovereign and superadded "upgrade" which select warrior-kings were vested with so as to exercise the guardianship and perform their "*aufhaltend*" duty. From then on, having lost its deterring sheen, "Empire" was downgraded to "Caesarism," "imperialism," i.e. mere (absolute) power.[17]

The medieval terms "Guelphs" and "Ghibellines" refer to Florentine factions, which respectively took their Italianized names after the Bavarian house of Welf and the Swabian estate of Waiblingen. The feud between these two elites over matters of succession began as a German affair pitting monarchy against nobility, which eventually elicited papal interference. But it was not until the reign of Frederick Barbarossa of Hohenstaufen, Holy Roman Emperor and Lord of Weiblingen (1122-1190), that the factional dispute came to reflect an all-out confrontation between the rival claims of spiritual superiority opposing the Germanic Emperor to the Roman Pope (the above-mentioned 13th century "breakdown"). The repercussion in Italian, particularly Tuscan, politics of so profound and far-reaching an antagonism occasioned the two labels: the Guelphs sided with the Papacy, the Ghibellines, with the Empire.

The first, most famous Ghibelline was, of course, Dante, who, in his positively underwhelming *De Monarchia,* tries to get to the bottom of the question of whether the authority of the monarch (the emperor) is directly dependent on God or on a vicar or minister of God, such as the pope, the successor of Peter. Through a sequence of shaky syllogisms, Dante ends up contending that the Church is to be nothing more than a charitable organization. The Church, he states, is to perform exclusively as the administrator (*dispensator*) of gifted riches "on behalf of the Church herself and Christ's poor." In this bearing, it appears that Dante's line runs chiefly on the prejudice that a practice may be rated superior to another simply because the one *predates* the other: because, historically, imperial power had been in full bloom (*Imperium habuit totam suam virtutem*) long before the Church appeared to radiate hers, the Empire, so Dante infers, may claim primacy. Yet, even granting that precedence is sufficient grounds for primacy, this is still not enough to convince one that the pope should confine himself to prayers and alms-giving if nothing guarantees that an irresponsible emperor irresponsibly elected will not lay waste to Christendom at large. And setting out in the finale to make his point stronger, Dante trips in yet another inconsistency that pulverizes the entire effort. Mankind, he avers, can (work on itself to) overcome its built-in greed only in a state of peace, the establishment of which the Prince alone can guarantee; i.e., only the emperor, as the world's steward (*curator*), can bring about this "earthly paradise." For this to happen, says Dante in the conclusion, let this earthly "curator" show some reverence to the vicar of Peter so that, "illuminated by the light of paternal grace, [the emperor] may more mightily irradiate the orb of the earth, over which he has been appointed by Him alone, who is the governor of all things spiritual and temporal."[18] The confutatitive objection is immediate: if the emperor has indeed been appointed by God, why should he bother to demand the papal chrism? Yet if, for some archaic yet unavoidable "tradition," the emperor *must* bow to papal authority so that the world may click into gear, then why can't the pope, who evidently knows no worse, dispense with imperial bureaucracy altogether, and dispatch the job himself as a full-fledged pontifex once again? As we shall see, such was exactly the thinking of Pius XI, the pope who sealed the Fascist Concordat of 1929.

Julius Evola and the Politology of (Fascist) "Traditionalism"

Between those days, of the Guelphs and Ghibellines, and today, there arose the Age of the Machine; the world was transformed. And with it came the modern centralized State. To so-called "Conservative Revolutionaries" or "traditionalists," whom (with a fair degree of approximation) one may cluster under the heading of "Fascists," the national State originated in a movement that brought the royalty to centralize and "to absorb in itself the powers that [belonged] collectively to all the nobility." To effect this goal, the royalty entered "into a struggle with the nobility and [worked] relentlessly toward the destruction of the very feudal system from which it had itself issued." Critical in this connection was "the support of the third-estate" (the bourgeoisie), which, in the caste structure of Hinduism, "corresponds to the Vaishyas (thus were modern nations born)."[19]

As known, during the momentary socio-political debacle unleashed by the aftermath of WWI, there emerged in Continental Europe (especially in Germany, Italy, and France) a reactionary current which saw (or deluded itself into seeing) in the chasms opened by the war an opportunity to defy the Age of the Machine and the reviled State erected thereon by turning back the clock to a mythical restoration of the traditional *imperium*. Part of this speculative activity came alive in the march of Nazi-Fascism. Though these thinkers – all of them associated in one form or another with esoteric initiation – might have had different ideas on the form by which the high-sacerdotal class ought to be related to that of the kingly warriors, they all seemed to subscribe to the saying of the Bhagavad-Gita that "Whatsoever the superior person does, that is followed by others. What he demonstrates by action, that, people follow"; they moreover believed that Modernity was a monstrous/titanic age of usurpation, which had, in Hindu terminology, delegitimized the noble classes of the warriors and priests – the Kshatryas and Brahmans – and, as was cited, propitiated in their sovereign stead the ignoble triumph of the Vaishyas and of the Sudras; that is to say, of the "merchant-class," on the one hand (with Liberalism), and of the unsightly toiling masses, on the other (with Socialism and Communism).

In Italy, the most notorious personage that gave full-bodied expression to this peculiar reactionary current was the Sicilian Julius Evola (1898-1974), "a weird sort of intellectual and Fascist."[20] In the thirties, Evola did encounter Mussolini, whom he tried, in vain, to charm; he was not a Party member and his writings had no impact on the discourse of the regime, nor, on the other hand, did he impress the Nazi intelligentsia either, which, according to a dossier of the SS, spurned his doctrine as that of a "Roman reactionary."[21]

Evola had fancied himself the bard of (Italian/Fascist) Ghibellinism, by which he did not intend that modern attitude against the intrusion of the Church in the affairs of the secular State – which is also very much the modern Democratic stance; Ghibellinism to him was rather the hostile and uncompromising opposition to Church and Catholicism "on the basis of an imperial claim to an equally sacred and transcendent form of authority"[22] – Dante's position, in short.[23] René Guénon, another "traditionalist" and one of the important names of European esotericism, thought that the central political challenge of modernity was to identify the proper consecration for the proper secular authority (i.e. what sort of religious body is to anoint what sort of king?), with a view to attempting to re-suture the "traditional unity" of Sword and Sun. Unlike Guénon, Evola was exclusively preoccupied, instead, with identifying "the second coming" of the Emperor, whose restoration would, of itself, have organically spawned the proper sacerdotal caste.[24]

According to this vision, the proximate danger, then, is the popes' "Guelphism," i.e. the Church's ungodly presumption that she can manage worldly things better than a God-sent Emperor: "at her height," writes Evola, "and in flagrant contradiction to her evangelical premises, [the Church] attempted to usurp the Empire's rights; thus arose the theocratic vision of Guelphism."[25] Evola intimates that it would be far more fitting for the Church to operate as a sort of Ministry of (spiritual) Health, as she did, in fact – and successfully so, in his view – under the Byzantine Empire. When the Guelph revolution exploded, in the 13th century, the Church came into her own by challenging royal incumbents; tactically, she schemed to divest politics of any spiritual connotation (i.e. pushing the vision that sovereignty is merely a "natural right") so that she could inveigle States into serving her as her secular (militarized) arm – as her "divisions," in short.[26]

At an even deeper level, for the Ghibellines, the ultimate insidiousness of Catholicism lies in its *anarchistic* core. It is thus to hide her occult nature, that, purportedly, the Church has traditionally resorted to presenting a façade of "mediocrity, compromise, ritualistic aestheticism, and prudence," which has enabled her to develop a formidable capacity for adaptation and absorption within a highly hierarchized yet externally impersonal structure. "The preaching of Christ," Evola contends, "was never aimed at constituting a new form of associative life or even a new religion. Such a preaching was at heart anarchistic, anti-social, defeatist, and subversively hostile to any rational order of things." Therefore, in order to restrain its insubordinate animus, and to begin to fashion itself as a viable organization, Catholicism has had to "incorporate the popular customs of the pagan world, to round off the more extreme and anti-political facets of its primitive complexion, and to avoid with colorless circumspection the logical conclusions of Protestantism [on the irrefragable impossibility of free-will] and mystical delirium." In the final analysis, the secret recipe of Christianity's success is its exclusive, quasi-monopolistic rapport with the "mass of cosmopolitan desperadoes."[27] Thus, from the moment it structured and militarized itself in hierarchical form, not only did Christianity betray its hallowed principle of peaceable equality but it also became *ipso facto* a *rival* of the Empire; as such, since there can only be *one* source of power, the Church must be either supplanted, defeated, and hollowed out, or at the very least subordinated, subjugated and absorbed.[28]

This labor of absorption may be facilitated by finessing Catholicism's "amphibious" and "virile" sensibilities; in other words, the Emperor may move to co-opt the Pope by appealing to Catholicism's most warrior-like and least compassionate traits, such as the Church's "crusading"[29] and "imperialistic" proclivities – viz. her partiality to the acquisition, other than souls, of territory and riches – on the one hand, and the highly politicized undertow of her vast missionary mobilization, on the other. [30] However, depending on the historical juncture at which they find themselves, there might be enemies of the Church for whom time is too short to attempt so daunting and so difficult a ruse with a player as consummate as the Roman *Curia*. Superstitiously, these partisans might have a better chance simply to wish the Church ill, hoping she would somehow commit a fatal blunder. It is curious, then, to notice how the same sort of anti-Roman hostility drawn from opposite ends of the political spectrum – which is but the byproduct of the same demented fight for world power – ends up leading two starkly different (Sicilian) types, such as Evola and Borgese, to formulate the same wishful scenario – Evola nearly a decade before Borgese – in nearly identical terms. In his youthful *Imperial Paganism* of 1928, Evola prophesied:

> Fascism faces two choices: either to recognize in the Church the bearer of an anti-nationalist and anti-Fascist universalism [...], or to wait and see whether the Church will take the anti-Christian step she has heretofore never dared to take: namely, to identify with Fascism, proclaim Italians the chosen people, and lead them on in a march for world conquest. Of course, the Church knows all too well how such a solution would assuredly lead to the complete collapse of the Church and of Italy herself. So all the more reason to wish that, one day, the "paladins of the Catholic tradition" will succeed in dragging the Church precisely into this sort of adventure – as long, that is, as Fascism does not awake to the reality and bring itself, in preparation of the true Counter-Reform and pagan restoration, to declare the absolute incompatibility between imperialism and Catholicism.[31]

The Anglo-American Vaishyas

None of this "traditionalist" nostalgia would have had reason to emerge had there not been afoot, in the cataclysmic aftermath of WWI, a very singular movement of spiritual revulsion against the consolidation of the "new structure," which was evidently "speaking" with the new dynamic idiom of Anglo-America. From the outset, and with militant vehemence, the Fascists took a snottily jaundiced view of Anglo-America's 'imperialism." They thought the latter a squalid "hypertrophy" of olden kingdoms and a vulgarian "leveling" of all excellence, which culminated in "monstrous banking and industrial trusts." The Anglo-Americans' love of gold, devotion to capital, and enslavement to the machine made their Commonwealth a horrid parody of true *imperium*: to Traditionalists, these new aspiring world-rulers that enslaved others chiefly by *economic* means were nothing but "commercial imperialists," Caesarist traffickers, having no honor, and thus deserving no respect, no awe. They were the laughable nouveaux riches and phony aristocrats of Empire.[32] Without "spiritual élan," censored Evola, "there can never be anything but an imperialist creature of brute violence or a mechanical, soulless, administrative superstructure": "traditionally," he continues, "it is unthinkable to define an empire exclusively in terms of the expanse of its overseas dominions and of its domination over, inferior, colored races."[33] A power aggregation of this sort, devoid as it completely is of sacral power, must then resort to the staged worship of "modern nationalism," which is an artificial ritualism wholly dependent on the manipulation and suggestibleness of the *masses*. These masses are fed "myths that are intended to galvanize them with fancies of imperialist primacy."

Verily, to Evola, Britain's oligarchic new world order is but the culmination of this modern drift: when true aristocratic values decay and the amorphous "mass" takes the upper hand, *nations disappear to be replaced by "great supranational aggregates, in the sign of a pseudo-Caesarism,"* i.e., of personal and centralized power unblessed by a condign *consecration* ("devoid of chrism").[34] As conveyed by the passage quoted at the beginning of this section, Evola deemed Anglo-America's oligarchical elites executive material unworthy of consecration. He observes, in this connection, that a *"President"* may at best be "greeted"; yet it is inconceivable that he can ever be worshiped, or feared like a Pharaoh; the warrior or the samurai may rightfully give his life for his liege; yet how would anyone pledge to offer his life "for the President!" without making a grotesque mockery of the ultimate sacrifice? One wonders, therefore, if America's mystique of Old Glory was not constructed precisely to sidestep this liturgical faux pas.

Extreme "super-organization, centralization and rationalization," such as contradistinguish the social and technical make-up of the modern and hyper-modern epoch are for Evola manifest symptoms of "the terminal, crepuscular phases of a given cycle of civilization." At this juncture, regimes morph into totalitarian structures characterized by a tightly organized and *flattening* central which towers over a "formless mass."[35] Already in the late 1920s, bearing Germany's recent rout vividly in mind, Evola knew that a military conflict against Anglo-America's imperialist, fearsome aberration was simply unthinkable; the Allies' powers of (industrial/martial) mobilization were simply insuperable. "To crush the enemy," he obscurely suggested, "one ought, instead, to unleash against him the very mechanical forces he himself has conjured up in the first place so as to see to it that he self-destructs."[36]

The "Pious" Nationalism of the *Action Française*: U.S. Neoconservatism *avant la lettre*

Evola's "Ghibelline" viewpoint is here discussed not only because it yields a fairly accurate and transparent exposition of the self-same vision that informs the contemporary politics of America's Neoconservative movement, but also because its critique of modernity evidences the weaknesses of Neoconservatism itself. Though Neocons would obviously dismiss Evola's quixotic glance at the past glories of China's, Persia's, or Japan's empires as the anachronistic raving of a crackpot, and a politically repulsive one at that (the vanquished dross of history), the fact nonetheless remains that they, as a movement, strive to uphold a wishfully sacral idea of the American Nation, whose ongoing implementation represents for all intents and purposes a cohesive and organized endeavor to erect a copy of traditional Empire in hyper-modern U.S. idiosyncratic form. And, indeed, being creatures of hyper-modernity, Neocons are challenged by the very constraints adumbrated by Evola, namely the absence of spiritual wonderment in the modern age and America's (unlike Britain's) utter lack of a royal/priestly tradition. Like Evola, the Neocons deride the Gospels, yet unlike Evola, who once thought that Italians and Germans possessed sufficient imperial pedigree to dispense with papal support altogether, the Neocon Ghibellines sufficiently appreciate both the influence and the *grandeur* of the Church as to make the capture/absorption of Rome a priority. The capture would afford the Techno-Empire the allegiance of an extra billion people, and the sacral cachet of the Roman pageantry would invest their structure with a semblance of *potestas* [power/authority], i.e. of sovereign majesty, which is apparently believed to be of great importance in further impressing and galvanizing the patriotic masses for the last stretch of "just wars" before the onset of "eternal peace."

In this sense, an exemplary precursor of sorts of the Neoconservative movement was the experiment of the Action Française (AF), the late Right-wing formation of France's Third Republic led by writer, publicist, and political activist Charles Maurras (1868-1952). The AF saw its heyday in the first three decades of the twentieth century. The movement, staunchly royalist, chauvinistic, pro-Fascist, acrimoniously anti-German, and ardently pro-Catholic eventually dissolved in France's political morass of the 1930s under the centrifugal pull of its various components, not least of which was its extremist, anti-Semitic fringe (the AF was never in power). Evola acknowledged how he shared Maurras' view on Christianity.[37] And it was precisely Pius XI's condemnation of the movement in December 1926 that most weakened it, in fact. The story is interesting because, in a way, the nature of the advances the AF made to the Church gave the game away: it blew the lid off the gearbox of this whole Ghibelline/Guelph tug-of-war between Pontifical expansionism and Totalitarian opportunism.

Maurras had been too candid; too naïve: he had overtly professed his atheism, while essentially lauding Catholicism, on the other hand, for "preserving and perfecting" the ideas that were dear to him and his movement, namely "order, tradition, discipline, hierarchy, authority, continuity, unity, labor, family, and guild socialism [...]." Even more forthrightly, he had extolled Catholicism's cult for self-immolation because such "an exaltation of sacrifice," as he put it, had steeled Catholics into the best and most motivated of soldiers. Yet the functional masterpiece of the Church – wrote Maurras, spewing out far more than was tactfully acceptable – was to have tamed and "subjected the 'Christian sentiment,' which is aboriginally *anarchistic and turbulent,*" to the (imperial) discipline she had inherited from the Roman empire.[38]

> The idea of God can also degenerate into anarchism. Too often does the individual, in open revolt against the general interest and the institutions of society (homeland, social milieu, city, family), surrender to this drift, typically by necessity or for fear of loneliness and destitution; yet if there took root in a mind so anarchically disposed the sentiment that it may establish a direct connection with God almighty, [such a mind] will be inclined to obey God more than men [...].[39]

Maurras thus identified Christianity with "a spiritual drift of mystical anarchy," a spirit that spreads like venom, the toxins of which only the Church knows how to neutralize. "The idea of God," he averred is a "politically dangerous" one and the social chaos it would ordinarily prompt is averted only thanks to the regimenting action of a "tutelary institution." On the greater plane, the Church has been able to immunize civilization against "this revolutionary mysticism," which result implies, in the end, that "neither God nor Christ lives in the Church," and that, for Maurras, was a felicitous state of affairs. It thus follows that, in a rigorously royalist conception of power, the Church can only aspire to being an "auxiliary body" of the Crown, though certainly one of the most important, if not *the* most important.

Needless to say, this sort of clumsy frankness – issuing to boot from a party not even in the ruling coalition – was, to the Church, an irritation of the first degree: the censure was total. The rotund suggestion of "auxiliarity" was rebuffed by French prelates as a "fundamental error"; it was a (Ghibelline) misconception that originated from an unpalatable "double discourse" having "two ideological keys of interpretation": for Rome, no ambivalence is tolerable: the Catholic's allegiance is to the pope first and foremost. Not that Maurras did not know such a thing, of course, yet the Church seemed to be intimating that the political discourse of laity cannot, in any event, afford to be perceived as an "amoral technique," by which Ghibellines – for that is what they do by default – are manifestly seeking "to use" the Church with "cynical utilitarianism."[40]

A penitent, but, by then, much debilitated AF was eventually rehabilitated in July 1939 by Pius XII shortly after his election;[41] there had been other, geo-political political reasons behind the condemnation of 1926, which will be mentioned in the following section. Clearly, American Neoconservatives, for their part, have not displayed the (atheistic) tactlessness of the AF in their dealings with the Vatican: their approaches have been, all and all, deferential, and, most importantly, the Neocons have assembled, over the years, a whole squadron of conservative Catholics and prestigious "converts," precisely for this purpose, namely to conduct the dialogue with no manifest intimation that "cynical utilitarianism," on either side, might be at play.[42]

The "Pope's Divisions": the Vatican between Fascism and Nazism

> *... When [Pope Pius XI] went on to say, "Rome is mine," the [Fascist] ambassador could not contain himself.*
>
> *"Rome," he sputtered, "is the capital of Italy, home of his Majesty the King and the government."*
>
> *"Rome," replied the Pontiff, "is my diocese."*
>
> *"Certainly," agreed the ambassador, "in matters of religion – "*
>
> *"Yes," the pope interrupted, "all the rest is just a matter of keeping the streets clean" [November 1929].*
>
> David I. Kertzer, *The Pope and Mussolini* [43]

> *"As far as the Papacy is concerned, let us be clear: the Vatican represents 400 million men scattered all over the world; an intelligent policy should see to it that this colossal force be harnessed to one's expansionist drive. I am, today, entirely foreign to any religion, but politics is politics. Nobody can assail [...] this spiritual sovereignty."*
>
> – Benito Mussolini, November 1921[44]

Joseph Stalin is said to have once exclaimed: "The Pope! How many divisions has he got?"[45] Whereby the Georgian, voicing conventional wisdom, implied that the Holy See, having no guns, could under no conditions be considered a full-bodied player on the grand chessboard. Of course, Stalin was wrong, not because the power of prayer outguns the world's guns – alas, it does not – but because the Papacy, by entering into tight alliances with secular States by way of special compacts – the "concordats" – might achieve such a symbiotic entente with these States' ruling elites on matters of domestic and especially foreign policy as to become factually, when its influence is extraordinarily strong, the spiritual handler of a (client) nation's armies. Such, indeed, is the intended design of the Holy See's "Guelph" strategy of indirect appropriation of a sovereign State's "divisions" for the launching of "crusades." And, from the evidence presented by French historian Annie Lacroix-Riz in *Le Vatican, l'Europe et le Reich* (2010),[46] which seems incontrovertible, it appears that such a strategy was deliberately and steadfastly pursued by Pius XI and his successor Pius XII from the 1920s through the salient phases of the Second World War. This story is here sketched out as an eloquent illustration of the conceptual frame woven thus far and as a "parallel" thread, on the politics of religion, to the narrative line of *New World Order.*

This story begins in 1870, when the young Kingdom of Italy annexed what had been theretofore the Pontifical State, which stretched over a large swath of land in central Italy. The papacy, then, was at its nadir: the former Pontifical territory was spoliated into quasi-nonexistence and the pope, claiming to be taken hostage by the anti-clerical godlessness of the new State, withdrew from public view to await better times. Meanwhile, the "Guelph" jewel of the old pontifical miter, the Habsburg Empire of Austria-Hungary, remained unshakably loyal to Rome, providing it, along with France, the Netherlands, and Bavaria, with the best part of its financial sustenance. Concurrently, America, with the ever-attentive imperial brokerage of Britain, set out on a manifest spiritual conquest of the world, reaching beyond the Atlantic. Prospects seemed to improve for the papacy when in 1882 Italy, which found her footing as a fully-dependent commercial colony of Germany, joined the latter and Austria in the so-called Triple Alliance *("La Triplice")*. It seemed, then, as though the Central Powers were on the verge of recreating a "Catholic space" in *Mittel-Europa* not unlike the area once covered by the Holy Roman Empire, which the incumbent pope, Leo XIII, would have assuredly blessed. But in May 1915, under Benedict XV, the Italians, bribed by the British with promises of miserable colonial concessions and territorial annexations at the expense of Austria (transacted with the "Treaty of London"), betrayed the *Triplice* to side with the Allies, who tasked her precisely with besieging and breaking through the southern flank of the Central Powers, that is, through Austria herself, the "Catholic State" *par excellence.* For this "Free-Masonic" infamy, the Vatican vowed never to forgive the Italian Statesmen behind the *Patto di Londra* and swore bitter revenge on them.[47] But in November 1918 the Central Powers collapsed and, with them, Rome's dream of the Holy Middle-European Kingdom. The dissolution of the Hapsburg Empire and the fall of her Austrian paladin came as a shocking and devastating blow to Rome. Tethered to the Allies, Italy "won," of course, but at so colossal and unaffordable a cost, both human (half-a-million dead) and financial, that she literally unraveled at the end of the war, precipitating into three years of socio-political chaos – the three years it took to put Mussolini in charge (1919-1922). Interestingly, at the postwar conferences of Versailles and Trianon (1919-1920), which were designed to redraw the map of vanquished *Mittel-Europa,* Austria suffered a far greater dismemberment than Germany: the message to the ultimate recipient was clear. By virtually annihilating the Church's chief supply of vicarious secular might, the "problem of Rome" from the victors' perspective could have been considered done and over with. The only mainstay of Vatican foreign policy that survived the epochal transformation of WWI – one that was going to have fateful consequences – was *hatred for Russia,* which the Church saw as an obstacle to the reunion of the Eastern Churches with the Holy See.[48]

It is now ascertained that Fascism was a political creation that had been, to a large extent, groomed and maneuvered by Free-Masonry not only to break Italy's postwar impasse with an authoritarian solution[49] but also to forestall the upsurge of a Catholic mass-party – the *partito popolare* – whose progressive ardor seemed to have repulsed the Vatican as well. Crucial in this regard was the international network of the Lodges, which enabled the *Massoni* to win the approval of the operation by their American brethren[50] in the U.S. Government.[51] Since the turn of the century, Italian Free-Masonry had been the spiritual engine of so-called "radical nationalism," an odd current of chauvinistic and bellicose yearning that preconized, god-only-knows upon which techno-military bases, a spiritual renascence for Italy and Italians through (stylized) violence, a carnivalesque throwback to *Romanitas,* and novel imperial incursions. Fascism was very much a product of this conjuration.[52]

The Lateran Pacts of 1929 between the two Romes were a marriage of convenience. Orphaned of Austria as Italy was of Germany, internationally semi-clandestine and hurting for cash, the Holy See needed a new temporal legitimization, something to jumpstart it with, and was evidently prepared to pay a good (political) price for it. Mussolini's Italy was likewise in dire need of secular acceptance, and, indeed, a "consecration" with a "reinstated" papacy would have conferred upon Fascism a not inconsiderable gloss to a player so unsubstantial, so insecure, and with such a tenuous hold on geopolitical reality. That the Church had ulterior motives there is no doubt: the plan to resume the prewar strategy of Guelph expansion was foremost in her mind and it clearly could not advance unless Versailles' (anti-German territorial) clauses were definitely scrapped. Because Austria seemed disfigured beyond repair, even though the old Hapsburg Empire could perhaps have been partially and painstakingly re-pieced together, a concordat at a time, the ready-made "divisions" to bet on were most assuredly Germany's. Hence the privileged and absolutely central role that this country would occupy in the foreign policy of the Vatican from the days immediately after the Great War through, as we shall see, the winter of 1941. Italy was merely a stepping-stone; she counted for little in the larger picture.

Elected in February 1922, Pius XI (Achille Ratti), also known as the "Pope of the Jesuits" and the "Pope of the *Azione Cattolica*" immediately set out to lay the groundwork for the relaunch of a Guelph "politics aimed at the defense and conquest of the 'Reign of Christ'." The vast and tightly articulated network of the *Azione Cattolica* (AC), i.e., the lay educational organization under the Vatican's bishopric, was used by the Church as the "domestic weapon" in the host country to establish ground traction and build thereon. Unsurprisingly the static that would flicker between the Church and Fascism on the one hand (1931), and Nazism on the other (1937), originated in the lower depths of this crucial fight for the mind of youth. What came to be ratified in Rome in February 1929 was in essence an alliance between two retrograde hierarchies sealed on the (superstitious) devoutness of Italy's peasant masses in the name of anti-modernism; it was called "Clerico-Fascism." And it was no accident that the Church, as she began to rally, had come to compromise with one of the very few, and very weak monarchies of the old kind that had survived the disfiguring fire of the Great War. The Lateran Pacts afforded the Church "temporal *invisible* power" to pursue her conquest of the "Reign of Christ," and, no less importantly, they mightily replenished the coffers of the Vatican (with Italian money, as compensation for the expropriations of 1870) at a time when, after having lost one traditional supplier after another, Rome had come to rely exclusively on American donations, which, however, were not sufficient. Catholicism was proclaimed State religion and the *Azione Cattolica* was granted special status, which shielded it from thorough fascistization. All in all, it was an armed truce. Politically, as is well known, Mussolini had been born a fanatically unbelieving and anti-clerical Socialist; merely five months after the Concordat, in a speech, he had sent a Ghibelline warning to the Vatican:

> We should be proud that Italy is the only European nation which contains the headquarters of a world religion. The religion was born in Palestine but became Catholic in Rome. If it had stayed in Palestine, then in all probability it would have shared the fate of the many sects, like the Essenes or the Therapeutae, which vanished without a trace.[53]

The death penalty was reintroduced in 1930 but the Vatican did not flinch. The Clerico-Fascist alliance had to hold for the time being.[54]

Meanwhile Germany had to be nurtured and blandished; the ideal envoy for the mission was Monsignor Eugenio Pacelli, the future Pope Pius XII (1939-1958), who had taken his decisive assignment in the affair first as apostolic nuncio (ambassador) to Bavaria in 1917 and subsequently as nuncio to the German Reich three years later, before becoming Cardinal Secretary of State in February 1930 and, finally, pope in March 1939. In the structure of Pacelli's strategy, the 1924 Concordat with Bavaria represented a first important step – a step which France read as a warning that she had better reconcile herself to the inevitability of the *Anschluss* (Germany's reunification with Austria) and with the Vatican's uncompromising determination to work, on Germany's behalf, toward abolishing the frontiers drawn at Versailles.[55] The virulent polemic initiated as a result by Maurras' vehemently anti-German *Action Française* revolved precisely around the (plausible) suspicion that the Vatican was scheming with Germany's Catholics to create, with each successive *Land*-concordat, a swelling Clerico-Nationalist majority wherewith to abolish the Weimar Constitution, which forbade Germany from undersigning a *national* concordat with the Vatican, and therewith midwife a new sort of *monarchy*. "Have Ghibellines been so rare in the Throne of Peter? Rome has been never arraigned," railed the *Maurrassiens,* "let alone taken to task, for this sort of Ghibellinism which we call pro-Germanism."[56] As early as 1923, Pius XI is said to have confided to the Belgian ambassador how, "despite their recent past as bitter enemies," he wished that France, Belgium, and Germany would form an alliance to stop the advance of Communism, which he indefatigably described as the chief ill of the times. By 1930, the Secretary of State's (Pacelli's) aversion to France and predilection for Germany had become, among diplomats, a commonplace.[57]

Concomitantly, the Holy See, in a two-track type of strategizing, sagaciously cultivated its crucial relationship with the United States, especially in anticipation of what it envisioned as the forthcoming, epochal "crusade" against Soviet Russia. Rome's rapport with America appeared to have been largely conducted in terms of gold and geopolitical discourse. Most notable, for the latter, was the inauguration, in November 1919, of the School of Foreign Service at Georgetown University, which was bound to evolve into America's most prestigious academy for International Relations. Originally, this was, wholly, a Jesuit production entrusted by the head of the order, Wlodimir Ledochowski (1866-1942) to the ardently patriotic soldier of Jesus, the American Edmund A. Walsh (1885-1956). Walsh was eventually sent to Russia in 1922 by his Vatican handlers who, after the suppression by the Bolsheviks of the Orthodox Church's monopoly over belief, were hoping "for a potential Catholic revival in Russia, where they had formerly been excluded. Indeed, Russia's small Catholic community had actually welcomed the overthrow of the Romanovs." Walsh's mission to Soviet Russia was a failure, however; the Vatican legation was withdrawn in November 1923. This signaled "the end of the Holy See's attempts at rapprochement with the Soviet government, [and] marked a shift toward 'absolute polarity and mutual repulsion'.

Although in 1926, the Jesuit oriental scholar Michel d'Herbigny was consecrated a bishop in Berlin by Archbishop Pacelli and sent to Russia, where he secretly ordained bishops, d'Herbigny [too] was expelled and the new bishops were imprisoned as soon as the Soviets discovered the nature of his mission, bringing Vatican-Soviet relations to a standstill." None the worse for disappointment, the inexhaustible Fr. Walsh, S.J., nevertheless soldiered on, confident in "his self-imposed role as anticommunist watchdog." At Georgetown – as well as in a multitude of other American academies, such as the War College – he preached, with a scholarly diction and around the clock, to civilian and military audiences (Dwight D. Eisenhower amongst them in 1928) against the blasphemous abominations of Soviet Russia. And speaking in 1924 of his experience in relief work, Walsh predicted that a "distinct Papal Relief organization of world-wide scope and similar in function to the Red Cross [would] be among the permanent agencies working for the success of mankind":[58] this was glimpsing into the future of *Caritas* (presently the Vatican's charitable strong-arm), which, expected like a bashful handmaiden to clean up the oligarchs' (strife-inducing) filth, stands, quite obviously, as that (subdued) institutionalization of Catholicism most appealing to One-Worlders.

Gold-wise the relationship between the Holy See and the United States had been an essential one since the green days of Italian Fascism, as we have seen. Starting in the early to mid-1920s, the invested patrimony of the Vatican would expand into a veritable financial empire which extended from the European portfolios of Italy, France, Belgium, Germany, Hungary, Britain, and Switzerland to faraway stakes in Latin America, and whose key terminus was in Wall Street – or, rather, in the investment banking trust of the J.P Morgan Company, to be specific. The Church's financial holding company was purportedly created in two stages: from

1929 to 1933, following the Lateran Accords, and from 1939 to 1945, on the lucrative coattails of WWII. Counseled by the financiers of the Morgan Bank, the Holy See gained access, e.g., to the trust of Anaconda Copper and to Iraq's oil wells.[59] These and a plethora of other ventures ended up being so fabulously remunerative for Rome that "Pius XI would confer upon both Jack and Tom Lamont [of J.P. Morgan Company] the Grand Cross of Saint Gregory the Great." The "alacrity" that the House of Morgan also displayed in helping Mussolini stabilize the Lira in 1926 and in doing good business with Fascism in general (with Washington's blessings, quite naturally) was very much linked to this USA-Vatican entente.[60] No less importantly, from the mid-1920s through the Great Depression, the Catholic Church of America, which was America's wealthiest private real estate owner, and the second holder, after the U.S. government, of all property broadly defined, began sharing that wealth with Rome, under the consenting and the enthusiastic gaze of America's private Catholic donors (such as Joe Kennedy, the Knights of Columbus, etc.). The hyper-active conveyor of this (Ghibelline) cascade of dollars upon the Holy See was originally Monsignor, and later Cardinal, Francis Spellman (1889-1967).[61] Already in 1924, "recognizing the growing importance of the Church in the United States, Pius XI had doubled the number of American cardinals."[62]

By the early 1930s, things were so set that the Vatican could placidly contemplate the possibility of forging a "Catholic Alliance stretching from Lisbon to Budapest, with its center in Rome" that "might shut out Communism [...] and constitute a new force of balance and social order in Europe." Much has been (tendentiously) written of the affinity presumably shared by Church and Fascism, and later Nazism, for authoritarian and anti-Semitic sentiment, with the intent of arguing that it was allegedly through the occult mediation of the paradigmatic bearers within the Church of such heinous prejudices – i.e., the Society of Jesus ("the Jesuits") – that the Clerico-Fascist alliance of 1929 and the Nazi Concordat of 1933 came into being. But that is not so. To claim that "Fascism had made any doctrinal inroads among these soldiers of Loyola" is to misjudge the situation entirely, for what was at work in those days was the line concerted by a House of experienced, and cynical, tacticians (the *Curia*) determined on seeing their Guelph Empire through. This meant composing with local dictators, of course, which was not without its difficulties (and mortal sins), in fact, for, in 1931, the Fascist regime and the Holy See came to lock horns, again, on the sensitive issue of the *Azione Cattolica*'s (AC) allowable radius of political interference – with particular regard, this time around, to trade-union activism. The perennial grinding tension between the two Romes gave way to another crisis, and the crisis degenerated into the customary scenes all across Italy of Fascist *squadristi* (punitive posses of Black-Shirts) assaulting and vandalizing various local branches of the AC and beating the activists. The Pope responded in June 1931 by resorting to the standard Vatican tactic of the plaintive encyclical – in this instance, *"Non abbiamo bisogno"* ("We Do not Need": "... How many acts of brutality and of violence there have been, even to the striking of blows and the drawing of blood!"), which was designed to arouse the ecumenical opprobrium of the world's faithful against a reviled persecutor, i.e., the Fascists.

But the Blackshirts' powers of harassment were presently too intense for Pius, who found himself forced to withdraw the troops of the AC from any sort of political engagement. Thus reined in, Rome's "White paladins" were asked to stand down and wait in silence (*"attendismo"*) for brighter days (which would only come with the regime's fall in 1943). "Peace" was made,[63] and Pius XI went on blessing Italy's horrid and brutally dissipative invasion of Ethiopia in 1935 – in the hope, that is, that Italian victory would present a new chance for [Jesuit] missionaries" – and Fascism's (dismally ineffectual) intervention in Spain, the following year, in support of Francisco Franco's conservative counter-revolution.[64]

But, politically speaking, Fascist Italy was, again, a *quantité négligeable*, which, aside from a half-earnest craving for more African dirt, possessed no foreign policy whatsoever.[65] In the scope of the Vatican's Guelph ambition, Germany's divisions, more than anything, mattered. As known, the pressure that Pacelli, as Secretary of State, brought to bear on Germany's Catholics was decisive in undermining the executive of von Schleicher – known as the "Red General" for his socialistic leanings and long-time association with Russia – and thereby in favoring the accession to the Chancellorship in January 1933 of Adolf Hitler, the most fanatically anti-Bolshevik agitator available on the foredoomed stage of Weimar.[66] The Concordat with Nazism was ratified in July 1933, and, unfailingly, the pivot of the entire "confrontation" between two factions not-so-secretly bent on using one another (as it customarily is between Guelphs and Ghibellines) consisted of the agreement on *education*. In this regard, Hitler had already made his agenda (à la Maurras) perfectly transparent in a conversation with the representatives of Germany's bishops three months before the ratification: "We need soldiers, devout soldiers. Devout soldiers are the most precious because they risk everything. Thus we will keep confessional schools so as to raise believers." No less revealingly, there were in this Concordat "spectacular secret clauses," as well, hinting at an eventual spiritual *conquista* by Catholicism of the Slav world (especially of the Ukraine), with the explicit understanding that such an evangelizing deployment would have occurred in the wake of a German onslaught against the Soviet arch-enemy in the East. News of this secret appendix was immediately leaked by the Poles in Paris and Moscow, and became common knowledge despite the Vatican's *démentis*.[67]

With remarkable parallelism to the Italian situation, and as manifest proof of Rome's not-so-hidden stubbornness in pursuing her very own goals, the Holy See, via the activity of the *Azione Cattolica*'s German extension, ran afoul of the swastika immediately. Like the Fascists three years before, the Nazis had likewise to sic their Brown-clad thugs on Germany's Catholic Youth and as the struggle, a fierce one, showed no sign of abatement on either side, the Nazis escalated by leveling at the Catholics a series of scandal-mongering broadsides in 1934. They started, first, by exposing with fanfare, and very efficaciously, several sensationally grotesque cases of fiscal fraud and embezzlement that featured pious little nuns laden with cash, concealed under their robes, restlessly shuttling like mules between Italy and Germany; and subsequently – after the break-down of a patched-up truce in 1936 – the offensive was sustained by hitting the Church hardest where she was most ignominiously weak: sex. In March 1937, Pius XI had, for his part, fomented the Church's "guerrilla warfare" against the Reich by firing, six years after the clash with Mussolini's Blackshirts, another plaintive encyclical – *Mit brennenden Sorge* ("With Burning Anxiety":"... The Church cannot wait to deplore the devastation of its altars, the destruction of its temples, if an education, hostile to Christ ..."). Pioneering the tactic that the U.S. Neoconservatives via the *Boston Globe* would adopt in January 2002 to discredit publicly and thus silence the Church in the run-up to the War on Terror, Goebbels and his Ministry of Propaganda counter-attacked, far more efficaciously, again, by unleashing packs of reporters tasked with the failsafe assignment of unearthing from Catholicism's clerical underground lurid stories of homosexuality, molestations, pedophilia, and sacristies and seminaries turned into bordellos. Searingly blasted by Goebbels' inquisitorial vituperations ("the horrifying rot" of "these monsters! ..."), the Holy See, again, retreated and capitulated humiliatingly by agreeing to the dissolution of all Catholic Youth Organizations in Germany. There followed the pacification of 1937-1938.

Meanwhile, accompanied by the Vatican's legendary "fund manager," Bernardino Nogara, Cardinal Secretary of State Pacelli traveled to America to talk money in November 1937. Ever cautious and keen on upholding their (strictly Guelph) policy of the "two irons in the fire" – i.e. one iron in Europe, or better, Germany, the other (steadily) in America – the Romans entrusted the omnipresent and financially omnipotent House of Morgan with $3.5 million of their money, which was invested in T-bills. When Germany marched into Poland in September 1939, Pacelli, who was, since March, Pope Pius XII, did not condemn the invasion. Polish

Catholics felt stabbed in the back thrice; the nomination of two German apostolic administrators in the occupied areas was bitterly understood as Rome's *de facto* recognition of the Nazi conquest. It must have been that Pacelli had kept his silence in the hope that France and Britain, whose solemn pledge to succor "poor Poland" had become the (tabooed) joke of the day, would come to better judgment, negotiate with Germany and, at long last, regroup against Soviet Russia.[68] The "good news" was finally delivered in March 1940, when Nazi Foreign Minister Ribbentrop personally assured the Pope that Operation Barbarossa, the invasion of Soviet Russia, was forthcoming; Pacelli is said to have received the information with satisfaction.[69]

One historiographic account situates roughly at this juncture (December 1939) the participation of Pius XII in a plot, organized by dissident circles of the *Reichswehr,* to assassinate, or at the very least to remove Hitler from power.[70] That the plot failed because Britain refused to endorse the coup and to offer any negotiatory guarantees in case of success, seems entirely logical, considering that Britain was determined to see this conflict through to the devastating end of Germany herself; that the pope took part in it is also plausible, though not because he sought thereby to end the conflict, but rather on account of his fear that the impending invasion of France, on which Hitler was hell-bent, as well as a confrontation with Britain, might have diverted precious resources away from what Rome obsessively saw as the common "Red Peril" in the East.

Be that as it may, when the armistice with France was signed in June 1940 and there opened a dizzying vista of "total victory," "the Roman *Curia,*" writes Annie Lacroix-Riz, "lost all sense of measure." In the Pope's Christmas address of 1940 and in the (unsigned) editorial of the Vatican's main organ, the *Osservatore Romano,* of March 12th 1941,[71] there then appeared deeply ambiguous, allusive, and de-contextualized references to a Catholic *"novus ordo"* (new world order) presided by a "fighting pope" *("Il Papa è un combattente").*

In April 1941, just two months prior to Germany's fateful penetration of Belarus, Pius XII, methodical and Guelph to a fault, summoned Cardinal Eugène Tisserant, the Vatican's foremost Orientalist, and the Father General of the Jesuits, Wlodimir Ledochowski to discuss, in strict adherence to the "secret clauses" of the Reich Concordat, concrete solutions for "re-Christianizing" the USSR. In doing so, not to outrage the patriotic and Orthodox sensibilities of the Russian people, Pacelli cautioned against any action that might convey the impression that there was an obvious connection between Barbarossa and the dispatch of Catholic priests in the occupied zones. Yet not even four months after the launch of the anti-Soviet "crusade," i.e. by late October 1941 and long before Stalingrad, the Vatican was informed by trusted sources at the highest level that the Axis Powers had already irremediably lost the war.[72] Thenceforth, the extrication of the Holy Roman Church from this devilish mess became the unquestionable priority. Had it not been for America, i.e., had it not been for the savvy cultivation of the strategy of the "two irons in the fire," the hexing of Evola and Borgese might have come true; and it is indeed difficult to imagine what would have befallen the Church had she wagered exclusively on Germany (and Italy).

Clearly, Rome had *completely* underestimated Britain. By misunderstanding that the latter was the absolutely central player and producer of both World Wars and of everything related to their preparation, including, in my view, the Bolshevik "Revolution"; and by having, in truth, utterly deceived herself into thinking that Communism's giant, truculent *bogusness* was a cosmic manifestation of "evil," the Church came rather close this one time to the brink of the precipice. Pacelli had thoroughly failed to intuit that Soviet Russia had been, from the outset, not ever "the enemy," but rather the secretly allied, and gargantuan, foil in East – only *propagandistically* hostile to the West – that was going to enable the British and America's Anglophiles to quash "Germany resurgent," which had been the source of all their geopolitical nightmares. It was not by coincidence that the United States established diplomatic relations with the USSR four days after Hitler's plebiscitary acclamation on November 12th, 1933. Of course, the trouble in all this was that, conditioned by a mental cast of eras gone by, Popes Ratti and Pacelli had precisely visualized "Germany resurgent" as their Guelph battering ram into the "new century" – a century the insidiousness of which they appeared not to have fully fathomed.

But Rome had hedged her bets and predisposed the American-padded fallback option at least since the fall of 1939, at which time, President Roosevelt, looking far ahead, and already entertaining vivid dreams of Ghibelline greatness for his country, had thought, after Dante's fashion, of offering Pius XII the role of charitable *"dispensator"* and "reverential" Father in the postwar stabilization of Europe. The Reverential Father was going to need money, which the United States would provide, far more abundantly than any other power, by drawing it, at first, chiefly from FDR's "secret funds."

To this effect, the intermediatory offices of Archbishop Spellman, Pacelli's long-time intimate, were given an additional boost and the former CFO of U.S. Steel, the *richissime* and Italy-loving Protestant Myron C. Taylor was sent in December 1939 to the Papal court as FDR's personal representative. Owing to the alertness of this former admirer of Mussolini's "public works," the Vatican was further able to secure in

May 1940 the fiduciary access to New York's banking grid, and to the managing offices of the Federal Reserve Bank, which, being thereupon given custody of a considerable amount of Vatican gold shipped from Europe, obliged, for the duration of the war, to settle the international payments of the Holy See.

When it finally dawned on her, in late 1941, what sort of grand scenario had been in the cards all along, Rome hurriedly lent Washington a hand in re-scripting the epilogue of the war's act, and proceeded thereon to lay the foundations and principles of the post-1945 "new" anti-Soviet Alliance. For this second act (the "Cold War"), making do with whatever props the stage afforded, the Holy See recycled Italy's whole kit and caboodle: the Clerico-Fascist bureaucracy, staffed to a significant extent with her "White" paladins, was transferred wholesale into Italy's new Republic (the "Demo-Christian" apparatus), and the Mafia was eagerly re-awakened to assist logistically in the landing of U.S. troops in Sicily in July 1943.

On the other side of the Atlantic, the Italian-American sinew – which could boast of a number of key personalities, such as Amedeo Giannini, the founder of Bank of America – was threaded into the bulging mass of this reinforced US-Vatican Anti-Communist amalgam, with further effusion of money, conveyed to the Throne of St. Peter as enthusiastically as ever by the ubiquitous Cardinal Spellman, who would rise to become the quintessential, hyper-bellicist[73] stars-and-stripes crusader of the Cold War.[74] The rhetorical terms of this new Ghibelline "consecration" found a pithy instance in the letter that FDR's successor, Harry "Give 'em Hell" Truman, addressed to Pius XII on August 6th, 1947. "Your Holiness," intoned the techno-knight of Hiroshima, "this is a Christian Nation [...]: I desire to do everything in my power to support and to contribute to a concert of all the forces striving for a moral world."[75]

In fine, in addressing the controversy of the papacy's responsibility in the Jewish persecution, Annie Lacroix-Riz contends that Pius knew everything and did nothing, directly or indirectly, to prevent the holocaust. To this one can add that the Allies – who certainly were no less informed of the killings than Pius XII, and who, unlike Pacelli, were on top of the game and had *direct* control of their own divisions – were even more culpable for not stopping the slaughter when they could have easily done so.[76] The truth is that they were tactically focused on standing pat for as long as it took – in fact, three whole years of undisturbed German campaigning (and butchery) in the East (from June 1941 to June 1944) – to see the Nazis routed before it was safe to close in on them from the West, and at long last raze Germany to the ground. But by then it was too late. The Jews had been nobody's concern but the Nazis'.

THE PAIN OF TECHNO-FASCISM

> *[The new spirit that has, for over a century, shaped our landscape], encroaches upon human resources as well: it exploits weaknesses and hardens the areas of resistance. We are for the time being in a condition in which we may still reckon the loss; we still sense the annulment of values, the flattening and simplification of the world. Yet newer generations are growing up already, wholly foreign to all the ancient traditions we were born with, and it gives an odd feeling to observe these young ones, many of whom will live to see the year 2000. It is likely that by then the last residues of the modern [...] era will have entirely vanished.*
>
> Ernst Jünger, *On Pain* (1934)[77]

The "Fascist" analysis of modern power, and of its relation to the management of devout belief, is, despite its manifest bias, suggestive. It undoubtedly fails, however, in one crucial aspect, and that is in its contention that modern-day, Anglo-American imperialism is but a vulgar and artificial surrogate of the ancient, "sacred and spiritual" *Imperium*. To have claimed, as Evola and others did, that modern power-structures are but the expression of petty mercantile and crassly pecuniary interests was itself a presumptuous snobbery which obscures the fact that, though its aesthetics might feel repulsive to a soul more or less imbued with essences of the past, the Age of the Machine does, in fact, carry considerable spiritual weight. It is the manifestation of a spiritual force of a different nature. The Nazi-Fascists lost the war, and they could not have lost it worse than they did. Their utter spiritual rout also stemmed from their crazed conceit of being the bearers of the "noble and sovereign" Way, when, truly, no Fascist bard could really tell what a return to "sovereignty" in the twentieth century might have actually signified, or prove convincingly that such a revival of sovereignty, possible as it might have been, would have been conducive to a moral plane in every way "superior" to that afforded by the modern Age of the Machine. The Fascists were "out of the world," in a way; they might have grasped that the United States had at its disposal unprecedented powers of military devastation, but they surprisingly failed to construe Anglo-America's manifest combination of commercial and financial hegemony, astounding powers of technological annihilation, and territorial expansion as a full-blown and novel incorporation of imperial sovereignty in its own right. Mussolini's geo-political appreciation of the United States, which he thought "uninterested in the evolution of the modern world, and thus a strategic player of minor importance,"[78] offers patent evidence of his spiritual unintelligence. Hitler was more perceptive than the Italian, but not much, convinced as he was in 1940 that, though one could clearly see that America had a ravenous appetite for imperial expansion, she would not become "a problem" for world peace until 1970 or 1980.[79]

Thus, before drawing conclusions from this whole exposition, there remains to dwell for a moment on the central notion of "the Machine." What is it really? And what propitiated its advent? Is it merely, as we have been taught, the fruit of a market-driven desire for saving labor, i.e., one of the benevolent faces of "progress"? Or, is it, following anti-modernism's conflict theory, the chief instrument by which a "centralizing and totalitarian collectivity" constrains and constricts refractory individuals, i.e., an evil "Matrix"?[80]

Or what if, on a deeper and different level (from these discursive commonplaces), our intoleration for *physical pain* was instead the true gauge of our technological fitness? In other words, what if humanity, having sensed it was about to be engulfed in an epochal transformation, and dreading the laceration that this shift would have wrought on its *flesh*, "reacted" collectively with an organized motion to segregate the forthcoming sufferance, and that the result of this segregative movement is what we call "technology"?

This insight is that of another "Fascist," the famous warrior/writer Ernst Jünger (1895-1998), a virtuoso and visionary once attuned to the deeper esoteric currents of Nazism, who developed it into an unconventional interpretation of the Age of the Machine in his 1934 essay *On Pain*. Jünger's point of departure in the 1920s is the standard Fascist one, namely the languorous yearning for the ancient "chivalry" (*Ritterlichkeit*) and its knights, all creatures of a heroic and magical world, which are found to be deplorably deprived of breathing room in the era of mobilized masses and "technique." Very much bound to the mystique of blood and soil, Jünger was, clearly, enamored of his *national* cradle. And having passionately fought in the Great War, he was also keenly aware of and profoundly perturbed by the unrelenting siege the Universalist spirit had been laying to his homeland. For young pro-Fascist nationalists like him, "the supranational powers," – i.e. Jewry, Free-Masonry, High-Finance, and the "Church's pursuit of power for the mere sake of power, which is customarily referred to as Jesuitism" – had coalesced into a conspiratorial nebula organically hostile to the aboriginal "will to fashion a community through blood-ties," which is nationhood. "Nations," wrote Jünger, "are cores of organic bonds of a higher substance; an internationalist aggregation [*Gruppierung*], on the other hand, is merely an instrumental abstraction which is concocted, behind the scenes, by an American brain." To him, when the time for settling scores would have come and native blood would have been given thereby occasion "to speak," the unreal constructs of these "internationalist" conceptualizations would have collapsed like houses of cards.[81] Interestingly, seeming to fear her most, Jünger stung the Church with relish (he would convert to Catholicism at the age of 101, two years before his death), and, again, like Borgese and Evola, wished her ill with yet another Neoconservative/Ghibelline curse: [82]

> We believe the Free-Masonry of Blood to be stronger and more fearsome than all the Lodges of the world. Which is to say that one may inflict upon Jesuitism the most damage by letting devout Catholics endorse the collaboration between nationalism and Catholicism.[83]

But, upon maturer reflection, Jünger found modernity's greatest insidiousness in the objectification of the body, that is to say, in modern society's transformative drive to *separate pain from life*. Whereas heroic societies sought to assimilate pain – either through (asceticism's) mortification of the flesh or knightly discipline – modern ones, which believe there is only body and no soul, strive instead to isolate, confine, bottle up the pain, as it were, away from the space of workday activity. They shove it "to the margins" (*nach den Ränden*). The (socio-existential) retribution in all this is that, thus compressed and away from sight, pain, when it strikes back, hits us all with extraordinarily magnified violence. Clearly, the more compressed and the more occulted the "bottling," the more brutal and cruel the explosion when the pain is inevitably released, "with arrears" as it were – according to patterns more or less predictable, depending on the phenomenon, viz. wars, crime waves, natural disasters, epidemics, etc. There is a price to pay for this segregation, regardless. And here comes into play the pivotal role of *technology*, i.e., the very means by which the bottling up of pain is systematically effected in ways that are indeed ever more sophisticated, ever more "advanced": the classic culminant instance of this progression is the atom bomb, of course. All of which has conversely engendered a whole set of social practices designed to exorcise the fear of the modern discharge of pain such as a particular use of the *uniform*, whose functionality is not just that of making, through "absorption," gashes and fatal wounds more palatable to our gaze, but also that of effacing the individual's gender, thus creating a "third sex."

Modern masses, too, are treated like objects that have come to be husbanded through new "disciplining structures," and shepherded by the new police apparatuses into areas where they are directed to acclaim their leaders. To separate pain from life, humanity has taught itself various manners of creating spaces in which pain may be taken to be an illusion, and this has led to those notorious instances of de-sensitization whereby we receive news, and watch images of hecatombs, drone strikes, and any other sort of mass annihilation without any trace of emotion, yet may faint at the sight of our torn flesh. For Jünger, the indifferent "silence" with which we greet the news of a plane crash is far more cruel and abstract than the frenzied cheers that punctuate the (sacrificial) slaying of bulls in "southern arenas." Rhetorically, the sinister underside of this new, monstrous ethos is that modernity's worship of technology is just as poignantly an ode to mayhem and to the self-righteous impunity of detonating nuclear devices, and killing *everything* in sight for miles, should it be "expeditious" to do so.

Hyper-modern man is meaner and crueler. And he now lives in what one may call the Techno-Structure, an apparatus combining high organizational efficiency with total moral blindness. The Techno-Structure appears to be driven by an icy will to entomologize society, i.e. of turning us into genderless and "virtuous" "ants" and "the global village" into a centralized cluster of mechanized anthills. The era of the Techno-Structure is an "era of transition" whose "new orders" (*neue Ordnungen*) have yet to appear, and, it is understandable, Jünger remarks, "why in an epoch so instrumental, the State is not acknowledged as the all-encompassing institution, but rather as a totem of sorts,[84] and why technique and ethos have surprisingly become synonymous."[85] The tract ends on a spectral note. The gestation of this titanic monstrosity is what lies in the future of our species and there is no point resisting it; the chivalrous heart, therefore, cannot but embrace this destiny, hoping to survive and witness the dawn, as Evola put it, of the "pagan restoration."

> It thus follows that, practically speaking, the individual has no choice but to partake in the rearmament, either because he discerns in the latter a preparation to the downfall, or because he believes he recognizes, upon those hills where crosses have rotten away and palaces decayed, that inquietude that usually forebodes the advent of a new lordship [*neue Feldherrenzeichen*].[86]

But this "new lordship": is it not the very technocratic and internationalist *imperium* that eventually brought about the "downfall" of the Nationalist "blood" – that native blood which miscarried so catastrophically when it had a chance to "speak" and scores were finally settled in WWII?

On Pain is a prophetic piece. We *are* living through the transition; verily, the year 2000 (actually, 2001) was a momentous divide; and we can indeed reckon some of the loss and intuit the shape of "new orders" to come – or that are doing their utmost to emerge. What America is presently manning is, truly, in seminal form, the Techno-Structure. It is an imperial bastion alright, and there would be no reason to suppose that its topmost technocratic cadre is not just as competent and (spiritually) dedicated as the knightly orders that administered the kingly estates of yore. And like the latter, America's new Techno-fascism is equally endowed with spiritual force, but of a different sort, as Jünger's essay sought to convey. It is an enormous force, which chiefly speaks through mechanized organization, and, in affirming itself, it indeed samples, synthesizes, and regurgitates "the old" within a process of ever-advancing, highly dynamic innovation that standardizes, flattens, and centralizes everything.

Morphologically, the transitional nature of our time is highlighted by the fact that the Anglo-American Commonwealth still presents itself as a hybrid compound. The Commonwealth comprises two nominally separate sovereign bodies, yet America pursues a foreign, imperial policy that has been, from the outset, Britain's. Britain, for her part, evidently favors for herself a low-profile in the muscular theatrics of power, though via finance and intelligence she is still very much at the console. Constitutionally, on the other hand, Britain can fuse with America – through language, culture, and Puritanical business-worship – only up to a point because traditionally, she already thrives in a self-contained nucleus of Crown, (Anglican) Church, and Sword. America has neither Church nor Crown, though her irrepressible imperial appetencey makes her crave both institutions all the more acutely. For the time being, therefore, the problem appears to have been composed in the following fashion: 1) Britain is presented to the masses as little more than America's loyal "partner"; 2) America denies her imperial nature and concurrently diverts the violent energy she restlessly secretes to a nationalist cult of "the flag"; and 3) considering that, at bottom, the Anglo-American "system" wishes to suppress all traditional religions and replace them, in the long-run, with a "universal" creed along the lines of "the Religion of Man," it presently endorses a two-pronged strategy. The informal church of the Religion of Man is already populous, immensely so: it is, as known, a product of modernity's disillusionment and pathological consumerism, and it presently encompasses a majority of westerners, many of them "fallen-away Christians," who have come to worship above and beyond all, not so much their rationality as their *psyche,* i.e. their power of self-awareness, which, in conjunction with rational cogitation, they mistake for the source of their putative compassion, soberness and "overall decency," as well as the source of their alleged meditative capacity to become "one with the cosmos." The informal church of the Religion of Man is also very much the church of Leftism, of the Democratic, (postmodern) Left, politically speaking. The system's two-pronged strategy is to continue to encourage this triumphant form of mass agnosticism, which coincides with the New-Ageish devotion preconized by Borgese, Mumford and all

One-Worlders, while proceeding, on the other hand, to attract, in Ghibelline fashion, the more "traditional" flocks – above all, Catholicism's – with a view to incorporate them, slowly but surely, into the "structure," within which, ultimately, all spiritual afflatus is to be extinguished, as if dealing, in point of fact, with "ants" in an anthill. For the system, "all that is required of the good Christian is chastity and a modicum of charity in immediate personal relations."[87] In the Soviet *imperium*, which was but a conspicuously inefficient prototype of Techno-Structure, the problem vis-à-vis Catholicism, in provinces such as Poland, was posited in the exact same terms:

> The rulers tolerate ["patriotic"] Catholics as a temporary and necessary evil, reasoning that the stage has not yet arrived at which one can utterly wipe out religion, and that it is better to deal with accommodating bigots than with refractory ones [...]. The masses in highly industrialized countries like England, the United States, or France are largely de-Christianized. Technology, and the way of life it produces, undermines Christianity far more effectively than do violent measures [i.e. by raising man, not as a "child of God," but as a purely social creature]. The core of the problem is to avoid galvanizing the forces of Christianity by some careless misstep. It would be an unforgivable carelessness, for example, to close the churches suddenly and prohibit all religious practice. Instead one should try to split the Church in two. Part of the clergy must be compromised as reactionaries and "foreign agents" – a rather easy task, given the utterly conservative mentality of many priests. The other part must be bound to the State as closely as the Orthodox Church is in Russia, so that it becomes a tool of the government. A completely submissive Church – one that may on occasion collaborate with the security police – loses authority in the eyes of the pious. Such a Church can be preserved for decades, until the moment when it dies a natural death due to a lack of adherents.[88]

The above passage, written in 1950 under Communism, describes fairly accurately the (Ghibelline) strategy presently pursued by America's Techno-Structure in relation to Catholicism. This is bound to be an articulated and long-term strategy for it will take time to "digest" that massive cohort of believers whose creedal custom "consists essentially in the cultivation of an intimate emotional relationship between the worshipper and a *personal* God or other divine being." In other words, this devotional custom teaches the believer to invoke a tutelary "spirit," something like a guardian angel, as he persuades himself that he is instead in direct contact with the One. This "emotional method, which is used by the majority of Christians" is known in India as "*bhakti-marga*, the path of devotional faith, as opposed to *karma-marga*, the path of duties or works, and *jñana-marga*, the path of knowledge."[89]

The Catholic Church is possibly the foremost administrator of *bhakti-marga*. With regard to the spiritual welfare of religious feeling at large, this sort of devotion, while edifying in certain respects, may be problematic because this "tendency to speak of as many gods as there are human beings on the earth" may lead to a generalized state of affairs whereby "the most absolute polytheism" can hide behind "the mask of monotheism."[90] The Techno-Structure, for its part, understands that this persistence of the desire to worship can work to its advantage and therefore sees to it that "the masses continue to tread the path of devotion; but [that] the objects of this *bhakti* [be] no longer saints and a personal God, [but rather] the personified nation or class, and the deified leader."[91]

At the present time, Empire and Church appear to be engaged in some other variant of their usual arm-wrestling match. As seen, the two have developed a rather intimate, and preferential, sort of symbiosis since the 1940s; they have further cemented their bond by play-acting together, spectacularly, during the Cold War, and, together, in the 1980s, they dropped the curtain on the Soviet circus, which was no longer needed. True, there had been a bloody hiccup in 1969, followed by a nasty decade of terrorism and low-intensity civil strife in Italy, with the Church very much in the eye of that storm, but the enthronement of John Paul II had "normalized" the situation.[92] All in all, one would think that the Vatican is nowadays wholly subdued to America's Techno-Structure, considering that:

> a) the bulk of Vatican funding is American;
>
> b) the bulk of "progressive" Catholics have become entirely subservient to the business ethos of the Liberal mainstream, which finances its parishes and schools – schools that are, by and large, posh, unaffordable establishments catering almost exclusively to the ultra-rich;
>
> c) U.S. Catholic reactionaries have, since 9/11, rallied with ferocious exhilaration to the Neocons' patriotic and war-mongering promise of a never-ending hyper-modern crusade against Islam(ism); and
>
> d) Catholic "anarchists" – Evola's, Maurras', and pretty much everybody else's nemesis – very few to begin with, can be said to have been successfully relegated to the appendices of esoteric codices amid unicorns and faeries.

But appearances can be deceptive. For one, it is patent that the Holy See has no liking whatsoever for the War on the Terror and that it did not fall for the Orientalist deceit of the "Clash of Civilizations." This has been a significant disappointment for One-Worlders. Secondly, the Church appears downright opposed to the Techno-Structure's entomologizing push, and this clash has been fought out, for years now, on the front of sexual, bio-, and family ethics. What the Techno-Structure wishes in this bearing is clear: it is the systematic enforcement of a policy of demographic management that relies on three levers: 1) a discretionary calibration of population growth through a systematized recourse to abortion and careful administration of contraception, in keeping with the overall economic constraints (energy, nutrition, employment) under its direct and centralized supervision; 2) the (progressive) de-differentiation of males and females for the purpose of unisex, standardized employment – limited and controlled (exploitative and mind-deadening, as well) – and the concomitant commitment of the couples' children to the care of "diverse others," by which the elite means, in Newspeak, nannies and generic slave-labor from provinces of "inferior technological status" – namely, Hispanics for the U.S., Slavs, East Asians, Filipinos, and Africans for the European block; and 3) migration laws that may guarantee at all times this constant supply of slave-hands from the indigent peripheries of the globe. In sum, the Structure demands: birth control, gender erasure and abolition of the familial nucleus, and a ceaseless supply of slave-hands through unrestricted migratory flows.

Discursively, the system's extraordinary emphasis on gender theory – and the associated campaign for the "erasure of gender," not to mention the late flurry of transgender narratives – all of which could have been dismissed as so many episodes of an ongoing surreal psychodrama, acquire a serious, functional significance when one interprets them in light of Jünger's intuition of the Structure's need for a "third sex," with which to operate, in fact, the mechanical beehive: men and women as undifferentiated toilers, breeders, and soldiers[93] all rolled into one. The show is said to be, at first blush, "surreal" because too few have wondered what suddenly brought elites theretofore known to be profoundly racist, misogynistic, elitist, and homophobic to turn overnight into gung-ho partisans and bankrollers of "feminism," "nativism," and "LGBT." The disingenuousness of their discursive flattery of "the different other" is part and parcel of Techno-fascism.

To summarize, the Church has not "bought" the War on Terror, nor has she espoused gender theory and the abolition of the family, of course, but being the latter theme tightly linked to sex and brandished with exceptional vehemence by the postmodern Globalists engaged in the fight, the Church has had "to play the game," as prelates will tell you in the higher reaches of the Vatican. Via this inquisitorial platform of vetting a person's, or a group's, "goodness" chiefly on the basis of their stance on same-sex unions and adoptions, postmodernists aim at sundering Catholicism, their ploy being to identify among Catholics the healthy, pro-gay grain and separate it from the homophobic chaff. The Church has parried by fielding one of her "brigades," mostly made up of American Jesuits, in the pro-gay rights camp. And so the game goes on. The area in which Rome has so far completely caved in to the exigencies of the Techno-Structure is that of immigration: incapable of appearing untrue to her charitable self, the Church has lately vigorously championed the cause of all war refugees and migrant workers seeking asylum in Europe and the United States. By doing so, aside from buttressing the Structure's political economics, the Church has given tacit and significant support to NATO's unceasing ravage of the Middle-East.

In conclusion, one may make the three following observations. The first is that, in essence, the stance of the One-Worlders is – despite, or rather, because of their lofty language and high-flown ideals of universal brotherhood – possibly the most dangerous and insidious of all conceivable political solutions at this time. Because they affirm, and know to be lying when they do so, that the notion of "nationality" is "a collective utopia" and "a social myth,"[94] the perniciousness of which only the New World Order can defuse; because they affirm this, it unequivocally means, given that these propagandists' political handlers are themselves oligarchs in charge of tangible *national* realities – viz. those of Britain and America – that this Universalist alliance may only be achieved, against all unsubmissive nations, through a season of prolonged and devastating wars on a *global* scale.

Secondly, from an imperialist standpoint, the distinction between Republicans and Democrats appears to have become spurious: both sides have been fully committed to the NWO, and having divided labor, each wages its half of the offensive in its own fashion. Versus Rome, the Structure has tactically split: as said, the Neocon fringe is tirelessly striving to swallow the traditionalist bastion of the Church by massaging the conservative, plutocratic tier of her faithful, and by appealing to their orthodoxy in point of liturgy and devotional etiquette. The Democrats, for their part, use gender theory and sexual leitmotifs as their weapon of choice in their protracted effort to provoke and embarrass the Church typically by denigrating as patriarchal overbearingness and homophobic hatred any counter-argument she may try to put forth in traditional defense of heterosexuality, marriage, and procreation. What is significant overall is that the work of both factions is perfectly complementary in their joint endeavor to weaken the Church by splitting her in two via the absorption of the conservatives in the overtly imperialist wing of the Structure, on the one hand, and, on the other, via the attempted fragmentation of the progressive body of the U.S. Church into a "postmodern" reticulation of State-dependent "ethnic" churches (with priests as "quasi-civil servants"), and, preferably an even larger residual of "fallen-away Catholics," justifiably disgusted by a clergy for the most part unequal to the flock's expectations and needs. These defectors may be safely expected to drift into the informal church of the Religion of Man. In sum, there is but one faction at work in America's Techno-Structure: it is made up of stewards committed to the English-speaking idea, who are staunch imperialists: Ghibelline Globalists all of them.

Third and final point: While these imposing bodies, of Guelphs and Ghibellines, are busy playing their games, in view of more terrible conflicts, and more environmental devastation, the rest of us cannot really afford to wait and see what happens. Our "third way," which clearly acknowledges national difference as a source of creative *union* among forces from all corners of the world will have to rally, organize itself territorially, study new ways to reform the economy through *cooperation*, and, hopefully, proceed to confederate this constellation of free-districts in the name of pacifism.

Guido Giacomo Preparata
Rome, 24 June, 2016

(Endnotes)

1. "Depuis cinquante ans, l'établissement définitif de la grande federation asiatico-américano-européenne et sa domination incontestée sur ce qui restait encore ça et là, en Océanie ou dans l'Afrique Centrale, de barbarie inassimilable, avait habitué tous les peuples, convertis en province, aux délices d'une paix universelle et désormais imperturbable. Il n'avait pas fallu moins de cent cinquante ans de guerres pour aboutir à ce dénouement merveilleux [...]. Ce n'est point comme on l'avait annoncé, une vaste république démocratique qui sortit de là. Tant d'orgueil en éruption ne pouvait ne pas soulever un trône nouveau, le plus haut, le plus fort, le plus radieux qui fût jamais," Gabriel Tarde, *Fragment d'histoire future* (Paris: Éditions Glyphe, 2015 [1896]), 11, 20.

2. Julian Huxley, *On Living in a Revolution* (London: Chatto & Windus, 1941), 152, emphasis added.

3. See, e.g., Lewis Mumford, "Authoritarian and Democratic Technics," in *Technology and Culture,* Vol.5 n. 1 (1964):1-8; and *Technics and Civilization* (New York: Harcourt, Brace, Jovanonich Publishers, 1963 [1934]).

4. Lewis Mumford, *The Conduct of Life* (New York: Harcourt, Brace, and Company, 1951), 117.

5. Giuseppe Antonio Borgese, *Una costituzione per il mondo* (Roma: Edizioni di Storia e Letteratura, 2103 [1949]), 15, 37, 47, 48, 51, 54-55, 56, 69, 74-77, 78.

6. Leonardo Sciascia, *Fine del carabiniere a cavallo. Saggi letterari (1955-1989)* (Milano: Adelphi Edizioni, 2016), 139, 140, 142, 143, 144.

7. Giuseppe Antonio Borgese, *Goliath. The March of Fascism* (New York: The Viking Press, 1937) 30, 59, 63, 75, 77, 135.

8. Ibid, 168, 218, 455, 457.

9. Ibid, 224-225, 340.

10. Ibid, 306, 310, 315.

11. Lewis Mumford, *The Story of Utopias* (New York: The Viking Press, 1962 [1922]), 75.

12. Borgese, *Goliath*, 396-412.

13. Ibid., 438.

14. René Guénon, *Spiritual Authority and Temporal Power* (Ghent, NY: Sophia Perennis, 2001 [1929]), 61.

15. Julius Evola, *Lo Stato Organico. Scritti sull'idea di Stato, 1934-1963* (Roma: Controcorrente, 2004), 96 ("Non è facile concepire il modo con cui una consacrazione possa conferire una nuova legittimità ad uomini nuovi, che si muovono nel mondo creato dalla tecnica e dalla macchina, mondo in larga misura disumanizzato e devastato spiritualmente, ma anche pervaso dall'elementare").

16. Giambattista Vico, *La scienza nuova* (Ed. Paolo Rossi) (Milano: Biblioteca Universale Rizzoli, 1977 [1744]), 189, 205, 212, 218, 418, 424, 643.

17. Carl Schmitt, *Il nomos della terra. Nel diritto internazionale dello "Jus Publicum Europaeum"* (Milano: Adelphi Edizioni, 1991 [1950]), 42, 43, 45, 46, 49.

18. Dante, *Monarchia* (Ed. Federico Sanguineti) (Milano: Garzanti, 1985 [1313]), 94, 128, 134, 140, 142, 144, 146 ("Illa igitur reverentia Cesar utatur ad Petrum qua primogenitus filius debet uti ad patrem: ut luce paterne gratie illustratus virtuosius orbem terre irradiet, cui ab Illo solo perfectus est, qui est omnium spiritualium et temporalium gubernator").

19. Guénon, *Spiritual Authority*, 59.

20. Renzo de Felice, *Mussolini il Duce. Lo stato totalitario, 1936-1940 (Vol. V)* (Torino: Einaudi, 1965-1995), 316.

21. Bruno Zoratto (Ed.), *Julius Evola nei documenti segreti dell'Ahnenerbe* (Roma: Fondazione Julius Evola, 1997), 42-43.

22. Julius Evola, *The Path of Cinnabar. An Intellectual Biography* (Milton Keynes: Integral Tradition Publishing, 2009 [1963]), 86, 147.

23. Nicola Cospito and Hans Werner Neulen (Eds.), *Julius Evola nei documenti segreti del Terzo Reich* (Roma: Europa, 1986), 55, 56.

24. René Guénon, *Lettere a Julius Evola, 1930-1950* (Reggio Emilia: SeaR Edizioni, 1996), 127.

25. Julius Evola, *The Mystery of the Grail. Initiation and Magic in the Quest for the Spirit* (Rochester, VT: Inner Traditions, 1994 [1934]), 120-123.

26. Julius Evola, *Gli uomini e le rovine – Orientamenti* (Roma: Edizioni Mediterranee, 2001 [1967]), 149-153.

27. Julius Evola, *Imperialismo pagano. Il fascismo dinanzi al pericolo euro-cristiano – Heidnischer Imperialismus* (Roma: Edizioni Mediterranee, 2004 [1928-1933]), 70, 129, 136, 137.

28. Julius Evola, *Il Federalismo imperiale. Scritti sull'idea di Impero 1926-1953* (Roma: Controcorrente, 2004), 67.

29. Julius Evola, *Europa Una: Forma e presupposti* (Roma: Fondazione Julius Evola, 1996 [1932-1955]), 16, 31.

30. Evola, *Federalismo imperiale*, 75.

31. Evola, *Imperialismo pagano*, 80-81 ("Quindi due sole possibilità, per il fascismo: o riconoscere nella Chiesa un universalismo anti-nazionale e antifascista almeno come quello massonico [...], oppure vedere se la Chiesa osa il passo anticristiano che mai ha osato: identificarsi al fascismo, proclamare il popolo d'Italia il popolo eletto e marciare alla testa di esso per la conquista del mondo. Ma sa bene la Chiesa, quante probabilità vi siano perché questa seconda soluzione concluda ad un'unica cosa: allo sfacelo della Chiesa e quello dell'Italia stessa. Ragion per cui è da augurarsi che i paladini della "tradizione cattolica" riescano appunto, un giorno, a trascinare la Chiesa in un'avventura di questo genere – se il fascismo non si decide a capire ciò che deve capire, epperò a dichiarare l'assoluta incompatibilità fra imperialismo e cattolicismo, preparando le forze per la vera controriforma – per la restaurazione pagana").

32. Ibid, 109; and *Federalismo Imperiale*, 72, 127.

33. Evola, *Federalismo Imperiale*, 102,

34. Evola, *Europa Una,* 12, 13, 29, 39, 40, 48.

35. Evola, *Stato organico,* 57, 58, 69.

36. Evola, *Imperialismo pagano*, 120.

37. Ibid., 169.

38. Paul Doncoeur, Marie-Vincent Bernadot, Etienne Lajeunie, Daniel Lallement, François-Xavier Maquart, and Jacques Maritain, *Pourquoi Rome a parlé* (Paris: Aux Éditions Spes, 1927), 35, 104, 105, 112, 113, 204.

39. Charles Maurras, *Romantisme et révolution* cited in Doncoeur et al., *Pouquoi Rome a parlé*, 122-123 ("[L'idée de Dieu] peut aussi tourner à l'anarchie. Trop souvent révolté contre les intérêts généraux de l'espèce et des sous-groupements humains (patrie, caste, cité, famille) l'individu ne si soumet, en beaucoup de cas, que par necessité, horreur de la solitude, crainte du dénûment: mais si, dans cette conscience naturellement anarchique, l'on fait germer le sentiment qu'elle peut nouer des relations directes avec l'Être absolu, infini, tout-puissant, l'idée de ce maître invisible et lointain l'aura vite éloignée du respect qu'elle doit à ses maîtres visibles et prochains: *elle aimera mieux obéir à Dieu qu'aux hommes*").

40. Doncoeur et al., *Pouquoi Rome a parlé*, 35, 125, 144, 220.

41. Stéphane Giocanti, *Maurras. Le chaos et l'ordre* (Paris: Flammarion: 2008), 409.

42. For a study on the relationship between Catholicism and U.S. Neoconservatism, see Jeffrey J. Langan, "The Neoconservative Influence on American Catholicism. Smothering Pacifism in the Cradle," in Guido G. Preparata (Ed.), *New Directions in Catholic Social and Political Research. Humanity vs. Hyper-Modernity* (New York: Palgrave Macmillan, September 2016).

43. David I. Kertzer, *The Pope and Mussolini. The Secret History of Pius XI and the Rise of Fascism in Europe* (New York: Random House, 2014), 127.

44. Renzo De Felice, *Mussolini il rivoluzionario, 1883-1920 (Vol. I)* (Torino: Einaudi, 1995 [1966]), 596-597

45. Allegedly, this was said either to French Prime Minister Pierre Laval in 1935 or to Churchill in 1944, or both.

46. Annie Lacroix-Riz, *Le Vatican, l'Europe et le Reich. De la Première Guerre Mondiale à la Guerre Froide* (Paris: Armand Colin Éditeur, 2010).

47. Ibid., 17.

48. Pierre Dominique, *La politique des Jésuites* (Paris: Grasset, 1955), 235, 246-247, 253.

49. Renzo De Felice, *Mussolini il rivoluzionario*, 535; and *Mussolini il fascista. La conquista del potere, 1921-1925 (Vol. II)* (Torino: Einaudi, 1995 [1966]), 349-353.

50. Gianni Vannoni, *Le società segrete. Dal Seicento al Novecento – Note e documenti* (Firenze: Sansoni Editore, 1985), 263-264.

51. Natale Mario Di Luca. *Arturo Reghini. Un intellettuale Neo-Pitagorico tra Massoneria e Fascismo* (Roma: Atanòr, 2003), 61, 77.

52. Fabio Venzi, *Massoneria e Fascismo. Dall'Intesa cordiale alla distruzione delle logge: come nasce una "guerra di religione," 1921-1925* (Roma: Castelvecchi, 2008), 30.

53. Benito Mussolini, *Opera Omnia* (Firenze: La Fenice, 1972) Vol. XXIV, 45-46.

54. Enzo Santarelli, *Storia del Fascismo, La dittattura capitalistica, Vol. II* (Roma: Editori Riuniti, 1967), 154, 162-163, 164, 168, 169, 170, 188-189, 193.

55. Lacroix-Riz, *Le Vatican*, 151-155, 259.

56. Léon Daudet and Charles Maurras, *La politique du Vatican sous la terreur, 20 septembre-15 novembre 1927* (Versailles: Bibliothèque des oeuvres politiques, 1927), 8-9, 191.

57. Kertzer, *The Pope and Mussolini*, 59, 156.

58. Patrick McNamara, *A Catholic Cold War. Edmund A. Walsh, S.J., and the Politics of American Anti-Communism* (New York: Fordham University Press, 2005), 2-4, 8, 25, 46, 54, 67.

59. Roger Garaudy, *L'Église, le Communisme et les Chrétiens* (Paris: Éditions Sociales, 1949), 159, 160-163.

60. Ron Chernow, *The House of Morgan. The Secret History of Money and Power* (New York: Simon & Schuster, 1990), 277-286.

61. Lacroix-Riz, *Le Vatican*, 206-209, 477-482.

62. Kertzer, *The Pope and Mussolini*, 130.

63. De Felice, *Mussolini: Lo Stato totalitario*, 130-134.

64. Richard A. Webster, *Christian Democracy in Italy, 1860-1960* (London: Hollis & Carter, 1961), 113, 122, 123.

65. De Felice, *Mussolini, Gli anni del consenso*, 340, 373.

66. Guido G. Preparata, *Conjuring Hitler. How Britain and America Made the Third Reich* (London: Pluto Press, 2005), 200-201.

67. Lacroix-Riz, *Le Vatican*, 257, 331-332.

68. Ibid., 344, 345, 350-360, 479, 497; and Garaudy, *L'Église*, 87.

69. Lacroix-Riz, *Le Vatican*, 504-505.

70. See , e.g., John Cornwell, *Hitler's Pope, The Secret History of Pius XII* (New York: Viking), 236-238.

71. *Osservatore romano*, "Due anni di Pontificato, due anni di combattimento," 12 March 1941.

72. Lacroix-Riz, *Le Vatican*, 515, 516, 527, 532.

73. McNamara, *Catholic Cold War*, 144, 147.

74. Lacroix-Riz, *Le Vatican*, 518-9, 520, 534, 551, 554; and Garaudy, *L'Église*, 138-139.

75. http://www.trumanlibrary.org/publicpapers/index.php?pid=1542&st=holiness&st1=

76. David S. Wyman, *The Abandonment of the Jews. America and the Holocaust, 1941-1945* (New York: Pantheon Books, 1984).

77. "[Der Geist, der seit über hundert Jahren an unserer Landschaft formt], drückt seine Spuren auch in menschlichen Bestande ab; er trägt die weichen Stellen ab und härtet die Fläche des Widerstandes. Wir befinden uns in einem Zustande, in dem wir noch fähig sind, den Verlust zu sehen; wir empfinden noch die Vernichting des Wertes, die Verflachung und Vereinfachung der Welt. Schon aber wachsen neue Generationen auf, sehr fern von allen Traditionen, mit denen wir noch geboren sind, und ist es ein wunderliches Gefühl, diese Kinder zu beobachten, von denen so manches das Jahr 2000 noch erleben wird. Dann wird wohl die letzte Substanz des modernen [...] Zeitalters entschwunden sein"), Ernst Jünger, "Über den Schmerz," in *Blätter und Steine* (Hamburg: Hanseatische Verlagsanstalt, 1941 [1934]), 213.

78. Renzo de Felice, *Mussolini il Duce. Gli anni del consenso, 1929-1936 (Vol. IV)* (Torino: Einaudi, 1965-1995), 394.

79. Saul Friedlander, *Hitler et les États-Unis, 1939-1941* (Paris: Éditions du Seuil, 1966), 171, 222.

80. Bernanos, *La liberté, pour quoi faire?* (Paris: Gallimard, 1995 [1947]), 100, 135.

81. Ernst Jünger, "Der Nationalismus," in *Politische Publizistik, 1919 bis 1933* (Stuttgart: Klett-Cotta, 2001 [1925]), 193-195.

82. Ernst Jünger, "Die Antinationale Mächte," in *Politische Publizistik* [1927], 293-294.

83. Ibid., 295 ("Wir halten die Freimauerei des Blutes für starker and furchterbar als alle Logen der Welt. Wir meinen dass man den Jesuitismus am schwersten schädigt, indem man überzeugte Katholiken für die Zusammenarbeit zwischen Nationalismus und Katholizismus sprechen lässt").

84. Literally, "a cultual magnitude" *(eine kultische Größe).*

85. Junger, "Über den Schmerz," 173, 174-175, 183, 191, 194, 202, 207, 215.

86. Ibid., 216.

87. Aldous Huxley, *Ends and Means. An Inquiry into the Nature of Ideals and into the Methods Employed for Their Realization* (London: Chatto & Windus, 1938), 209.

88. Czeslaw Milosz, *The Captive Mind* (New York: Vintage Books, 1981 [1951), 73, 212.

89. Huxley, *Ends and Means*, 234-235.

90. Rudolf Steiner, *The Karma of Untruthfulness. Secret Societies, the Media, and Preparations for the Great War, Vol. I* (Forrest Row: Rudolf Steiner Press, 2005 [1916]), 212-213.

91. Huxley, *Ends and Means*, 244.

92. For a reflection on the dynamics of the Cold War (the "Cold Game"), see Guido G. Preparata, "A Study in Gray: The *Affaire Moro* and Notes for a Reinterpretation of the Cold War and the Nature of Terrorism," in Eric Wilson (Ed.), *The Dual State: Parapolitics, Carl Schmitt, and the National Security* Complex (Farnham, Surrey: Ashgate, 2012), 213-272.

93. "Pentagon Ends Ban on Transgender Troops in Military," Associated Press, June 30, 2016. "Saying it's the right thing to do, Defense Secretary Ash Carter announced Thursday that transgender people will be allowed to serve openly in the U.S. military, ending one of the last bans on service in the armed forces [...]."

https://www.yahoo.com/news/us-officials-military-concerned-transgender-timeline-075734316--politics.html

94. Mumford, *Utopias*, 221

Index

A

B

C

S

T